HUMAN-CENTRIC MACHINE VISION

Edited by **Manuela Chessa,
Fabio Solari** and **Silvio P. Sabatini**

INTECHOPEN.COM

Human-Centric Machine Vision

Edited by Manuela Chessa, Fabio Solari and Silvio P. Sabatini

CBS, Edition **2016**

Published by InTech

Janeza Trdine 9, 51000 Rijeka, Croatia

Publishing Process Manager Martina Blecic

Technical Editor Teodora Smiljanic

Cover Designer InTech Design Team

Additional hard copies can be obtained from orders@intechopen.com

Human-Centric Machine Vision,
Edited by Manuela Chessa, Fabio Solari and Silvio P. Sabatini
p. cm.
ISBN 978-953-51-0563-3

Contents

Preface

In the last decade, the algorithms for the processing of the visual information have greatly evolved, providing efficient and effective solutions to cope with the variability and the complexity of real-world environments. These achievements yield to the development of Machine Vision systems that overcome the typical industrial applications, where the environments are controlled and the tasks are very specific, towards the use of innovative solutions to face with everyday needs of people. In particular, the Human-Centric Machine Vision can help to solve the problems raised by the needs of our society, e.g. security and safety, health care, medical imaging, human machine interface, and assistance in vehicle guidance. In such applications it is necessary to handle changing, unpredictable and complex situations, and to take care of the presence of humans.

This book focuses both on human-centric applications and on bio-inspired Machine Vision algorithms. Chapter 1 describes a method to detect the 3D orientation of human eyes for possible use in biometry, human-machine interaction, and psychophysics experiments. Features' extraction based on wavelet moments and moment invariants are applied in different fields, such as face and facial expression recognition, and hand posture detection in Chapter 2. Innovative tools for assisting medical imaging are described in Chapters 3 and 4, where a texture classification method for the detection of calcification clusters in mammography and a technique for the screening of the retinopathy of the prematurity are presented. A real-time mice scratching detection and quantification system is described in Chapter 5, and a tool that reliably determines the presence of micro-organisms in water samples is presented in Chapter 6. Bio-inspired algorithms are used in order to solve complex tasks, such as the robotic cognitive autonomous navigation in Chapter 7, and the transformation of image filters by using complex-value neural networks in Chapter 8. Finally, the potential of Machine Vision and of the related technologies in various application domains of critical importance for economic growth is reviewed in Chapter 9.

Dr. Fabio Solari, Dr. Manuela Chessa and Dr. Silvio P. Sabatini
PSPC-Group, Department of Biophysical and Electronic Engineering (DIBE)
University of Genoa
Italy

The Perspective Geometry of the Eye: Toward Image-Based Eye-Tracking

Andrea Canessa, Agostino Gibaldi, Manuela Chessa,
Silvio Paolo Sabatini and Fabio Solari
University of Genova - PSPC Lab
Italy

1. Introduction

Eye-tracking applications are used in large variety of fields of research: neuro-science, psychology, human-computer interfaces, marketing and advertising, and computer science. The commonly known techniques are: contact lens method (Robinson, 1963), electro-oculography (Kaufman et al., 1993), limbus tracking with photo-resistors (Reulen et al., 1988; Stark et al., 1962), corneal reflection (Eizenman et al., 1984; Morimoto et al., 2000) and Purkinje image tracking (Cornsweet & Crane, 1973; Crane & Steele, 1978).

Thanks to the recent increase of the computational power of the normal PCs, the eye tracking system gained a new dimension, both in term of the technique used for the tracking, and in term of applications. In fact, in the last years raised and expanded a new family of techniques that apply passive computer vision algorithms to elaborate the images so to obtain the gaze estimation. Regarding the applications, effective and real-time eye tracker can be used coupled with a head tracking system, in order to decrease the visual discomfort in an augmented reality environment (Chessa et al., 2012), and to improve the capability of interaction with the virtual environment. Moreover, in virtual and augmented reality applications, the gaze tracking can be used with a display with variable-resolution that modifies the image in order to provide a high level of detail at the point of gaze while sacrificing the periphery (Parkhurst & Niebur, 2004).

Grounding the eye tracking on the image of the eye, the pupil position is the most outstanding feature in the image of the eye, and it is commonly used for eye-tracking, both in corneal reflections and in image-based eye-trackers. Beside, extremely precise estimation can be obtained with eye tracker based on the limbus position (Reulen et al., 1988; Stark et al., 1962). Limbus is the edge between the sclera and the iris, and can be easily tracked horizontally. Because of the occlusion of the iris done by the eyelid, limbus tracking techniques are very effective in horizontal tracking, but they fall short in vertical and oblique tracking. Nevertheless, the limbus proves to be a good feature on which to ground an eye tracking system.

Starting from the observation that the limbus is close to a perfect circle, its projection on the image plane of a camera is an ellipse. The geometrical relation between a circle in the 3D space and its projection on a plane can be exploited to gather an eye tracking technique that resorts on the limbus position to track the gaze direction on 3D. In fact, the ellipse and the circle are two sections of an elliptic cone whose vertex is at the principal point of the camera. Once the points that define the limbus are located on the image plane, it is possible to fit the conic equation that is a section of this cone. The gaze direction can be obtained computing which is the orientation in space of the circle that produces that projection (Forsyth et al., 1991; Wang et al., 2003). From this perspective, the more the limbus detection is correct, the most the estimation of gaze comes to be precise and reliable. In image based techniques, a common way to detect the iris is first to detect the pupil in order to start from a guess of the center of the iris itself, and to resort on this information to find the limbus (Labati & Scotti, 2010; Mäenpää, 2005; Ryan et al., 2008).

Commonly in segmentation and recognition the iris shape on the image plane is considered to be circular, (Kyung-Nam & Ramakrishna, 1999; Matsumoto & Zelinsky, 2000) and to simplify the search for the feature, the image can be transformed from a Cartesian domain to a polar one (Ferreira et al., 2009; Rahib & Koray, 2009). As a matter of fact, this is true only if the iris plane is orthogonal to the optical axis of the camera, and few algorithms take into account the projective distortions present in off-axis images of the eye and base the search for the iris on an elliptic shape (Ryan et al., 2008). In order to represent the image in a domain where the elliptical shape is not only considered, but also exploited, we developed a transformation from the Cartesian domain to an "elliptical" one, that transform both the pupil edge and the limbus into straight lines. Furthermore, resorting on geometrical considerations, the ellipse of the pupil can be used to shape the iris. In fact, even though the pupil and the iris projections are not concentric, their orientation and eccentricity can be considered equal. From this perspective, a successful detection of the pupil is instrumental for iris detection, because it allows for a domain to be used for the elliptical transformation, and it constrains the search for the iris parameters.

The chapter is organized as follows: in Sec. 3 we present the eye structure, in particular related to pupil and iris, and the projective rule on the image plane; in Sec. 4 we show how to fit the ellipse equation on a set of points without any constraint or given its orientation and eccentricity; in Sec. 5 we demonstrate how to segment the iris, resorting on the information obtained by the pupil and we show some results achieved on an iris database and on the images acquired by our system; in Sec. 6 we show how the fitted ellipse can be used for gaze estimation and in Sec. 7 we introduce some discussions and we present our conclusion.

2. Related works

The study of eye movements anticipates the actual wide use of computers by more than 100 years, for example, Javal (1879). The first methods to track eye movements were quite invasive, involving direct mechanical contact with the cornea. A first attempt to develop a not invasive eye tracker is due to Dodge & Cline (1901) which exploited light reflected from the cornea. In the 1930s, Miles Tinker and his colleagues began to apply photographic techniques to study eye movements in reading (Tinker, 1963). In 1947 Paul Fitts and his colleagues began using motion picture cameras to study the movements of pilots' eyes as they used cockpit controls and instruments to land an airplane (Fitts et al., 1950). In the same tears Hartridge & Thompson (1948) invented the first head-mounted eye tracker. One reference work in the gaze tracking literature is that made by Yarbus in the 1950s and 1960s (Yarbus, 1959). He studied eye movements and saccadic exploration of complex images, recording the eye movements performed by observers while viewing natural objects and scenes. In the 1960s, Shackel (1960) and Mackworth & Thomas (1962) advanced the concept of head-mounted eye tracking systems making them somewhat less obtrusive and further reducing restrictions on participant head movement (Jacob & Karn, 2003).

The 1970s gave an improvement to eye movement research and thus to eye tracking. The link between eye tracker and psychological studies got deeper, looking at the acquired eye movement data as an open door to understand the brain cognitive processes. Efforts were spent also to increase accuracy, precision and comfort of the device on the tracked subjects. The discovery that multiple reflections from the eye could be used to dissociate eye rotations from head movement (Cornsweet & Crane, 1973), increased tracking precision and also prepared the ground for developments resulting in greater freedom of participant movement (Jacob & Karn, 2003).

Historically, the first application using eye tracking systems was the user interface design. From the 1980s, thanks to the rapid increase of the technology related to the computer, eye trackers began to be used also in a wide variety of disciplines (Duchowski, 2002):

- human-computer interaction (HCI)
- neuroscience
- psychology
- psycholinguistics
- ophthalmology
- medical research
- marketing research
- sports research

Even if commercial applications are quite uncommon, a key application for eye tracking systems is to enable people with severe physical disabilities to communicate and/or interact with computer devices. Simply by looking at control keys displayed on a computer monitor screen, the user can perform a broad variety of functions including speech synthesis, control, playing games, typing Eyetracking systems can enhance the quality of life of a disabled person, his family and his community by broadening his communication, entertainment, learning and productive capacities. Additionally, eyetracking systems have been demonstrated to be invaluable diagnostic tools in the administration of intelligence and psychological tests. Another aspect of eye tracking usefulness could be found in the cognitive and behavioural therapy, a branch of psychotherapy specialized in the treatment of anxiety disorders like phobias, and in diagnosis or early screening of some health problems. Abnormal eye movement can be an indication of diseases in balance disorder, diabetic retinopathy, strabismus, cerebral palsy, multiple sclerosis. Technology offers a tool for quantitatively measuring and recording what a person does with his eyes while he is reading. This ability to know what people look at and don't look at has also been widely used in a commercial way. Market researchers want to know what attracts people's attention and whether it is good attention or annoyance. Advertisers want to know whether people are looking at the right things in their advertisement. Finally, we want to emphasize the current and prospective aspect of eye and gaze tracking in game environment, either in rehabilitation, an entertainment or an edutainment context.

A variety of technologies have been applied to the problem of eye tracking.

Scleral coil

The most accurate, but least user-friendly technology uses a physical attachment to the front of the eye. Despite the older generation and its invasivity, the scleral coil contact lens is still one of the most precise eye tracking system (Robinson, 1963). In this table-mounted systems, the subject wears a contact lens with two coils inserted. An alternate magnetic field allows for the measurement of horizontal, vertical and torsional eye movements simultaneously. The real drawback of this technique is its invasivity respect to the subject, in fact it can decrease the visual acuity, increase the intraocular pressure, and moreover it can damage the corneal and conjunctival surface.

Electro-oculography

One of the least expensive and simplest eye tracking technologies is recording from skin electrodes, like those used for making ECG or EEG measurements. This method is based on the electrical field generated by the corneo-retinal potential, that can be measured on the skin of the forehead (Kaufman et al., 1993). The orientation of this field changes with the rotation of the eyes, and can be measured by an array of electrodes placed around the eyes. The electrical changes are subsequently processed to relate them with the movements of the eyes. Beyond the limited precision of this technique, there are some problems to be faced, as the contraction other than the eye muscles (like facial or neck) and eye blinking, that affect the electric potential related to eye movements, or as a correct and stable coupling of the electrodes, that ensures a measure of the field that is constant and reliable over time.

Most practical eye tracking methods are based on a non-contacting camera that observes the eyeball plus image processing techniques to interpret the picture.

Optical reflections

A first category of camera based methods use optical features for measuring eye motion. Light, typically infrared (IR), is reflected from the eye and sensed by a video camera or some other specially designed optical sensor. The information is then analyzed to extract eye rotation from changes in reflections. We refer to them as the reflections based systems.

- *Photo-resistor measurement*

  This method is based on the measurement of the light reflected by the cornea, in proximity of the vertical borders of iris and sclera, *i.e.* the limbus. The two vertical borders of the limbus are illuminated by a lamp, that can be either in visible light (Stark et al., 1962) or in infra-red light (Reulen et al., 1988). The diffuse reflected light from the sclera (white) and iris (colored) is measured by an array of infra-red light photo-transducers, and the amount of reflected light received by each photocell are functions of the angle of sight. Since the relative position between the light and the photo-transducers needs to be fixed, this technique requires a head-mounted device, like that developed by (Reulen et al., 1988). The authors developed a system that, instead of measuring the horizontal movements only, takes into account the vertical ones as well. Nevertheless, the measures can not be effectuated simultaneously, so they are performed separately on the two eyes, so that one is used to track the elevation (that can be considered equal for both the eyes), and one for the azimuth.

- *Corneal reflection*

  An effective and robust technique is based on the corneal reflection, that is the reflection of the light on the surface of the cornea (Eizenman et al., 1984; Morimoto et al., 2000). Since the corneal reflection is the brightest reflection, its detection is simple, and offers a stable reference point for the gaze estimation. In fact, assuming for simplicity that the eye is a perfect sphere which rotates rigidly around its center, the position of the reflection does not move with the eye rotation. In such a way, the gaze direction is described by a vector that generates from the corneal reflection to the center of the pupil or of the iris, and can be mapped to screen coordinates on a computer monitor after a calibration procedure. The drawback of this technique is that the relative position between the eye and the light source must be fixed, otherwise the reference point, *i.e.* the corneal reflection, would move, voiding the reliability of the system. This technique, in order to be more robust and stable, requires an infrared light source to generate the corneal reflection and to produce images with a high contrast between the pupil and the iris.

- *Purkinje images*

  The corneal is the brightest reflection created by the eye, but it is not the only one. The different layers of the eye produce other reflections, the Purkinje images, that are used in a very accurate eye tracking techniques (Cornsweet & Crane, 1973; Crane & Steele, 1978). From the first image to the fourth, the Purkinje images are respectively the reflection from the outer surface of the cornea, from the inner surface of the cornea, from the anterior surface of the lens, and finally the reflection from the posterior surface of the lens. Special hardware is required to detect the Purkinje images beyond the first, but such image allow the estimation of the three-dimensional point of regard.

In the last decades, another type of eye tracking family became very popular, thanks to the rapid increase of the technology related to the computer, together with the fact that it is completely remote and non-intrusive: the so called image based or video based eye tracker.

Image based

These systems are based on digital images of the front of the eye, acquired from a video camera and coupled with image processing and machine vision hardware and software. Two types of imaging approaches are commonly used: visible and infrared spectrum imaging (Li et al., 2005). This category of eye tracker algorithms is based on the geometric structure of the eye and on the tracking of its particular features: the pupil - the aperture that lets light into the eye, the iris - the colored muscle group that controls the diameter of the pupil, and the sclera, the white protective tissue that covers the remainder of the eye. A benefit of infrared imaging is that the pupil, rather than the limbus, is the strongest feature contour in the image. Both the sclera and the iris strongly reflect infrared light while only the sclera strongly reflects visible light. Tracking the pupil contour is preferable given that the pupil contour is smaller and more sharply defined than the limbus. Furthermore, due to its size, the pupil is less likely to be occluded by the eyelids. Pupil and iris edge (or limbus) are the most used tracking features, in general extracted through the computation of the image gradient (Brolly & Mulligan, 2004; Ohno et al., 2002; Wang & Sung, 2002; Zhu & Yang, 2002), or fitting a template model to the image and finding the best one consistent with the image (Daugman, 1993; Nishino & Nayar, 2004).

3. Perspective geometry: from a three-dimensional circle to a two-dimensional ellipse

If we want to resort on the detection of the limbus for tasks like iris segmentation and eye tracking, it is necessary good knowledge of the geometrical structure of the eye, in particular of the iris, and to understand how the eye image is projected on the sensor of a camera.

3.1 Eye structure

As it is evident from Fig. 1, the human eye is not exactly a sphere, but it is composed of two parts with different curvatures. The rear part is close to a sphere with radius ranging from 12 to 13 mm, according to anthropomorphic data. The frontal part, where the iris resides, is formed by two chambers, the anterior and the posterior one which are divided by iris and lens. The iris, the pupil, and the anterior chamber are covered by the cornea, that is a transparent lens with fixed focus. The crystalline lens is a lens with variable curvature that changes the focal distance of the eye in order to obtain on focus image of the object of interest on the retina. The cornea (about 8 mm in radius) is linked to a larger unit called the sclera (about 12 mm in radius) by a ring called the limbus, that is the external edge of the iris. The most important

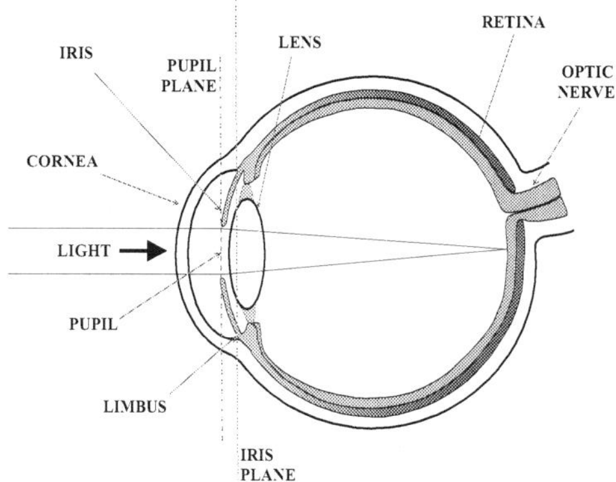

Fig. 1. Structure of the human eye. In the image the main parts related to the presented algorithm, and in particular the pupil plane (magenta line) and the iris plane (green line) are highlighted.

function of the iris is to work as a camera diaphragm. The pupil, that is the hole that allows light to reach the retina, is located in its center. The size of the pupil is controlled by the sphincter muscles of the iris, that adjusts the amount of light which enters the pupil and falls on the retina of the eye. The radius of the pupil consequently changes from about 3 to 9 mm, depending on the lighting of the environment.

The anterior layer of the iris, the visible one, is lightly pigmented, its color results from a combined effect of pigmentation, fibrous tissue and blood vessels. The resulting texture of the iris is a direct expression of the gene pool, thus is unique for each subject like fingerprints. The posterior layer is very darkly pigmented, contrary to the anterior one. Since the pupil is a hole in the iris, is the most striking visible feature of the eye, because its color, except for corneal reflections, is dark black. Pigment frill is the boundary between the pupil and the iris. It is the only visible part of the posterior layer and emphasizes the edge of the pupil.

The iris portion of the pigment frill is protruding respect to the iris plane of a quantity that depends on the actual size of the pupil. From this perspective, even if the iris surface is not planar, the limbus can be considered lying on a plane (see Fig. 1, green line). Similarly, the pupil edge lies on a plane that is a little bit further respect to the center of the eye, because of the protrusion of the pupil (see Fig. 1, magenta line). For what concerns the shape of the pupil edge and the limbus, for our purpose we consider them as two co-axial circles.

3.2 Circle projection

Given an oriented circle C in 3D world space, this is drawn in perspective as an ellipse. This means that if we observe an eye with a camera, the limbus, being approximated by a circle, will project a corresponding perspective locus in terms of the Cartesian coordinates of the camera image plane which satisfy a quadratic equation of the form:

$$f(x_1, x_2) = z_1 x_1^2 + z_2 x_1 x_2 + z_3 x_2^2 + z_4 x_1 + z_5 x_2 + z_6 =$$
$$= \left[x_1^2;\ x_1 x_2;\ x_2^2;\ x_1;\ x_2;\ 1 \right]^T [z_1;\ z_2;\ z_3;\ z_4;\ z_5;\ z_6] =$$
$$= \mathbf{d}^T \mathbf{z} = 0 \tag{1}$$

in which the column vectors $\mathbf{d}$ and $\mathbf{z}$ are, respectively, termed the dual-Grassmannian and Grassmannian coordinates of the conics, and where $4z_1 z_3 - z_2 > 0$ to be an ellipse. In the projective plane it is possible to associate to the affine ellipse, described by Eq.1, its homogeneous polynomial $w^2 f(x/w, y/w)$ obtaining a quadratic form:

$$\mathbf{Q}(x, y, w) = w^2 f(x/w, y/w) = z_1 x^2 + z_2 xy + z_3 x^2 + z_4 xw + z_5 yw + z_6 w^2 . \tag{2}$$

Posing Eq.2 equal to zero gives the equation of an elliptic cone in the projective space. The ellipse in the image plane and the limbus circle are two sections of the same cone, whose vertex is the origin, that we assume to be at the principal point of the camera. The quadratic form in Eq.2 can also be written in matrix form. Let $\mathbf{x}$ be a column vector with components $[x; y; w]$ and $\mathbf{Z}$ the 3x3 symmetric matrix of the Grassmannian coordinates:

$$\mathbf{Z} = \begin{bmatrix} z_1 & z_2/2 & z_4/2 \\ z_2/2 & z_3 & z_5/2 \\ z_4/2 & z_5/2 & z_6 \end{bmatrix}$$

Then:

$$\mathbf{Q}(\mathbf{x}) = \mathbf{Q}_{\mathbf{Z}}(\mathbf{x}) = \mathbf{x}^T \mathbf{Z} \mathbf{x} \tag{3}$$

where the subscript means that the associated matrix to the quadratic form is $\mathbf{Z}$. Together with its associated quadratic form coefficients, an ellipse is also described, in a more intuitive way, through its geometric parameters: center (x_c, y_c), orientation φ, major and minor semiaxes $[a, b]$. Let see how to recover the geometric parameters knowing the quadratic form matrix $\mathbf{Z}$.

The orientation of the ellipse can be computed knowing that this depends directly from the xy term z_2 of the quadratic form. From this we can express the rotation matrix $\mathbf{R}_\varphi$:

$$\mathbf{R}_\varphi = \begin{bmatrix} \cos\varphi & -\sin\varphi & 0 \\ \sin\varphi & \cos\varphi & 0 \\ 0 & 0 & 1 \end{bmatrix}$$

If we apply the matrix $\mathbf{R}_\varphi^T$ to the quadratic form in Eq.3, we obtain:

$$\begin{aligned} Q_Z(\mathbf{R}_\varphi^T \mathbf{x}) &= \left(\mathbf{R}_\varphi^T \mathbf{x}\right)^T \mathbf{Z}\left(\mathbf{R}_\varphi^T \mathbf{x}\right) \\ &= \mathbf{x}^T \mathbf{R}_\varphi \mathbf{Z}\mathbf{R}_\varphi^T \mathbf{x} \\ &= \mathbf{x}^T \mathbf{Z}' \mathbf{x} \\ &= Q_{Z'}(\mathbf{x}) . \end{aligned}$$

We obtain the orientation of the ellipse computing the transformation $\mathbf{Z}' = \mathbf{R}_\varphi \mathbf{Z}\mathbf{R}_\varphi^T$ which nullifies the xy term in $\mathbf{Z}$, resulting in a new matrix $\mathbf{Z}'$:

$$\mathbf{Z}' = \begin{bmatrix} z_1 & 0 & z_4'/2 \\ 0 & z_3' & z_5'/2 \\ z_4'/2 & z_5'/2 & z_6' \end{bmatrix}$$

This is characterized by the angle φ:

$$\varphi = \begin{cases} \frac{1}{2}\arctan\left(\frac{z_2}{z_1 - z_3}\right) & (z_1 - z_3) > 0 \\ \frac{1}{2}\arctan\left(\frac{z_2}{z_1 - z_3}\right) + \frac{\pi}{2} & (z_1 - z_3) < 0 \end{cases}$$

Once we computed $\mathbf{Z}'$, we can obtain the center coordinates of the rotated ellipse resolving the system of partial derivative equations of $Q_{Z'}(\mathbf{x})$ with respect to x and y, obtaining:

$$\begin{cases} \partial_x Q_{Z'}([x';y';1])|_{x'=x_c'} = 0 \\ \partial_y Q_{Z'}([x';y';1])|_{y'=y_c'} = 0 \end{cases}$$

$$\begin{cases} 2z_1 x_c' + z_4 = 0 \\ 2z_3 y_c' + z_5 = 0 \end{cases}$$

resulting in

$$\begin{cases} x_c' = -\dfrac{z_4'}{2z_1'} \\ y_c' = -\dfrac{z_5'}{2z_3'} \end{cases}$$

Then, we can translate the ellipse through the matrix $\mathbf{T}$,

$$\mathbf{T} = \begin{bmatrix} 1 & 0 & x_c' \\ 0 & 1 & y_c' \\ 0 & 0 & 1 \end{bmatrix}$$

to nullify the x and y term of the quadratic form:

$$\mathbf{Z}'' = \mathbf{T}^T \mathbf{Z}' \mathbf{T}$$

$$\mathbf{Z}'' = \begin{bmatrix} z_1'' & 0 & 0 \\ 0 & z_3'' & 0 \\ 0 & 0 & z_6'' \end{bmatrix}$$

$\mathbf{Z}''$ represents the canonical form of the ellipse:

$$z_1'' x^2 + z_3'' y^2 + z_6'' = 0 .$$

Now the major and minor semiaxes of the ellipse will be:

$$a = \sqrt{-\frac{z_6''}{z_1''}}$$

$$b = \sqrt{-\frac{z_6''}{z_3''}}$$

and the (xc, yc) are the center coordinates in the original reference frame (x, y):

$$\begin{bmatrix} x_c \\ y_c \\ 1 \end{bmatrix} = \mathbf{R}_\varphi \begin{bmatrix} x_c' \\ y_c' \\ 1 \end{bmatrix}$$

3.3 Pupil and Iris projection

Pupil and iris move together, rotating with the eye, so are characterized by equal orientation in the space. As shown in Fig.2, the slight difference in position between the pupil and iris plane cause the two projective cones to be not coaxial. Though this difference is relatively small, this fact reflects directly on the not geometrical correspondence between the center coordinates of the two projected ellipses on the image plane: pupil and limbus projections are not concentric. From Fig.2, it is also evident that, for obvious reasons, the dimensions of the two ellipse, i.e. the major and minor semiaxes, are very different (leaving out the fact that pupil changes its aperture with the amount of light). On the other side, if we observe the shape of the two ellipses, we can see that there are no visible differences: one seems to be the scaled version of the other. This characteristic is enclosed in another geometric parameter of the elliptic curve (and of the conic section in general): the eccentricity. The eccentricity of the ellipse (commonly denoted as either e or ϵ) is defined as follow:

$$e = \varepsilon = \sqrt{\frac{a^2 - b^2}{a^2}} = \sqrt{1 - \left(\frac{b}{a}\right)^2}$$

where a and b are the major and minor semiaxes. Thus, for ellipse it assumes values in the range $0 < \varepsilon < 1$. This quantity is independent of the dimension of the ellipse, and acts as a scaling factor between the two semiaxes, in such a way that we can write one semiaxis as

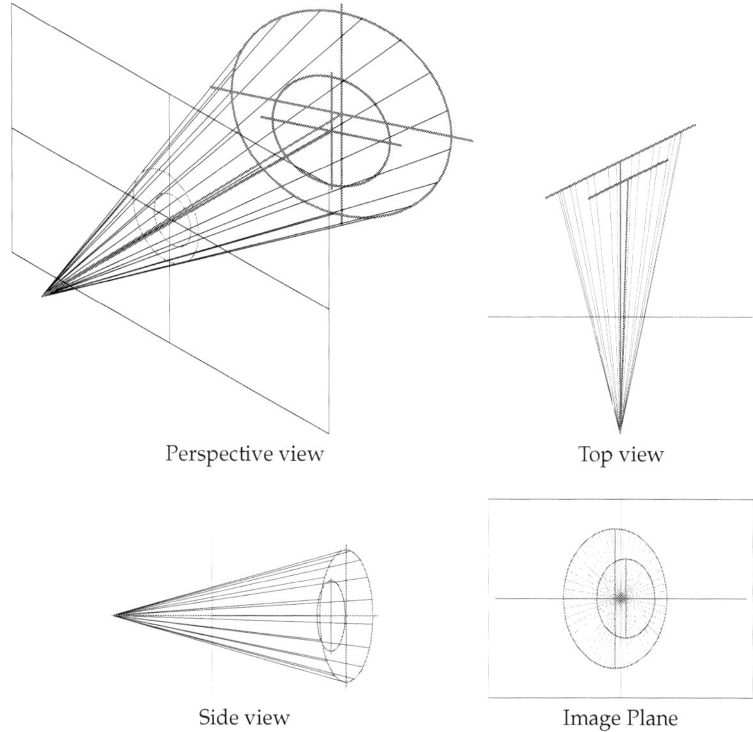

Fig. 2. Cone of projection of limbus (red) and pupil (blue) circles. For sake of simplicity, the limbus circle is rotated about its center, that lies along the optical axis of the camera. The axis of rotation is vertical, providing a shrink of the horizontal radius on the image plane. On the image plane, the center of the limbus ellipse, highlighted by the major and minor semiaxes, is evidently different from the actual center of the limbus circle, that is the center of the image plane, and is emphasized by the projection of the circle radii (gray lines).

function of the other: $a = b\sqrt{1 - \varepsilon^2}$. In our case, pupil and limbus ellipses have, in practical, the same eccentricity: we speak about differences in the order of 10^{-2}. It remains to take into account the orientation φ. Also in this case, as for the eccentricity, there are no essential differences: we can assume that pupil and limbus share the same orientation, unless errors in the order of $0.01°$.

4. Ellipse fitting on the image plane

4.1 Pupil ellipse fitting

The ellipse fitting algorithms presented in literature can be collected into two main groups: voting/clustering and optimization methods. To the first group belong methods based on the Hough transform (Leavers, 1992; Wu & Wang, 1993; Yin et al., 1992; Yuen et al., 1989), on RANSAC (Rosin, 1993; Werman & Geyzel, 1995), on Kalman filtering (Porrill, 1990;

Rosin & West, 1995), and on fuzzy clustering (Davé & Bhaswan, 1992; Gath & Hoory, 1995). All these methods are robust to occlusion and outliers, but are slow, heavy from the memory allocation point of view and not so accurate. In the second group we can find methods based on the Maximum Likelihood (ML) estimation (Chojnacki et al., 2000; Kanatani & Sugaya, 2007; Leedan & Meer, 2000; Matei & Meer, 2006). These are the most accurate methods, whose solution already achieves the theoretical accuracy Kanatani-Cramer-Rao (KCR) limit. First introduced by Kanatani (1996; 1998) and then extended by Chernov & Lesort (2004), KCR limit is for geometric fitting problems (or as Kanatani wrote "constraint satisfaction problems") the analogue of the classical Cramer-Rao (CR) limit, traditionally associated to linear/nonlinear regression problems: KCR limit represents a lower bound on the covariance matrix of the estimate. The problem related to these algorithms is that they require iterations for non linear optimization, and in case of large values of noise, they often fail to converge. They are computationally complex and they do not provide a unique solution. Together with ML methods, there is another group of algorithms that, with respect to a set of parameters describing the ellipse, minimizes a particular distance measure function between the set of points to be fitted and the ellipse. These algorithms, also referred as "algebraic" methods, are preferred because they are fast and accurate, notwithstanding they may give not optimal solutions. The best known algebraic method is the least squares, or algebraic distance minimization or direct linear transformation (DLT). As seen in Eq.1, a general ellipse equation can be represented as a product of vectors:

$$\mathbf{d}^T \mathbf{z} = [x^2;\ xy;\ y^2;\ x;\ y;\ 1]^T [a;\ b;\ c;\ d;\ e;\ f] = 0 .$$

Given a set of N point to be fitted, the vector $\mathbf{d}$ becomes the $N \times 6$ design matrix $\mathbf{D}$

$$\mathbf{D} = \begin{bmatrix} x_1^2 & x_1 y_1 & y_1^2 & x_1 & y_1 & 1 \\ \vdots & \vdots & \vdots & \vdots & \vdots & \vdots \\ x_N^2 & x_N y_N & y_N^2 & x_N & y_N & 1 \end{bmatrix}$$

The least square fitting implies to minimize the sum of the squared distance (or algebraic distance) of the curve to each of the N points:

$$\mathrm{argmin}_\mathbf{z} \left\{ \|\mathbf{Dz}\|^2 \right\} . \tag{4}$$

Obviously, Eq.4 is minimized by the null solution $\mathbf{z} = 0$ if no constraint is imposed. The most cited DLT minimization in eye tracking literature is (Fitzgibbon et al., 1996). Here the fitting problem is reformulated as:

$$\mathrm{argmin}_\mathbf{z} \left\{ \mathbf{z}^T \mathbf{Sz} \right\} \ \text{subject to}\ \mathbf{z}^T \mathbf{Cz} = 1 \tag{5}$$

where $\mathbf{S} = \mathbf{D}^T \mathbf{D}$ is the scatter matrix, and $\mathbf{C}$ the 6×6 constraint matrix:

$$\mathbf{C} = \begin{bmatrix} 0 & 0 & -2 & 0 & 0 & 0 \\ 0 & 1 & 0 & 0 & 0 & 0 \\ -2 & 0 & 0 & 0 & 0 & 0 \\ 0 & 0 & 0 & 0 & 0 & 0 \\ 0 & 0 & 0 & 0 & 0 & 0 \\ 0 & 0 & 0 & 0 & 0 & 0 \end{bmatrix}$$

The problem is solved by a quadratically constrained least squares minimization. Applying the Lagrange multipliers and differentiating, we obtain the system:

$$\begin{cases} \mathbf{S}\mathbf{z} - \lambda \mathbf{C}\mathbf{z} = 0 \\ \mathbf{z}^T \mathbf{C}\mathbf{z} = 1 \end{cases} \tag{6}$$

solved by using generalized eigenvectors. Halir & Flusser (1998) found some problems related to the Fitzgibbon et al. (1996) algorithm:

- the constraint matrix $\mathbf{C}$ is singular
- the scatter matrix $\mathbf{S}$ is also close to be singular, and it is singular when ideally the points' set lies exactly on an ellipse
- finding eigenvectors is an unstable computation and can produce wrong solutions.

Halir & Flusser (1998) proposed a solution to these problems breaking up the design matrix $\mathbf{D}$ into two blocks, the quadratic and the linear components:

$$\mathbf{D} = [\mathbf{D}_1 \,|\, \mathbf{D}_2]$$

Next, the scatter matrix $\mathbf{S}$ becomes:

$$\mathbf{S} = \left[\begin{array}{c|c} \mathbf{S}_1 & \mathbf{S}_2 \\ \hline \mathbf{S}_2^T & \mathbf{S}_3 \end{array} \right]$$

The constrained matrix $\mathbf{C}$:

$$\mathbf{C} = \left[\begin{array}{c|c} \mathbf{C}_1 & 0 \\ \hline 0 & 0 \end{array} \right]$$

The Grassmanian coordinate vector $\mathbf{z}$ of the conic is split in:

$$\mathbf{z} = \left[\begin{array}{c} \mathbf{z}_1 \\ \mathbf{z}_2 \end{array} \right]$$

Similarly the eigensystem problem presented in Eq. 6 can be divided into two equation:

$$\begin{aligned} \mathbf{S}_1 \mathbf{z}_1 + \mathbf{S}_2 \mathbf{z}_2 &= \lambda \mathbf{C}_1 \mathbf{z}_1 \\ \mathbf{S}_2^T \mathbf{z}_1 + \mathbf{S}_3 \mathbf{z}_2 &= 0 \end{aligned} \tag{7}$$

from which we have:

$$\mathbf{z}_2 = -\mathbf{S}_3^{-1}\mathbf{S}_2^T \mathbf{z}_1$$

and, substituting in Eq. 7, obtaining:

$$\begin{aligned} (\mathbf{S}_1 - \mathbf{S}_2 \mathbf{S}_3^{-1}\mathbf{S}_2^T)\mathbf{z}_1 &= \lambda \mathbf{C}_1\, \mathbf{z}_1 \\ \mathbf{C}_1^{-1}(\mathbf{S}_1 - \mathbf{S}_2 \mathbf{S}_3^{-1}\mathbf{S}_2^T)\mathbf{z}_1 &= \lambda\, \mathbf{z}_1 \\ \mathbf{M}\mathbf{z}_1 &= \lambda\, \mathbf{z}_1 \ . \end{aligned} \tag{8}$$

It was shown that there is only one elliptical solution $\mathbf{z}_1^e$ of the eigensystem problem in Eq.8, corresponding to the unique negative eigenvalue of $\mathbf{M}$. Thus, the fitted ellipse will be described by the vector:

$$\mathbf{z}^e = \left[\frac{\mathbf{z}_1^e}{-\mathbf{S}_3^{-1}\mathbf{S}_2^T\mathbf{z}_1^e} \right] \qquad (9)$$

or equivalently, by the matrix associated to the quadratic form:

$$\mathbf{Z} = \begin{bmatrix} z_1^e & z_2^e/2 & z_4^e/2 \\ z_2^e/2 & z_3^e & z_5^e/2 \\ z_4^e/2 & z_5^e/2 & z_6^e \end{bmatrix}$$

Recently, Harker et al. (2008) increased the numerical stability by introducing a translation and scaling factor on the data, to yield a so-called mean free coordinates, and improving the matrix partitioning. Once obtained the quadratic form coefficients of the ellipse it remains only to recover the geometric parameters as seen in Sec.3: the center of the coordinates (x_c, y_c), major and minor semiaxes (a, b), and the angle of rotation from the x-axis to the major axis of the ellipse (φ).

4.2 Iris ellipse fitting

Once we have fitted the pupil ellipse in the image plane, we can think, as suggested at the end of Sec.3, to exploit the information obtained from the previous fitting: the geometric parameters of the pupil ellipse. Now, let see how we could use the orientation and eccentricity information derived from the pupil. Knowing the orientation φ, we could transform the (x_i, y_i) data points pairs through the matrix $\mathbf{R}_\varphi$, obtaining:

$$\begin{bmatrix} x_i' \\ y_i' \end{bmatrix} = \mathbf{R}_\varphi^T \begin{bmatrix} x_i \\ y_i \end{bmatrix}$$

This transformation allow us to write the ellipse, in the new reference frame, without taking into account the xy term of the quadratic form. Thus, if we write the expression of a generic ellipse in (x', y') reference frame, centered in (x_c', y_c'), with major semiaxes oriented along the x' axis, we have:

$$b^2(x' - x_c')^2 + a^2(y' - y_c')^2 - a^2 b^2 = 0$$
$$a^2(1 - \varepsilon^2)(x' - x_c')^2 + a^2(y' - y_c')^2 - a^4(1 - \varepsilon^2) = 0 \,.$$

If we assume $x'' = x'\sqrt{1 - \varepsilon^2}$ and $y'' = y'$, reordering the terms in x'' and y'' we have:

$$a^2(x'' - x_c'')^2 + a^2(y'' - y_c'')^2 - a^4(1 - \varepsilon^2) = 0$$
$$z_1''(x''^2 + y''^2) + z_4''x'' + z_5''y'' + z_6'' = 0$$

that is the equation of a circle translated from the origin. This mean that the fitting of an ellipse in (x, y) becomes the fitting of a circle in (x'', y''). The four parameters vector $\mathbf{z}'' = [z_1''; z_4''; z_5''; z_6'']$ of the circle can be obtained using the "Hyperaccurate" fitting methods explained by Al-Sharadqah & Chernov (2009). The approach is similar to that of Fitzgibbon et al. (1996). The objective function to be minimized is always the algebraic distance $\|\mathbf{Dz}\|^2$, in which the design matrix $\mathbf{D}$ becomes an $N \times 4$ matrix:

$$\mathbf{D} = \begin{bmatrix} (x_1''^2 + y_1''^2) & x_1'' & y_1'' & 1 \\ \vdots & \vdots & \vdots & \vdots \\ (x_N''^2 + y_N''^2) & x_N'' & y_N'' & 1 \end{bmatrix}$$

subject to a particular constraint expressed by the matrix $\mathbf{C}$. This leads the same generalized eigenvalue problem seen in Eq. 6, that is solvable choosing the solution with the smallest non-negative eigenvalue. The matrix $\mathbf{C}$ takes into account, with a linear combination, two constraints, introduced by Taubin and Pratt (Pratt, 1987; Taubin, 1991):

- Taubin: $\frac{1}{N} \|\nabla(\mathbf{Dz}'')\|^2 = 1$
- Pratt: $z_4''^2 + z_5''^2 - 4z_1'' z_6'' = 1$.

The Pratt constraint, as seen in the Fitzgibbon method, can be put in a quadratic form

$$\mathbf{z}''^T \mathbf{C}_P \mathbf{z}'' = 1$$

constructing the matrix $\mathbf{C}_P$ as follow:

$$\mathbf{C}_P = \begin{bmatrix} 0 & 0 & 0 & -2 \\ 0 & 1 & 0 & 0 \\ 0 & 0 & 1 & 0 \\ -2 & 0 & 0 & 0 \end{bmatrix}$$

For the Taubin constraint, tougher mathematics is needed to make the quadratic form explicit:

$$\begin{aligned} &\frac{1}{N} \|\nabla(\mathbf{Dz}'')\|^2 \\ &= \frac{1}{N} \|\partial_x(\mathbf{Dz}'')\|^2 + \frac{1}{N} \|\partial_y(\mathbf{Dz}'')\|^2 \\ &= \frac{1}{N} \mathbf{z}''^T \mathbf{D_x}^T \mathbf{D_x} \mathbf{z}'' + \frac{1}{N} \mathbf{z}''^T \mathbf{D_y}^T \mathbf{D_y} \mathbf{z}'' \\ &= \mathbf{z}''^T \left[\frac{\mathbf{D_x}^T \mathbf{D_x} + \mathbf{D_y}^T \mathbf{D_y}}{N} \right] \mathbf{z}'' \\ &= \mathbf{z}''^T \mathbf{C}_{Tb} \mathbf{z}'' \end{aligned}$$

where $\mathbf{D_x}$ and $\mathbf{D_y}$ are, respectively, the partial derivatives of the design matrix with respect to x'' and y''. Thus $\mathbf{C}_{Tb}$ is

$$\mathbf{C}_{Tb} = \begin{bmatrix} 4(\overline{x''^2 + y''^2}) & 2\overline{x''} & 2\overline{y''} & 0 \\ 2\overline{x''} & 1 & 0 & 0 \\ 2\overline{y''} & 0 & 1 & 0 \\ 0 & 0 & 0 & 0 \end{bmatrix}$$

where $\bar{x}$ represents the standard sample mean notation $\bar{x} = \frac{1}{N} \sum_{i=1}^{N} x_i$. Besides, in (Al-Sharadqah & Chernov, 2009), deriving the variance of the Taubin and Pratt algebraic fit, they verified that expressing the constraint matrix $\mathbf{C}$ as follow:

$$\mathbf{C} = 2\mathbf{C}_{Tb} - \mathbf{C}_P$$

produces an algebraic circle fit with essential bias equal to zero. For this reason they called it *hyperaccurate*. Once we have obtained the solution $\mathbf{z}''$, we must scale it to the (x', y') reference frame with the scaling matrix $\mathbf{T}_{ecc}$:

$$\mathbf{T}_{ecc} = \begin{bmatrix} \sqrt{1-\varepsilon^2} & 0 & 0 \\ 0 & 1 & 0 \\ 0 & 0 & 1 \end{bmatrix}$$

to obtain

$$\mathbf{Z}' = \mathbf{T}_{ecc}^{T}\mathbf{Z}''\mathbf{T}_{ecc}$$

$$= \mathbf{T}_{ecc}^{T} \begin{bmatrix} z_1'' & 0 & z_4''/2 \\ 0 & z_1''^e & z_5''/2 \\ z_4''/2 & z_5''/2 & z_6'' \end{bmatrix} \mathbf{T}_{ecc}$$

$$= \begin{bmatrix} (1-\varepsilon^2)z_1'' & 0 & \sqrt{1-\varepsilon^2}z_4''/2 \\ 0 & z_1''^e & z_5''/2 \\ \sqrt{1-\varepsilon^2}z_4''/2 & z_5''/2 & z_6'' \end{bmatrix}$$

and then again, rotate $\mathbf{Z}'$ to the original frame (x, y), applying to rotation matrix $\mathbf{R}_{\varphi}$:

$$\mathbf{Z} = \mathbf{R}_{\varphi}^{T}\mathbf{Z}'\mathbf{R}_{\varphi}$$

$$= \begin{bmatrix} z_1 & z_2/2 & z_4/2 \\ z_2/2 & z_3 & z_5/2 \\ z_4/2 & z_5/2 & z_6 \end{bmatrix}$$

5. Iris and pupil segmentation

A proper segmentation of the iris area is essential in applications such iris recognition and eye tracking. In fact it defines in the first case, the image region used for feature extraction and recognition, while in the second case is instrumental to detect the size and shape of the limbus, and consequently an effective estimation of the eye rotation. The first step to be achieved for this purpose is to develop a system that is able to obtain images of the eye that are stable to different lighting conditions of the environment.

5.1 Pupil detection

- **Reflex removal**
  In order to be able to find correctly both the center of the pupil and the edge between

the pupil and the iris, it is fundamental to remove effectively the light reflections on the corneal surface. Working with IR or near IR light, the reflection on the corneas are considerably reduced, because the light in the visible power spectrum (artificial lights, computer monitor, etc.) is removed by the IR cut filter. The only sources of reflections are the natural light and the light from the illuminator, but working in indoor environment, the first is not present. The illuminators, posed at a distance of $\approx$ 10 cm from the corneal surface, produce reflections of circular shape that can be removed with a morphological open operation. This operation performed on the IR image I, and it is composed of an erosion followed by a dilation:

$$I_{OP} = A \circ d = (A \ominus d) \oplus d$$

where d is the structuring element and is the same for both operations, *i.e.* a disk of size close to the diameter of the reflections. The operation, usually used to remove small islands and thin filaments of object pixels, with this structuring elements has also the effect of removing all the reflections smaller than the disk. The reflections position is individuated thresholding the image resulting from the subtraction of the original image I with the opened one I_{OP}. In order not to flatten the image and to preserve the information, the new image I_r is equal to the original one, except for the pixels above the threshold, that are substituted with a low-passed version of the original image. Once the corneal reflection regions are correctly located on the image, they are ignored in the next steps of the algorithm.

- **Detection of the pupil center**
  The second step in the processing of the eye image is to roughly locate the center of the iris so to properly center the domain for the pupil edge detection. The I_r is transformed into a binary image where the darkest pixels, defined by a threshold at the 10% of the image maximum, are set to 0, while the others are set to 1. In this way the points belonging to the pupil are segmented, since they are the dark part of the image. In this part of the image, are eventually present points belonging to the eyelashes, to the glasses frame and to and other elements that are as dark as the pupil (See Fig. 5).

  From the binary image, we calculate the chamfer distance, considering that the pixel farthest from any white pixel is the darkest one. The dark points due to other than the pupil, are usually few in number (as for eyelashes) or not far from the white ones (as for glasses frame). On the other side, the pupil area is round shape and quite thick, so that the position of the darkest pixel is usually found to be inside the pupil, and it is approximately the center of the pupil $C = [x_c, y_c]$. From this perspective, a diffuse and uniform illumination is helpful to isolate the correct points and thus to find the correct pupil center.

- **Detection of the edge between pupil and iris**
  Starting from a plausible pupil center, the capability to correctly locate the pupil edge is subtended to the domain that we define for the research. From the chamfer distance it is possible to evaluate the maximum radius R_{max} where the pupil is contained. In fact it is composed of a large number of pupil points centered around (x_c, y_c), with some points belonging to eyelashes and other, spread in the image. From this perspective, the R_{max} is computed as the first minimum of the histogram of the chamfer distance. Once the search domain is defined, the edge between the pupil and the iris can be located computing the

derivative of the intensity of the image along a set of rays, originating from the center of the pupil. In such way each ray $\mathbf{r}$ can be written with the parametric equation:

$$\mathbf{r}(\rho, t) = \begin{bmatrix} x - x_c \\ y - y_c \end{bmatrix} = \rho \begin{bmatrix} \cos(t) \\ \sin(t) \end{bmatrix} = \rho \mathbf{u}(t)$$

where t varies between 0 and 2π, and ρ between 0 and R_{max}. The directional derivative along a particular direction $t = t^*$ on a ray $\mathbf{r}(\rho, t^*)$ is:

$$D_\rho I_r = \frac{dI_r(\mathbf{r}(\rho, t^*))}{d\rho}$$

For each ray, the edge is identified as the maximum of the derivative. Since it considers the intensity value of the image along the ray, this method can be sensitive to noise and reflections, finding false maxima, and detecting false edge points. In order to prevent the sensitivity to noise, instead of computing the derivative along the rays' direction, it is possible to compute the spatial gradient of the intensity, obtaining a more stable and effective information on the pupil edge. The gradient is computed on the smoothed image $\tilde{I} = G * I_r$, where $*$ is the convolutional product between G and I_r, and G is the 2D Gaussian kernel used to smooth the image:

$$\nabla \cdot (G * I_r) = \nabla \cdot \tilde{I} = (\frac{\partial \tilde{I}}{\partial x}, \frac{\partial \tilde{I}}{\partial y}) \tag{10}$$

Exploiting the properties of the gradient, the Eq. 10 can be written as $\nabla G * I_r$, that means that the spatial gradient is computed through the gradient of a Gaussian kernel. Since the feature we want to track with the spatial gradient is a curve edge, the ideal filter to locate is not like those obtained by ∇G, but a filter with the same curvature of the edge. Moreover, since the exact radius of the circle is unknown, and its curvature depends on it, also the size of the filter changes with the image location. Following this considerations it is possible to design a set of spatio-variant filters that take into account both the curvature and the orientation of the searched feature, at each image location, with the consequence of increasing drastically the computational cost. The solution adopted to obtain a spatio-variant filtering using filters of constant shape and size, is to transform the image from a Cartesian to a polar domain. The polar transform of I_r, with origin in (x_c, y_c) is:

$$I_w(\rho, t) = \mathcal{F}\{I_r(x, y); (x_c, y_c)\}$$

where $\mathcal{F}$ is defined by the mapping from (x, y) to (ρ, t) such that:

$$\begin{cases} \rho(x, y) = \sqrt{(x - x_c)^2 + (y - y_c)^2} \\ t(x, y) = \arctan \frac{y - y_c}{x - x_c} \end{cases}$$

where I_w is the warped image in the polar domain. The transform $\mathcal{F}$ is invertible, and defined by the mapping in Eq. 5.1. In such way the searched feature is transformed from a circle to a straight horizontal line, as for the normalization of the iris image (Ferreira et al., 2009; Rahib & Koray, 2009), and can be effectively detected considering only the first component of the spatial gradient (See Fig. 3a), i.e. $(\nabla G)_\rho * I_w = \partial \tilde{I}_w / \partial \rho$. Nevertheless, as introduced in Sec. 3, the shape of the pupil edge is a circle only when the plane that lies on the pupil's edge is perpendicular to the optical axis of the camera, otherwise its projection on the image plane is an ellipse. In this case, a polar domain is not the ideal to represent the feature, because the edge is not a straight line (See Fig. 3b). In order to represent the image in a domain where the feature is a straight line, *i.e.* it can be located with a single component of the spatial gradient, we developed a transformation from the Cartesian to an "elliptical" domain:

$$\begin{cases} \rho(x,y) = \sqrt{(x'-x_c)^2 + \frac{(y'-y_c)^2}{\sqrt{1-e^2}}} \\ t(x,y) = \arctan(\frac{y'-y_c}{x'-x_c}\frac{1}{\sqrt{1-e^2}}) \end{cases}$$

where (x',y') is the (x,y) domain, rotated of an angle φ in such way:

$$\begin{cases} x' = x\cos(\varphi) - y\sin(\varphi) \\ y' = x\sin(\varphi) + y\cos(\varphi) \end{cases}$$

And from the elliptic domain to the Cartesian one:

$$\begin{cases} x(\rho,t) = a\cos(t)\cos(\varphi) - b\sin(t)\sin(\varphi) + x_c \\ y(\rho,t) = a\cos(t)\sin(\varphi) + b\sin(t)\cos(\varphi) + y_c \end{cases} \tag{11}$$

where φ is the orientation of the ellipse, and $a = \rho$ is the major semi-axis, and $b = a\sqrt{1-e^2}$ is the minor one.

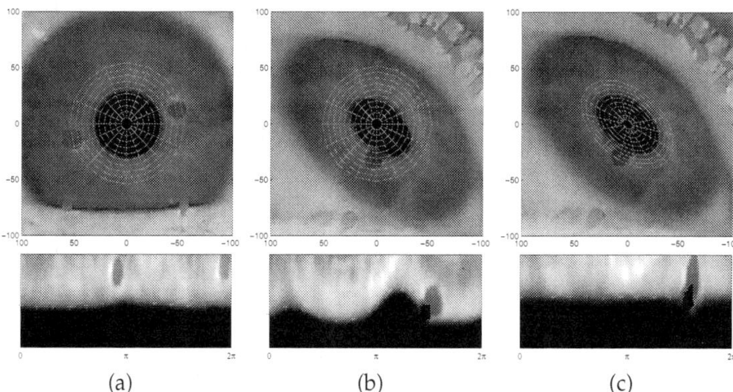

(a)   (b)   (c)

Fig. 3. Image of the pupil in Cartesian domain (top row) and transformed in polar (bottom row, a-b) and "elliptic" domain (bottom row, c). In image (a) the eye is looking almost toward the camera producing a circular limbus and pupils edge, while in image (b) and (c) it is looking at an extreme gaze, producing an elliptical pupil and iris. In the Cartesian images it is shown the transformed domain (magenta grid), while in the transformed images it is shown the position of the pupil edge (magenta crosses).

- **Pupil fitting**

  Since at this step no information is known about the orientation φ and eccentricity ε of the ellipse that describes the edge of the pupil, the points found are used to compute the ellipse parameters without any constraint, as explained in Sec. 4.1 from Eq. 8-9.

  At the first step the two axes are initialized to R_{max} and φ to zero. Once the maxima have been located in the warped image I_w, *i.e.* in the (ρ, t) domain, the Eq. 11 can be used to transform the points into the Cartesian coordinates system, in order to obtain a fitting for the ellipse equation of the pupil. In order to exploit the "elliptical" transformation and to obtain a more precise estimation of the ellipse, the fitting is repeated in a cycle where at each step the new domain is computed using the a, b and φ obtained by the fitting achieved at the previous step.

5.2 Iris detection

Analyzing both the images in the Cartesian domain I_r and in the warped one I_w (see Fig. 3), it is evident the high intensity change between the pupil and the iris points. With such a variation, the localization of the pupil edge is precise and stable even if a polar domain is used. Much more complicated is the detection of the limbus, for different reasons: first, the edge between iris and sclera is larger and less defined respect to the edge between pupil and iris, second, the pupil edge is almost never occluded, except during blinks, while the limbus is almost always occluded by the eyelids, even for small gaze angles. With the purpose of fitting the correct ellipse on the limbus, it is mandatory to distinguish the points between iris and sclera from the points between iris and eyelids.

- **Iris edge detection**

  Following the same procedure used to locate the points of the pupil edge, the image where the reflections are removed I_r, is warped with an elliptical transformation using Eq. 11. Differently from the pupil, the domain is designed with a guess of the parameters, because, as presented in Sec. 3, the perspective geometry allows to use the same φ and e found for the pupil. The only parameter that is unknown is ρ, that at the first step of the iteration is defined to be within $[R_{pupil}, 3R_{pupil}]$. In such way it is ensured that the limbus is inside the search area, even in case of a small pupil.

  As in for the pupil edge, the ellipse equation that describes the limbus is obtained by the maxima of the gradient computed on the warped image. As explained in Sec. 4.2, the fitting is limited to the search of (x_c, y_c) and a, because φ and ε are those of the pupil. In order to prevent deformations of the ellipse due to false maxima that can be found in correspondence of eyelashes or eyebrows, we compute the euclidean distance between the maxima and the fitted ellipse. The fitting is then repeated not considering the points that are more than one standard deviation distant from the ellipse.

  In order to obtain a more precise identification of the iris edge, no matter if the points belong to the limbus or to the transition between the iris and the eyelids, the search is repeated in a loop where the parameters used to define the domain at the current step are those estimated at the previous one. Differently from the pupil search, the size of the parameter ρ is refined step by step, halving it symmetrically respect to the fitted ellipse.

- **Removal of eyelid points**

  Once the correct points of the edge of the iris are found, in order to obtain correctly the limbus, it is necessary to remove the maxima belonging to the eyelids. Starting from the consideration that the upper and lower eyelid borders can be described by parabola segments (Daugman, 1993; Stiefelhagen & Yang, 1997), it is possible to obtain the parameters that describe the parabolas. With the specific purpose of removing the eyelid points, and without requiring to precisely locate the eyelids, it is possible to make some assumptions.

First, the parabolas pass through the eyelid corners, that slightly move with the gaze and with the aperture of the eyelids. If the camera is fixed, as in our system, those two points can be considered fixed and identified during the calibration procedure. Second, the maxima located at the same abscissa on the Cartesian image respect to the center of the iris, can be considered belonging to the upper and lower eyelids. The (x_i, y_i) pairs of these points can be used in a least square minimization:

$$\text{argmin}_{\mathbf{z}} \left\{ \|\mathbf{y} - \mathbf{Dz}\|^2 \right\}$$

where $\mathbf{D}$ is the N $\times$ 3 design matrix:

$$\mathbf{D} = \begin{bmatrix} x_1^2 & x_1 & 1 \\ \vdots & \vdots & \vdots \\ x_N^2 & x_N & 1 \end{bmatrix}$$

$\mathbf{z} = [a; b; c]$ is the parameters column vector that describe the parabola's equations, and $\mathbf{y} = [y_1; \ldots; y_N]$ is the ordinate column vector. The solution can be obtained solving the linear equation system of the partial derivative of Eq. 12 with respect to $\mathbf{z}$:

$$\mathbf{z} = \mathbf{S}^{-1} \mathbf{D}^T \mathbf{y}$$

where $\mathbf{S} = \mathbf{D}^T \mathbf{D}$ is the scatter matrix.

This first guess for the parabolas provides not a precise fitting of the eyelids, but a very effective discrimination of the limbus maxima. In fact it is possible to remove the points that have a positive ordinate respect to the upper parabola, and those that have a negative ordinate respect to the lower parabola, because they probably belong to the eyelids (See Fig. 6, white points). The remaining points can be considered the correct points of the edge between the iris and the sclera (See Fig. 6, red points), and used for the last fitting of the limbus ellipse (See Fig. 6, green line).

5.3 A quantitative evaluation of iris segmentation

In order to evaluate the reliability of the proposed algorithm in a large variety of cases, we performed an extensive test on the CASIA Iris Image Database (CASIA-IrisV1, 2010). After that, the algorithm was tested on images taken from a hand-made acquiring system, designed to obtain images where the eye centered in the image, with the minor number of corneal reflections possible, and taken in a indoor environment with artificial and diffuse light so to have an almost constant pupil size.

5.3.1 CASIA Iris Database

CASIA Iris Image Database is a high quality image database realized to develop and to test iris segmentation and recognition algorithms. In particular, the subset CASIA-Iris-Thousand contains 20.000 iris images taken in IR light, from 1.000 different subjects. The main sources of variations in the subset are eyeglasses and specular reflections.

Since the eye position in the image changes from subject to subject, it is not possible to define the eyelid corner position used to fit the eyelids parabolas. The algorithm was slightly modified to make it work with CASIA-Iris-Thousand, positioning the "fixed" points at the same ordinate of the pupil center, and at an abscissa that is $\pm5R_{pupil}$ respect to the pupil center as well.

The correct segmentation of the iris and the pupil may fail for different reasons (See Fig 5). Concerning the pupil, the algorithm may fail in the detection of its center if in the image are present dark areas, like in case of non uniform illumination and if the subject is wearing glasses (a-b). One other source of problems is if the reflexes are in the pupil area and are not properly removed, because they can be detected as pupil edges, leading to a smaller pupil (c). Moreover the pupil edge can be detected erroneously if a part of its edge is occluded by the eyelid or by the eyelashes (d-f). Concerning the iris, since its fitting is constrained by the pupil shape, if the pupil detection is wrong consequently the iris can be completely wrong or deformed. Even if the pupil is detected correctly, when the edge between the iris and the sclera come to have low contrast, for reasons like not uniform illumination, not correct camera focus, or bright color of the eye, the algorithm may fail in finding the limbus (g-h).

Over the whole set of images, the correct segmentation rate is $94,5\%$, attesting a good efficacy of the algorithm. In fact it is able to segment properly the iris area (See Fig 4) with changhing size of the puil, in presence of glasses and heavy reflexes (a-c), bushy eyelashes (d-e), iris and pupil partially occluded (f).

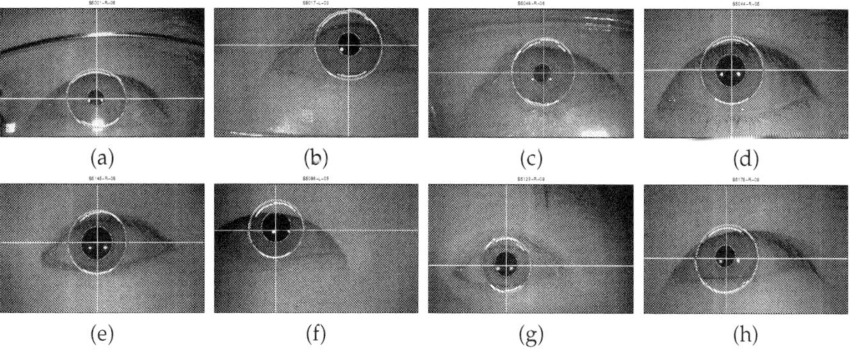

(a)   (b)   (c)   (d)

(e)   (f)   (g)   (h)

Fig. 4. Examples of correct segmentation on the CASIA Iris Database, on the Thousand subset. The magenta ellipse defines the pupil contour, while the green one is the limbus. The red dots represent the points used to compute the limbus ellipse equation, while the white ones are those removed for their possible belonging to the eyelashes or to wrong estimation of the edge.

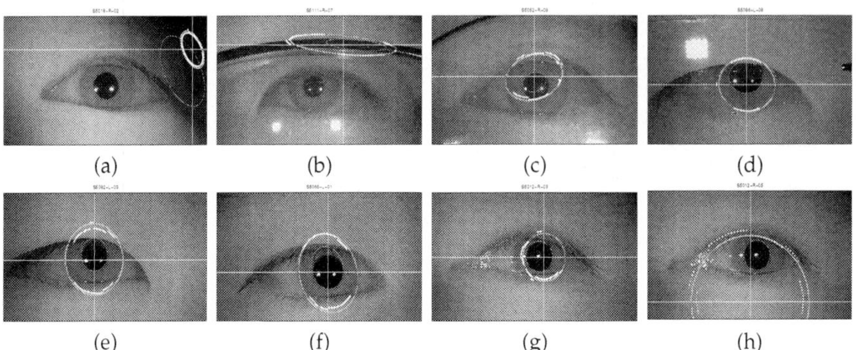

Fig. 5. Examples of wrong segmentation on the CASIA Iris Database, on the Thousand subset. The magenta ellipse defines the pupil contour, while the green one is the limbus. The red dots represent the points used to compute the limbus ellipse equation, while the white ones are those removed for their possible belonging to the eyelashes or to wrong estimation of the edge.

5.4 The proposed system

The images available in the CASIA-Iris-Thousand are characterized by a gaze direction that is close to the primary, and are taken by a camera positioned directly in front of the eye. The images provided by such a configuration are characterized by a pupil and an iris whose edge is close to a perfect circle. In fact, since the normal to the plane that contains the limbus is parallel to the optical axis of the camera, the projected ellipse has eccentricity close to zero. While the feature to be searched in the image has a circular shape, the technique of re-sampling the image with a transformation from Cartesian to polar coordinates is an effective technique (Ferreira et al., 2009; Lin et al., 2005; Rahib & Koray, 2009). In such domain, starting from the assumption that its origin is in the center of the iris, the feature to be searched, *i.e.* the circle of limbus, is transformed to a straight line, and thus it is easier to be individuated than in the Cartesian domain.

On the other side, considering not only the purpose of biometrics but also the eye tracking, the eye can be rotated by large angles respect to the primary position. Moreover, in our system, the camera is positioned some centimeters lower than the eye center in order to prevent as much as possible occlusions in the gaze direction. The images obtained by such a configuration are characterized by the pupil and the iris with an eccentricity higher than zero, that increases the more the gaze direction differs from the optical axis of the camera (see for example Fig. 6, top-right).

Since the presented eye-tracking system is based on the perspective geometry of the pupil and iris circle on the image plane, it is important for the system that the relative position between the eye and the camera stay fixed. On the oder side, for a good easiness of use and freedom of movement of the subject it is important the the system allows free head movement. For this purpose, we developed an head mounted device, in order to guarantee both these features.

5.4.1 Hardware implementation

The head-mounted device is endowed with two cheap USB web cams (Hercules Deluxe Optical Glass) that provide images at a resolution of 800×600 pixels, with a frame rate of 30 fps. The cameras were mounted in the inner part of a chin strap, at a distance of ≈ 60 mm from the respective eye. At this distance, the field of view provided by the cameras, is $[36°, 26°]$, that is more than enough to have a complete view of the eyes. To make them work in infra-red light, the IR-cut filter were removed from the optics, and substituted with a IR-pass filter, with cut frequency of 850 nm. To have a constant illumination of the images, both in daylight or in indoor environments and during night time, the system were endowed with three IR illuminators, that help to keep constant the contrast and the illumination of the stream of images.

In fact, the illuminators produce visible corneal reflexes, that are used as reference feature in other kinds of eye trackers (Eizenman et al., 1984; Morimoto et al., 2000). In our case, since we are seeking to use the limbus position to track the eye, if the reflex, depending on the position of the eye falls in its correspondence, it can lead to the detection of a wrong edge, thus to a wrong gaze estimation. To prevent this case, and considering that the points affected by the reflexes are few respect to the entire limbus edge, these points are removed at the beginning of the image elaboration.

5.4.2 Image acquisition and segmentation

The developed algorithm was tested on three sets of images, taken from different subjects. In each set, the subjects were asked to fixate a grid of points, in order to have the gaze ranging from $-30°$ and $-30°$ of azimuth, and from $-20°$ and $20°$ of elevation, with a step of $5°$. In this way each set is composed by 117 images where the gaze direction is known. The azimuth and elevation angles were defined following a Helmholtz reference frame (Haslwanter, 1995). The use of a transformation of the image from a Cartesian to an elliptic domain allows the algorithm to work properly on the segmentation of the pupil and consequently, as explained in Sec 3, on the segmentation of the iris, even in the cases where the iris is drastically occluded (see for example Fig. 6, center-right).

Considering that the images are captured in an optimal condition, *i.e.* in an indoor environment where the only sources of IR light are the illuminators and the subjects do not wear glasses, and with the eye correctly centered in the image, the algorithm is able to segment properly the pupil and the iris in the 100% of the cases.

6. Eye-tracking

Once the iris circle is detected steadily on the image plane, and its edge is fitted with an ellipse, knowing the coefficient matrix $\mathbf{Z}$ of the quadratic form, it remains to estimate the gaze direction. This can be obtained computing which is the orientation in space of the circle that produces that projection.

6.1 Tracking

Because $\mathbf{Z}$ is a symmetric matrix, it can be diagonalized, leading to a matrix:

$$\mathbf{\Sigma} = \mathrm{diag}(\lambda_1, \lambda_2, \lambda_3)$$

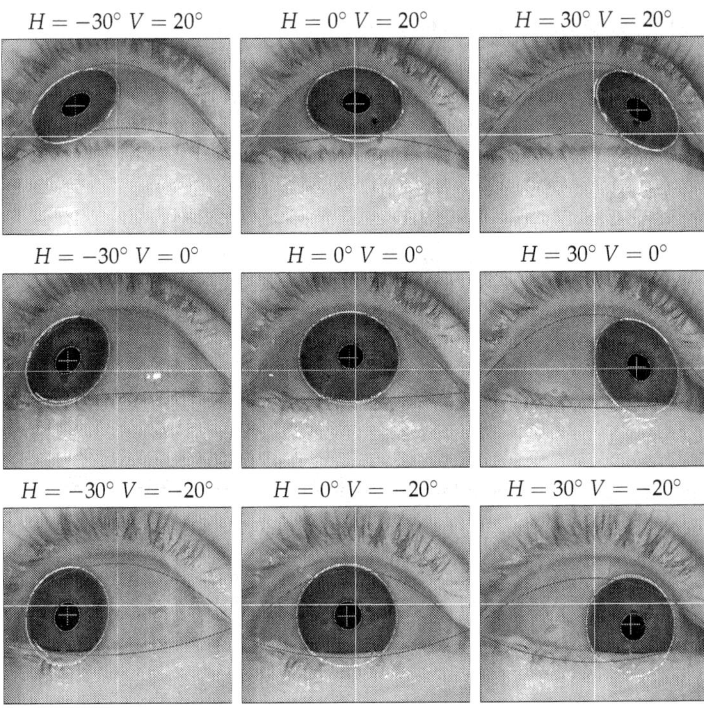

Fig. 6. Subset of the images taken from a subject with the IR camera. The subject is fixating to a grid of nine points at the widest angles of the whole set. The magenta ellipse defines the pupil contour, while the green one is the limbus. The red dots represent the points used to compute the limbus ellipse equation, while the white ones are those removed for their possible belonging to the eyelashes or to wrong estimation of the edge. The blue lines represent the parabolas used to remove the possible eyelashes points.

with $\lambda_1, \lambda_2, \lambda_3 \in \mathbb{R}$. This transformation from $\mathbf{Z}$ to $\mathbf{\Sigma}$ is just a change of basis, and thus $\mathbf{\Sigma}$ may be expressed as $\mathbf{\Sigma} = \mathbf{R}^{-1}\mathbf{Z}\mathbf{R}$, where $\mathbf{R}$ is the matrix changing between the actual orthonormal basis to a new one, formed by three eigenvectors of $\mathbf{Z}$. The columns of $\mathbf{R}$ are the components of the eigenvectors $\mathbf{e}_1, \mathbf{e}_2, \mathbf{e}_3$, and the elements $\lambda_1, \lambda_2, \lambda_3$ of the diagonal of $\mathbf{\Sigma}$ are the associated eigenvalues. For the Sylvester's Law of inertia the signature of $\mathbf{\Sigma}$ is equal to that of $\mathbf{Z}$, $(-, +, +)$; thus only one eigenvalue is negative, and the other are positive. We assume $\lambda_3 < 0$ and $\lambda_2 > \lambda_1 > 0$. If we apply the transformation matrix $\mathbf{R}$ to $\mathbf{Q}_{\mathbf{Z}}(\mathbf{x})$, we obtain:

$$\begin{aligned}
\mathbf{Q}_{\mathbf{Z}}(\mathbf{R}\mathbf{x}) &= (\mathbf{R}\mathbf{x})^T \mathbf{Z}(\mathbf{R}\mathbf{x}) \\
&= \mathbf{x}^T \mathbf{R}^T \mathbf{Z}\mathbf{R}\mathbf{x} \\
&= \mathbf{x}^T \mathbf{\Sigma}\mathbf{x}
\end{aligned}$$

and consider $\mathbf{x}' = \mathbf{R}^T\mathbf{x}$, the equation of the projective cone in the new basis is:

$$\lambda_1 x'^2 + \lambda_2 y'^2 + \lambda_3 w'^2 = 0 \tag{12}$$

which is a cone expressed in canonical form, whose axis is parallel to $\mathbf{e}_3$. Now, look for a while at the intersection of the cone with the plane $w = \frac{1}{\lambda_3^2}$. This is the ellipse:

$$\lambda_1 x'^2 + \lambda_2 y'^2 = 1$$

whose axes are parallel to $\mathbf{e}_1$ and $\mathbf{e}_2$, and semiaxis length are $\sqrt{\lambda_1}$ and $\sqrt{\lambda_2}$. If we consider to cut the cone in Eq.12 with a plane tilted along $\mathbf{e}_1$ there exist a particular angle θ which makes tha plane to intersect the cone in a circle: this circle will be the limbus and θ its tilt angle in the basis described by the rotation matrix $\mathbf{R}$. As suggested in Forsyth et al. (1991), to find θ it is possible to exploit the properties of circle to have equal semiaxes or, equivalently, to have equal coefficient for the x'^2 and y'^2 terms in the quadratic form. Equality of the x'^2 and y'^2 coefficients is achieved by a rotation along the x' axis by an angle $\theta = \pm\arctan\left(\sqrt{\frac{\lambda_2-\lambda_1}{\lambda_1-\lambda_3}}\right)$, which set both the coefficients equal to λ_1. The normal to the plane that intersects the cone in a circle, expressed in the camera coordinate system, is $\mathbf{n} = \mathbf{R}_{cam}\mathbf{R}\mathbf{R}_\theta[0;\ 0;\ -1]$, where:

$$\mathbf{R}_\theta = \begin{bmatrix} 1 & 0 & 0 \\ 0 & \cos\theta & -\sin\theta \\ 0 & \sin\theta & \cos\theta \end{bmatrix}$$

and $\mathbf{R}_{cam}$ is the matrix describing the rotation of the camera with respect the fixed world reference frame.

6.2 Calibration

Since it is not possible to measure with the desired precision the relative position between the center of the eye and nodal point of the camera, and particularly the relative orientation, we developed a calibration procedure with the purpose of estimating the implicit parameters. The subject is asked to fixate a calibration grid of 25 points in a known position. The grid of points is designed to make the subject fixate with an azimuth angle between $-30°$ and $30°$ with steps of $15°$, and with an elevation angle between $-20°$ and $20°$ with steps of $10°$.

The calibration procedure is based on a functional whose minimization provides: (1) the eye position respect to the camera, (2) the camera orientation respect to a fixed reference frame, (4) the radius of the eye.

6.3 Estimation of the gaze direction

In order to have a validation of the algorithm, the estimation of the fixation angle is computed over a different set of points respect to the calibration grid. The grid of point used for the test is designed to make the subject fixate with an azimuth angle between $-20°$ and $20°$ with steps of $5°$, and with an elevation angle between $-10°$ and $10°$ with steps of $5°$.

The error is measured as the angle between the estimated gaze direction and the actual direction of the calibration points. Over the whole set of 45 points, the algorithm is able to provide a mean error of $\approx 0.6°$.

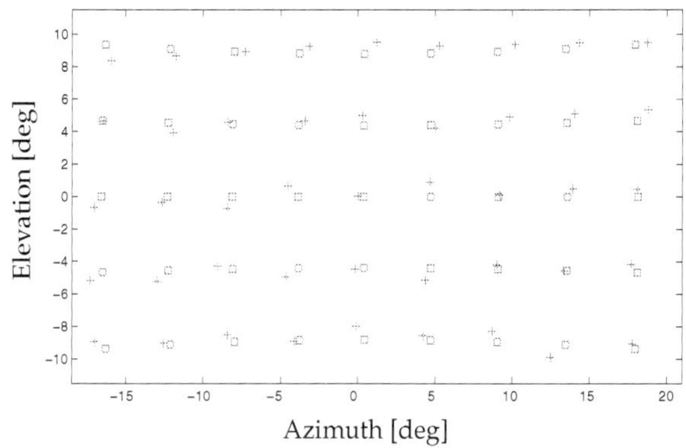

Fig. 7. Azimuthal (horizontal) and elevation (vertical) angles of the grid of fixational points (blue squares), with respect to the angles estimated by the proposed algorithm (red crosses).

7. Discussion and conclusion

We developed a novel approach for iris segmentation and eye tracking that resorts on the geometrical characteristics of the projection of the eye on the image plane.

Once that the pupil center is roughly located and the ellipse that describes the pupil is fitted, the parameters of the pupil ellipse can be exploited to improve the search of the limbus. We developed a transformation of the image to an elliptical domain, that is shaped by the pupil, in order to transform the limbus in a straight line, thus easier to be detected. The points that do not belong to the limbus are removed considering that the border of the superior and inferior eyelids is well described by two parabolas intersecting at the eyelids intersections. The similarity of the projections of iris and pupil allows a proper segmentation even if large parts of the iris are occluded by eyelids. We developed a method that takes into account the orientation and eccentricity of the pupils ellipse in order to fit the limbus ellipse. The iris segmentation algorithm is able to work both on an iris image database and on the images acquired by our system. Since the limbus can be considered a perfect circle oriented in 3D with respect to the image plane, its imaged ellipse is used to compute the gaze direction finding the orientation in space of the circle that projects the fitted ellipse.

Even though the iris segmentation demonstrates a good effectiveness in a large variety of cases and a good robustness to perturbations due to reflections and glasses, the gaze tracking part is in a preliminary implementation, and many improvements can be implemented in the current algorithm. In order to restrain the wrong matching of the pupil center, the pupil search area can be constrained to a circle defined by the pupil points found during the calibration procedure. In fact, considering to calibrate the algorithm over the range of interest for the tracking of the eye, the pupil is searched in an area where it is likely to be, preventing to detect the initial point on the glasses frame or on other dark regions of the image. Moreover, since the system is not endowed with a frontal scene camera, it comes to be more difficult both to calibrate correctly the algorithm and to test it. Currently for the calibration, the subject is posed manually in the desired position respect to the grid, without any chin rest, and she/he is asked to remain steady all along the procedure. Without any visual feedback from where the subject is fixating, any movement between the subject and the grid (due to undesired rotations and translations of the head, or to physiologic nystagmus) becomes an unpredictable and meaningful source of error. The next steps of our research are to implement of a more comfortable and precise calibration procedure, as through a chin rest or a scene camera, and to extend the system from monocular to binocular tracking.

In conclusion, the proposed method, resorting on visible and salient features, like pupil and limbus, and exploiting the known geometry of the structure of the eye, is able to provide a reliable segmentation of the iris that can be in principle used both for non-invasive and low-cost eye tracking and for iris recognition applications.

7.1 Acknowledgment

Portions of the research in this paper use the CASIA-IrisV4 collected by the Chinese Academy of Sciences' Institute of Automation (CASIA).

This work has been partially supported by the Italian MIUR (PRIN 2008) project "Bio-inspired models for the control of robot ocular movements during active vision and 3D exploration".

8. References

Al-Sharadqah, A. & Chernov, N. (2009). Error analysis for circle fitting algorithms, *Electron. J. Stat.* 3: 886–911.

Brolly, X. & Mulligan, J. (2004). Implicit calibration of a remote gaze tracker, *IEEE Conference on CVPR Workshop on Object Tracking Beyond the Visible Spectrum.*

CASIA-IrisV1 (2010). *http://biometrics.idealtest.org.*

Chernov, N. & Lesort, C. (2004). Statistical efficiency of curve fitting algorithms, *Comput. Statist. Data Anal.* 47: 713-728.

Chessa, M., Garibotti, M., Canessa, A., Gibaldi, A., Sabatini, S. & Solari, F. (2012). A stereoscopic augmented reality system for the veridical perception of the 3D scene layout, *International Conference on Computer Vision Theory and Applications (VISAPP 2012).*

Chojnacki, W., Brooks, M., van den Hengel, A. & Gawley, D. (2000). On the fitting of surfaces to data with covariances, *IEEE Trans. Patt. Anal. Mach. Intell.* 22(11): 1294–1303.

Cornsweet, T. & Crane, H. (1973). Accurate two-dimensional eye tracker using first and fourth purkinje images, *J. Opt. Soc. Am.* 63(8): 921–928.

Crane, H. & Steele, C. (1978). Accurate three-dimensional eyetracker, *J. Opt. Soc. Am.* 17(5): 691–705.

Daugman, J. (1993). High confidence visual recognition of persons by a test of statistical independence, *Pattern Analysis and Machine Intelligence, IEEE Transactions on* 15(11): 1148–1161.

Davé, R. N. & Bhaswan, K. (1992). Nonparametric segmentation of curves into various representations, *IEEE Trans. Neural Networks* 3: 643–662.

Dodge, R. & Cline, T. (1901). The angle velocity of eye movements, *Psychological Review*.

Duchowski, A. (2002). A breadth-first survey of eye-tracking applications, *Behav. Res. Methods. Instrum. Comput.* 34(4): 455–470.

Eizenman, M., Frecker, R. & Hallett, P. (1984). Precise non-contacting measurement of eye movements using the corneal reflex, *Vision Research* 24(2): 167–174.

Ferreira, A., Lourenço, A., Pinto, B. & Tendeiro, J. (2009). Modifications and improvements on iris recognition, *BIOSIGNALS09*, Porto, Portugal.

Fitts, P. M., Jones, R. E. & Milton, J. L. (1950). Eye Movements of Aircraft Pilots during Instrument-Landing Approaches., *Aeronautical Engineering Review* (2(9)): 24–29.

Fitzgibbon, A. W., Pilu, M. & Fischer, R. (1996). Direct least squares fitting of ellipses, *Proc. of the 13th International Conference on Pattern Recognition*, Vienna, pp. 253–257.

Forsyth, D., Mundy, J., Zisserman, A., Coelho, C., Heller, A. & Rothwell, C. (1991). Invariant descriptors for 3-D object recognition and pose, *IEEE Trans. Patt. Anal. Mach. Intell.* 13(10): 971–991.

Gath, I. & Hoory, D. (1995). Fuzzy clustering of elliptic ring-shaped clusters, *Pattern Recognition Letters* 16: 727–741.

Halir, R. & Flusser, J. (1998). Numerically stable direct least squares fitting of ellipses, *Sixth International Conference in Central Europe on Computer Graphics and Visualization*, pp. 59–108.

Harker, M., O'Leary, P. & Zsombor-Murray, P. (2008). Direct type-specific conic fitting and eigenvalue bias correction, *Image Vision and Computing* 26: 372–381.

Hartridge, H. & Thompson, L. (1948). Methods of investigating eye movements, *British Journal of Ophthalmology* .

Haslwanter, T. (1995). Mathematics of three-dimensional eye rotations, *Vision Res.* 35(12): 1727–1739.

Jacob, R. J. K. & Karn, K. S. (2003). Eye Tracking in Human-Computer Interaction and Usability Research: Ready to Deliver the Promises, *The Mind's eye: Cognitive The Mind's Eye: Cognitive and Applied Aspects of Eye Movement Research* pp. 573–603.

Javal, E. (1879). Essai sur la Physiologie de la Lecture, *Annales D'Oculistique* .

Kanatani, K. (1996). *Statistical Optimization for Geometric Computation: Theory and Practice*, Elsevier Science Inc., New York, NY, USA.

Kanatani, K. (1998). Cramer-rao lower bounds for curve fitting, *Graph. Models Image Proc.* 60: 93-99.

Kanatani, K. & Sugaya, Y. (2007). Performance evaluation of iterative geometric fitting algorithms, *Comp. Stat. Data Anal.* 52(2): 1208–1222.

Kaufman, A., Bandopadhay, A. & Shaviv, B. (1993). An eye tracking computer user interface, *Virtual Reality, 1993. Proceedings., IEEE 1993 Symposium on Research Frontiers in*, pp. 120–121.

Kyung-Nam, K. & Ramakrishna, R. (1999). Vision-based eye-gaze tracking for human computer interface, *Systems, Man, and Cybernetics, 1999. IEEE SMC '99 Conference Proceedings. 1999 IEEE International Conference on*, Vol. 2, pp. 324–329.

Labati, R. D. & Scotti, F. (2010). Noisy iris segmentation with boundary regularization and reflections removal, *Image and Vision Computing* 28(2): 270 – 277.

Leavers, V. (1992). *Shape Detection in Computer Vision Using the Hough Transform*, Springer-Verlag.

Leedan, Y. & Meer, P. (2000). Heteroscedastic regression in computer vision: Problems with bilinear constraint, *Int. J. Comput. Vision.* 37(2): 127–150.

Li, D., Winfield, D. & Parkhurst, D. (2005). Starburst: A hybrid algorithm for video-based eye tracking combining feature-based and model-based approaches, *Computer Vision and Pattern Recognition - Workshops, 2005. CVPR Workshops. IEEE Computer Society Conference on*, pp. 79-86.

Lin, C., Chen, H., Lin, C., Yeh, M. & Lin, S. (2005). Polar coordinate mapping method for an improved infrared eye-tracking system, *Journal of Biomedical Engineering-Applications, Basis and Communicatitons* 17(3): 141–146.

Mackworth, N. & Thomas, E. (1962). Head-mounted eye-marker camera, *J. Opt. Soc. Am.* 52(6): 713–716.

Matei, B. & Meer, P. (2006). Estimation of nonlinear errors-in-variables models for computer vision applications, *IEEE Trans. Patt. Anal. Mach. Intell.* 28(10): 1537–1552.

Matsumoto, Y. & Zelinsky, A. (2000). An algorithm for real-time stereo vision implementation of head pose and gaze direction measurement, *Automatic Face and Gesture Recognition, 2000. Proceedings. Fourth IEEE International Conference on*, pp. 499 –504.

Mäenpää, T. (2005). An iterative algorithm for fast iris detection, *in* S. Li, Z. Sun, T. Tan, S. Pankanti, G. Chollet & D. Zhang (eds), *Advances in Biometric Person Authentication*, Vol. 3781 of *Lecture Notes in Computer Science*, Springer Berlin/Heidelberg, pp. 127–134.

Morimoto, C., Koons, D., Amir, A. & Flickner, M. (2000). Pupil detection and tracking using multiple light sources, *Image and Vision Computing* 18(4): 331–335.

Nishino, K. & Nayar, S. (2004). Eyes for relighting, *ACM SIGGRAPH* 23(3): 704–711.

Ohno, T., Mukawa, N. & Yoshikawa, A. (2002). Freegaze: a gaze tracking system for everydaygaze interaction, *Eye Tracking Research and Applications Symposium.*

Parkhurst, D. & Niebur, E. (2004). A feasibility test for perceptually adaptive level of detail rendering on desktop systems, *Proceedings of the 1st Symposium on Applied perception in graphics and visualization*, ACM, New York, NY, USA, pp. 49–56.

Porrill, J. (1990). Fitting ellipses and predicting confidence envelopes using a bias corrected kalman filter, *Image Vision and Computing* 8(1): 1140–1153.

Pratt, V. (1987). Direct least-squares fitting of algebraic surfaces, *Computer Graphics* 21: 145–152.

Rahib, A. & Koray, A. (2009). Neural network based biometric personal identification with fast iris segmentation, *International Journal of Control, Automation and Systems* 7: 17–23.

Reulen, J., Marcus, J., Koops, D., de Vries, F., Tiesinga, G., Boshuizen, K. & Bos, J. (1988). Precise recording of eye movement: the iris technique part 1, *Medical and Biological Engineering and Computing* 26: 20–26.

Robinson, D. A. (1963). A method of measuring eye movemnent using a scleral search coil in a magnetic field, *Bio-medical Electronics, IEEE Transactions on* 10(4): 137–145.

Rosin, P. (1993). Ellipse fitting by accumulating five-point fits, *Pattern Recognition Letters* 14: 661–699.

Rosin, P. L. & West, G. A. W. (1995). Nonparametric segmentation of curves into various representations, *IEEE Trans. PAMI* 17: 1140–1153.

Ryan, W., Woodard, D., Duchowski, A. & Birchfield, S. (2008). Adapting starburst for elliptical iris segmentation, *Biometrics: Theory, Applications and Systems, 2008. BTAS 2008. 2nd IEEE International Conference on*, pp. 1–7.

Shackel, B. (1960). Note on mobile eye viewpoint recording, *J. Opt. Soc. Am.* 50(8): 763–768.

Stark, L., Vossius, G. & Young, L. R. (1962). Predictive control of eye tracking movements, *Human Factors in Electronics, IRE Transactions on* 3(2): 52–57.

Stiefelhagen, R. & Yang, J. (1997). Gaze tracking for multimodal human-computer interaction, *Acoustics, Speech, and Signal Processing, 1997. ICASSP-97., 1997 IEEE International Conference on*, Vol. 4, pp. 2617–2620.

Taubin, G. (1991). Estimation of planar curves, surfaces and nonplanar space curves defined by implicit equations, with applications to edge and range image segmentation, *IEEE Trans. Patt. Anal. Mach. Intell.* 13: 1115–1138.

Tinker, M. (1963). *Legibility of Print*, Iowa State University, Ames, IA, USA.

Wang, J. & Sung, E. (2002). Study on eye gaze estimation, *IEEE Transactions on Systems,Man and Cybernetics* 32(3): 332-350.

Wang, J., Sung, E. & Venkateswarlu, R. (2003). Eye gaze estimation from a single image of one eye, *Computer Vision, 2003. Proceedings. Ninth IEEE International Conference on*, Vol. 1, pp. 136 –143.

Werman, M. & Geyzel, G. (1995). Fitting a second degree curve in the presence of error, *IEEE Trans. Patt. Anal. Mach. Intell.* 17(2): 207–211.

Wu, W. & Wang, M. (1993). Elliptical object detection by using its geometric properties, *Pattern Recognition* 26: 1499–1509.

Yarbus, A. (1959). *Eye movements and vision*, Plenum Press, New York.

Yin, R., Tam, P. & Leung, N. (1992). Modification of hough transform for circles and ellipses detection using 2-d array, *Pattern Recognition* 25: 1007–1022.

Yuen, H., Illingworth, J. & Kittler, J. (1989). Detecting partially occluded ellipses using the hough transform, *Image Vision and Computing* 7(1): 31–37.

Zhu, J. & Yang, J. (2002). Subpixel eye gaze tracking, *IEEE Conference on Automatic Faceand Gesture Recognition*.

Feature Extraction Based on Wavelet Moments and Moment Invariants in Machine Vision Systems

G.A. Papakostas, D.E. Koulouriotis and V.D. Tourassis
Democritus University of Thrace,
Department of Production Engineering and Management
Greece

1. Introduction

Recently, there has been an increasing interest on modern machine vision systems for industrial and commercial purposes. More and more products are introduced in the market, which are making use of visual information captured by a camera in order to perform a specific task. Such machine vision systems are used for detecting and/or recognizing a face in an unconstrained environment for security purposes, for analysing the emotional states of a human by processing his facial expressions or for providing a vision based interface in the context of the human computer interaction (HCI) etc..

In almost all the modern machine vision systems there is a common processing procedure called *feature extraction*, dealing with the appropriate representation of the visual information. This task has two main objectives simultaneously, the compact description of the useful information by a set of numbers (features), by keeping the dimension as low as possible.

Image moments constitute an important *feature extraction method* (FEM) which generates high discriminative features, able to capture the particular characteristics of the described pattern, which distinguish it among similar or totally different objects. Their ability to fully describe an image by encoding its contents in a compact way makes them suitable for many disciplines of the engineering life, such as image analysis (Sim et al., 2004), image watermarking (Papakostas et al., 2010a) and pattern recognition (Papakostas et al., 2007, 2009a, 2010b).

Among the several moment families introduced in the past, the orthogonal moments are the most popular moments widely used in many applications, owing to their orthogonality property that comes from the nature of the polynomials used as kernel functions, which they constitute an orthogonal base. As a result, the orthogonal moments have minimum information redundancy meaning that different moment orders describe different parts of the image.

In order to use the moments to classify visual objects, they have to ensure high recognition rates for all possible object's orientations. This requirement constitutes a significant operational feature of each modern pattern recognition system and it can be satisfied during the feature extraction stage, by making the moments invariant under the basic geometric transformations of rotation, scaling and translation.

The most well known orthogonal moment families are: Zernike, Pseudo-Zernike, Legendre, Fourier-Mellin, Tchebichef, Krawtchouk, with the last two ones belonging to the discrete type moments since they are defined directly to the image coordinate space, while the first ones are defined in the continuous space.

Another orthogonal moment family that deserves special attention is the *wavelet moments* that use an orthogonal wavelet function as kernel. These moments combine the advantages of the wavelet and moment analyses in order to construct moment descriptors with improved pattern representation capabilities (Feng et al., 2009).

This chapter discusses the main theoretical aspects of the wavelet moments and their corresponding invariants, while their performance in describing and distinguishing several patterns in different machine vision applications is studied experimentally.

2. Orthogonal image moments

A general formulation of the $(n+m)^{th}$ order orthogonal image moment of a NxN image with intensity function $f(x,y)$ is given as follows:

$$M_{nm} = NF \times \sum_{i=1}^{N} \sum_{j=1}^{N} Kernel_{nm}\left(x_i, y_j\right) f\left(x_i, y_j\right) \qquad (1)$$

where $Kernel_{nm}(.)$ corresponds to the moment's kernel consisting of specific polynomials of order n and repetition m, which constitute the orthogonal basis and NF is a normalization factor. The type of Kernel's polynomial gives the name to the moment family by resulting to a wide range of moment types. Based on the above equation (1) the image moments are the projection of the intensity function $f(x,y)$ of the image on the coordinate system of the kernel's polynomials.

The first introduction of orthogonal moments in image analysis, due to Teague (Teague, 1980), made use of Legendre and Zernike moments in image processing. Other families of orthogonal moments have been proposed over the years, such as Pseudo-Zernike, Fourier-Mellin etc. moments, which better describe the image in process and ensure robustness under arbitrarily intense noise levels.

However, these moments present some approximation errors due to the fact that the kernel polynomials are defined in a continuous space and an approximated version of them is used in order to compute the moments of an image. This fact is the source of an approximation error (Liao & Pawlak, 1998) which affects the overall properties of the derived moments and mainly their description abilities. Moreover, some of the above moments are defined inside the unit disc, where their polynomials satisfy the orthogonality condition. Therefore, a prior coordinates' transformation is required so that the image coordinates lie inside the unit disc. This transformation is another source of approximation error (Liao & Pawlak, 1998) that further degrades the moments' properties.

The following Table 1, summarizes the main characteristics of the most used moment families.

| Moment | Properties | | | |
Family	Kernel Form	Normalization Factor (NF)	Type	Coordinate System
Zernike (Mukundan, & Ramakrishnan, 1998)	$Kernel_{nm}(r,\theta) = \left(\sum_{s=0}^{\frac{n-|m|}{2}} (-1)^s \dfrac{(n-s)!}{s!\left(\dfrac{n+|m|}{2}-s\right)!\left(\dfrac{n-|m|}{2}-s\right)!} r^{n-2s} \right) e^{-jm\theta}$	$\dfrac{n+1}{\pi}$	continuous	Unit disc polar coordinates
Pseudo-Zernike (Mukundan, & Ramakrishnan, 1998)	$Kernel_{nm}(r,\theta) = \left(\sum_{s=0}^{n-|m|} (-1)^s \dfrac{(2n+1-s)!}{s!(n+|m|+1-s)!(n-|m|-s)!} r^{n-s} \right) e^{-jm\theta}$	$\dfrac{n+1}{\pi}$	continuous	Unit disc polar coordinates
Fourier-Mellin (Mukundan, & Ramakrishnan, 1998)	$Kernel_{nm}(r,\theta) = \left(\sum_{k=0}^{n} (-1)^{n+k} \dfrac{(n+k+1)!}{(n-k)!k!(k+1)!} r^k \right) e^{-jm\theta}$	$\dfrac{n+1}{\pi}$	continuous	Unit disc polar coordinates
Legendre (Mukundan, & Ramakrishnan, 1998)	$Kernel_{nm}(x,y) = P_n(x)\ P_m(y)\ \ with\ \ P_n(x) = \dfrac{1}{2^n n!}\dfrac{d^n(x^2-1)^n}{dx^n}$	$\dfrac{(2n+1)(2m+1)}{4}$	continuous	[-1,1]
Tchebichef (Mukundan et al., 2001)	$Kernel_{nm}(x,y) = t_n(x)\ t_m(y)\ \ with\ \ t_n(x) = \sum_{k=0}^{n} (-1)^{n-k} \binom{N-1-k}{n-k}\binom{n+k}{n}\binom{x}{k}$	$F(n,N)*F(m,N)$ $where$ $F(n,N) = \dfrac{N^{-2n}}{(2n)!\binom{N+n}{2n+1}}$	discrete	image dimensions
Krawtchouk (Yap et al., 2003)	$Kernel_{nm}(x,y) = K_n(x;p,N)\ K_m(y;p,N)\ \ with\ \ K_n(x;p,N) = \sum_{k=0}^{N} a_{k,n,p}\, x^k$	1	discrete	image dimensions

Table 1. Orthogonal moments' characteristics.

Apart from some remarkable attempts to compute the theoretical image moment values (Wee & Paramesran, 2007), new moment families with discrete polynomial kernels (Tchebichef and Krawtchouk moments) have been proposed, which permit the direct computation of the image moments in the discrete domain.

It is worth pointing out that the main subject of this chapter is the introduction of a particular moment family, the *wavelet moments* and the investigation of their classification capabilities as compared to the traditional moment types.

However, before introducing the wavelet moments, it is useful to discuss two important properties of the moments that determine their utility in recognizing patterns.

2.1 Information description

As it has already been mentioned in the introduction, the moments have the ability to carry information of an image with minimum redundancy, while they are capable to enclose distinctive information that uniquely describes the image's content. Due to these properties, once a finite number of moments up to a specific order n_{max} is computed, the original image can be reconstructed by applying a simple formula, inverse to (1), of the following form:

$$\hat{f}(x,y) = \sum_{n=0}^{n_{max}} \sum_{m=0}^{n} Kernel_{nm}(x,y) M_{nm} \tag{2}$$

where $Kernel_{nm}(.)$ is the same kernel of (1) used to compute moment M_{nm}.

Theoretically speaking, if one computes all image moments and uses them in (2), the reconstructed image will be identical to the original one with minimum reconstruction error.

2.2 Invariant description

Apart from the ability of the moments to describe the content of an image in a statistical fashion and to reconstruct it perfectly (orthogonal moments) according to (2), they can also be used to distinguish a set of patterns belonging to different categories (classes). This property makes them suitable for many artificial intelligence applications such as biometrics, visual inspection or surveillance, quality control, robotic vision and guidance, biomedical diagnosis, mechanical fault diagnosis etc. However, in order to use the moments to classify visual objects, they have to ensure high recognition rates for all possible object's orientations. This requirement constitutes a significant operational feature of each modern pattern recognition system and it can be satisfied during the feature extraction stage, where discriminative information of the objects is retrieved.

Mainly, two methodologies used to ensure invariance under common geometric transformations such as rotation, scaling and translation, either by image coordinates normalization and description through the geometric moment invariants (Mukundan & Ramakrishnan, 1998; Zhu et al., 2007) or by developing new computation formulas which incorporate these useful properties inherently (Zhu et al., 2007).

However, the former strategy is usually applied for deriving the moment invariants of each moment family, since it can be applied in each moment family in a similar way.

According to this method and by applying coordinates normalization (Rothe et al., 1996) the *Geometric Moment Invariants (GMIs)* of the following form, are constructed:

$$GMI_{nm} = GM_{00}^{-\gamma} \sum_{x=0}^{M-1} \sum_{y=0}^{N-1} \left[(x - \bar{x})\cos\theta + (y - \bar{y})\sin\theta \right]^{n}$$

$$\left[(y - \bar{y})\cos\theta - (x - \bar{x})\sin\theta \right]^{m} f(x,y) \tag{3}$$

with

$$\gamma = \frac{n+m}{2} + 1, \quad \bar{x} = \frac{GM_{10}}{GM_{00}}, \quad \bar{y} = \frac{GM_{01}}{GM_{00}},$$

$$\theta = \frac{1}{2}\tan^{-1}\left(\frac{2\mu_{11}}{\mu_{20} - \mu_{02}} \right) \tag{4}$$

where $(\bar{x}, \bar{y})$ are the coordinates of the image's centroid, GM_{nm} are the geometric moments and μ_{nm} are the central moments defined as:

$$GM_{nm} = \sum_{x=0}^{N-1} \sum_{y=0}^{N-1} x^{n}y^{m} f(x,y) \tag{5}$$

$$\mu_{nm} = \sum_{x=0}^{N-1} \sum_{y=0}^{N-1} (x - \bar{x})^{n} (y - \bar{y})^{m} f(x,y) \tag{6}$$

which are translation invariant. The value of angle θ is limited to $-45^{\circ} \le \theta \le 45^{\circ}$ and additional modifications (Mukundan & Ramakrishnan, 1998) have to be performed in order to extent θ into the range $0^{\circ} \le \theta \le 360^{\circ}$.

By expressing each moment family in terms of geometric moment invariants the corresponding invariants can be derived. For example, Zernike moments are expressed (Wee & Paramesran, 2007) in terms of GMIs as follows:

$$ZMI_{nm} = \frac{n+1}{\pi} \sum_{k=m}^{n} B_{nmk} \sum_{l=0}^{s} \sum_{j=0}^{m} w^{i} \binom{s}{i}\binom{m}{j} GMI_{k-2i-j,2i+j} \tag{7}$$

where n is a non-negative integer and m is a non zero integer subject to the constraints n-|m| even and $|m| \le n$ and

$$w = \begin{cases} -i & , m > 0 \\ +i & , m \le 0 \end{cases} \quad with \quad i = \sqrt{-1}, \quad s = \frac{1}{2}(k-m)$$

$$B_{nmk} = \frac{(-1)^{\frac{(n-k)}{2}} \left(\dfrac{n+k}{2} \right)!}{\left(\dfrac{n-k}{2} \right)! \left(\dfrac{k+m}{2} \right)! \left(\dfrac{k-m}{2} \right)!} \tag{8}$$

3. Wavelet-based moment descriptors

In the same way as the continuous radial orthogonal moments such as Zernike, Pseudo-Zernike and Fourier-Mellin ones are defined in a continuous form (9), one can define the *wavelet moments* by replacing the function $g_n(r)$ with a wavelet basis functions.

$$M_{nm} = \iint g_n(r)e^{-jm\theta} f(r,\theta)\,r\,dr\,d\theta \tag{9}$$

Based on Table 1 it can be deduced that by choosing the appropriate function $g_n(r)$, the Zernike, Pseudo-Zernike and Fourier moments are derived. If one chooses wavelet basis functions of the following form

$$\psi_{a,b}(r) = \frac{1}{\sqrt{a}}\psi\left(\frac{r-b}{a}\right) \tag{10}$$

where $a \in \Re_+, b \in \Re$ are the dilation and translation parameters and $\psi(\cdot)$ the *mother wavelet* that is used to generate the whole basis.

Two widely used mother wavelet functions are the *cubic B-spline* and the *Mexican hat* functions defined as follows:

$$\text{Cubic B-spline Mother Wavelet } \psi(r) = \frac{4a^{n+1}}{\sqrt{2\pi(n+1)}}\sigma_w\cos(2\pi f_0(2r-1))\times e^{\left(-\frac{(2r-1)^2}{2\sigma_w^2(n+1)}\right)} \tag{11}$$

where

$$\begin{cases} n = & 3 \\ a = & 0.697066 \\ f_0 = & 0.409177 \\ \sigma_w^2 = & 0.561145 \end{cases} \tag{12}$$

$$\text{Mexican Hat Mother Wavelet } \psi(r) = \frac{2}{\sqrt{3\sigma}}\pi^{-1/4}\left(1-\frac{r^2}{\sigma^2}\right)\times e^{\left(-\frac{r^2}{2\sigma^2}\right)} \tag{13}$$

with $\sigma=1$.

The main characteristic of the above wavelet functions is that by adjusting the a,b parameters a basis functions consisting of dilated (scaled) and translated versions of the mother wavelets can be derived.

The graphical presentation of the above two mother wavelet functions for the above set of their parameters, is illustrated in the following Fig.1

Since the a,b parameters are usually discrete (this is mandatory for the case of the resulted moments), a discretization procedure needs to be applied. Such a common method (Shen & Ip, 1999) that also takes into consideration the restriction of $r \leq 1$, applies the following relations.

$$a = a_0{}^m = 0.5^m, \qquad\qquad m = 0,1,2,3...$$
$$b = b_0 \times n \times a_0{}^m = 0.5 \times n \times 0.5^m, \quad n = 0,1,...,2^{m+1} \tag{14}$$

With the above the wavelet basis is constructed by a modified formula of (10) having the form:

$$\psi_{mn}(r) = 2^{m/2}\psi\left(2^m r - 0.5n\right) \tag{15}$$

It has to be noted that the selection of b_0 to 0.5 causes oversampling, something which adds significant information redundancy when the wavelet moments are used to reconstruct the initial image, but it doesn't seriously affect their recognition capabilities. Moreover, in order to reduce this affection a feature selection procedure can be applied to keep only the useful features, by discarding the redundant ones.

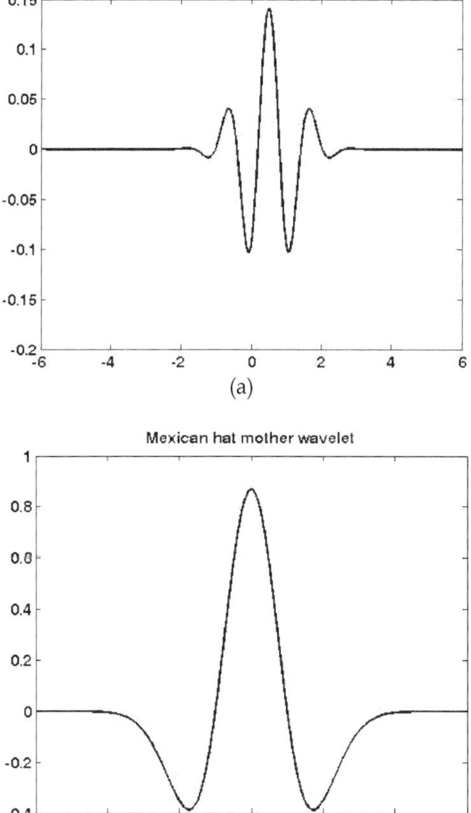

Fig. 1. Plots of (a) cubic B-spline and (b) Mexican hat mother wavelet functions.

Based on the previous analysis and by following the nomenclature of Table 1, the wavelet moments of a NxN image $f(x,y)$ are defined in the unit disc ($r \leq 1$) as follows:

$$W_{mnq} = \sum_{x=1}^{N}\sum_{y=1}^{N} \psi_{mn}(r)e^{-jq\theta}f(r,\theta) \qquad (16)$$

with $r = \sqrt{x^2 + y^2}$, $\theta = \arctan(y/x)$.

The corresponding wavelet moment invariants can be derived by applying the methodologies presented in section 2.2. An important property of the radial moments defined by (9) is that their amplitudes are rotation invariant. The translation invariants are achieved by moving the origin to the mass center (x_0,y_0) of the image, while scaling invariance is obtained by resizing the image to a fixed size having a predefined area (by a factor $a = \sqrt{M_{00}/area}$) by using the zero[th] geometric moment order (M_{00}).

The inherent properties of the wavelet moments coming from the wavelet analysis (Strang & Nguyen, 1997), according to which a signal is breaking up into shifted and scaled versions of the base wavelet (mother wavelet), make them appropriate in describing the coarse and fine information of an image. This description has the advantage to study a signal on a *time-scale* domain by providing time and frequency (there is a relation between scale and frequency), useful information of the signal simultaneously.

4. Experimental study

In order to investigate the discrimination power of the wavelet moments, four machine vision experiments have been arranged by using some well-known benchmark datasets. The following Table 2, summarizes the main characteristics of the datasets being used, from different application fields (object, face, facial expression and hand posture recognition). Moreover, Fig. 2, illustrates six pattern samples from each dataset.

Dataset		Type	Num. Classes	Instances / Class	Total Instances
ID	Name				
D1	COIL (Nene et al., 1996)	computer vision	10	12	120
D2	ORL (Samaria & Harter, 1994)	face recognition	40	10	400
D3	JAFFE (Lyons et al., 1998)	facial expression recognition	7	30,29,32,31,30,31,30	213
D4	TRIESCH I (Triesch & von der Malsburg, 1996)	hand posture recognition	10	24 (only the dark background)	240

Table 2. Characteristics of the benchmark datasets.

Since the wavelet moment invariants are constructed by applying the same methods as in the case of the other moment families and therefore their performance in recognizing geometrical degraded images is highly depended on the representation capabilities of the wavelet moments, it is decided to investigate only the discrimination power of the wavelet moments under invariant conditions.

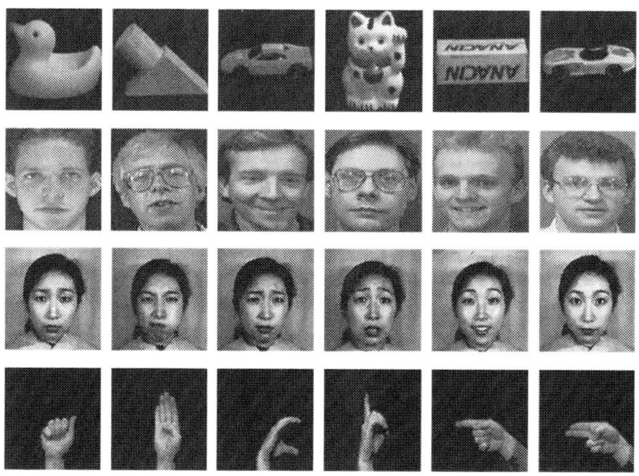

Fig. 2. Six pattern samples of the D1 (1st row), D2 (2nd row), D3 (3rd row) and D4 (4th row) datasets.

The performance of the wavelet moments (WMs) is compared to this of the well-known Zernike (ZMs), Pseudo-Zernike (PZMs), Fourier-Mellin (FMs), Legendre (LMs), Tchebichef (TMs) and Krawtchouk (KMs) ones. In this way, for each dataset, a set of moments up to a specific order per moment family is computed, by resulting to feature vectors of the same length. It is decided to construct feature vectors of 16 moments length which correspond to different order per moment family (ZMs(6th), PZMs(5th), FMs(3rd), LMs(3rd), TMs(3rd), KMs(3rd), WMs(1st)). Moreover, the wavelet moments are studied under two different configurations in relation to the used mother wavelet (WMs-1 uses the cubic B-spline and WMs-2 the Mexican hat mother wavelets respectively).

Furthermore, the *Minimum Distance* classifier (Kuncheva, 2004) is used to compute the classification performance of each moment feature vector. This classifier operates by measuring the distance of each sample from the patterns that represent the classes' centre. The sample is decided to belong to the specific class having less distance from its pattern. For the purpose of the experiments the *Euclidean* distance is used to measure the distance of the samples from the centre classes, having the following form:

$$Euclidean\ Distance\ d(\mathbf{p}, \mathbf{s}) = \sqrt{\sum_{i=1}^{n}(p_i - s_i)^2} \tag{17}$$

The above formula measures the distance between two vectors the pattern $\mathbf{p}=[p_1, p_2, p_3, ... p_n]$ and the sample $\mathbf{s}=[s_1, s_2, s_3, ..., s_n]$, which are defined in the R^n space. The following Table 3 and Table 4, summarize the classification rates (18) of the studied moment families for different set of training data used to determine the classes' centres (percent of the entire data – 25%, 50%, 75%, 100%).

$$CRate = \frac{number\ of\ correct\ classified\ samples}{total\ number\ of\ samples} \tag{18}$$

Moment Family	Datasets							
	D1		D2		D3		D4	
	25%	*50%*	*25%*	*50%*	*25%*	*50%*	*25%*	*50%*
ZMs	0.6370	0.7235	0.6576	0.6964	0.2004	0.2055	0.0857	0.1014
PZMs	0.5912	0.6305	0.6247	0.6657	0.2130	0.2257	0.0906	0.1001
FMs	0.5720	0.6000	0.6068	0.6354	0.1837	0.1965	0.0746	0.0872
LMs	0.4713	0.5158	0.7770	0.8124	0.2392	0.2547	0.0686	0.0678
TMs	0.4688	0.5055	0.7772	0.8073	0.2385	0.2557	0.0689	0.0678
KMs	0.5079	0.5915	0.3999	0.4193	0.2090	0.2348	0.0759	0.0823
WMs – 1	0.2829	0.2862	0.2252	0.2228	0.1521	0.1616	0.0715	0.0758
WMs – 2	0.2723	0.2807	0.2206	0.2219	0.1532	0.1643	0.0682	0.0790

Table 3. Classification performance of the moment descriptors.

Moment Family	Datasets							
	D1		D2		D3		D4	
	75%	*100%*	*75%*	*100%*	*75%*	*100%*	*75%*	*100%*
ZMs	0.7543	0.8083	0.7289	0.8175	0.2060	0.2723	0.1150	0.2625
PZMs	0.6683	0.7417	0.6857	0.7675	0.2385	0.3333	0.1154	0.2958
FMs	0.6207	0.7000	0.6396	0.7525	0.2098	0.2723	0.0983	0.2792
LMs	0.5457	0.7833	0.8319	0.8975	0.2562	0.3192	0.0681	0.1625
TMs	0.5287	0.7833	0.8241	0.8900	0.2719	0.3192	0.0727	0.1583
KMs	0.5940	0.7250	0.4206	0.5550	0.2383	0.3146	0.0854	0.2750
WMs – 1	0.2887	0.3000	0.2146	0.2425	0.1717	0.1784	0.0844	0.1542
WMs – 2	0.2960	0.3083	0.2136	0.2425	0.1702	0.1784	0.0846	0.1500

Table 4. Classification performance of the moment descriptors.

From the above results it is deduced that the percent of the dataset used to determine the classes' centres is crucial to the recognition performance of all the moment families. The performance of the wavelet moments is very low when compared to the other families. This behaviour is justified by the chosen order (1st) that produces less discriminant features. It seems that the existence of the third parameter ($n=0,1,\ldots,2m+1$) does not add significant discriminative information to the feature vector, compared to that enclosed by the m and q parameters. As far as the performance of the other moment families is concerned, the experiments show that each moment family behaves differently in each dataset (highest rates: D1(ZMs), D2(LMs), D3(PZMs), D4(PZMs)) with the Pseudo-Zernike moments being the most efficient.

It is worth mentioning that the above rates are not optimized and they can be increased by using a more sophisticated classification scheme (e.g. neural classifier) or by constructing larger or appropriate selected feature vectors.

Besides the classification performance of the compared moment families discussed previously, it is also interesting to analyse their computational load. In almost all the non wavelet moment families (PZMs, FMs, LMs, TMs and KMs) the number of independent moments that are computed up to the pth order is equal to $(p+1)^2$, while in the case of ZMs is $(p+1)*(p+2)/2$ due to some constraints. On the other hand the number of wavelet moments that is computed for the pth order is $(p+1)^2 * (2^{p+1}+1)$ due to the third parameter (n) of (16) defined in (14). From this analysis it is obvious that if a common computation algorithm is applied to all the moment families, the time needed to compute the wavelet moments up to a specific order (p) is considerable higher.

5. Discussion – Open issues

The previous analysis constitutes the first study of the wavelet moments' classification performance in well-known machine vision benchmarks. The experimental results highlight an important weakness of the wavelet moments; the computation of many features for a given order (due to the third parameter), which do not carry enough discriminative information of the patterns. On the other hand, this additional parameter adds an extra degree of freedom to the overall computation which needs to be manipulated appropriately. The usage of a feature selection mechanism can significantly improve the classification capabilities of the wavelet moments by keeping only the useful features from a large pool. In this way, the multiresolution nature of the wavelet analysis can be exploited in order to capture the discriminative information in different discrimination levels.

Moreover, it has to be noted that a fast and accurate algorithm for the computation of the wavelet moments need to be developed, since their computation overhead is very high, compared to the other moment families, due to the presence of the third configuration parameter.

6. References

Feng, Z. ; Shang-qian, L.; Da-bao, Wang & Wei, G. (2009). Aircraft recognition in infrared image using wavelet moment invariants. *Image and Vision Computing*, Vol. 27, No. 4, pp. 313-318.

Kuncheva, L.I. (2004). *Combining pattern classifiers: methods and algorithms*. Wiley-Interscience Publiching.

Liao, S.X. & Pawlak, M. (1998). On the accuracy of Zernike moments for image analysis. *IEEE Trans. Pattern Analysis and Machine Intelligence*, Vol. 20, No. 12, pp. 1358-1364.

Lyons, M.J., Akamatsu, S., Kamachi, M. & Gyoba, J. (1998) Coding facial expressions with Gabor wavelets. Proceedings of the 3rd IEEE International Conference on Automatic Face and Gesture Recognition (pp. 200-205). Nara, Japan.

Mukundan, R. & Ramakrishnan, K.R. (1998). *Moment functions in image analysis*. World Scientific Publisher.

Mukundan, R.; Ong, S.H. & Lee, P.A. (2001). Image analysis by Tchebichef moments. *IEEE Transactions on Image Processing*, Vol. 10, No. 9, pp. 1357-1364.

Nene, S.A.; Nayar, S.K. & Murase, H. (1996). Columbia Object Image Library (COIL-20). Technical Report No. CUCS-006-96.

Papakostas, G.A.; Boutalis, Y.S.; Karras, D.A. & Mertzios, B.G. (2007). "A new class of Zernike moments for computer vision applications. *Information Sciences*, Vol. 177, No.13, pp. 2802-2819.

Papakostas, G.A.; Boutalis, Y.S.; Karras, D.A. & Mertzios, B.G. (2009a). Pattern classification by using improved wavelet compressed Zernike moments. *Applied Mathematics and Computation*, Vol. 212, No. 1, pp. 162-176.

Papakostas, G.A.; Tsougenis, E.D. & Koulouriotis, D.E. (2010a). Near optimum local image watermarking using Krawtchouk moments", *IEEE International Workshop on Imaging Systems and Techniques (IST'10)*, pp. 459-462, Thessaloniki – Greece.

Papakostas, G.A.; Karakasis, E.G. & Koulouriotis, D.E. (2010b). Novel moment invariants for improved classification performance in computer vision applications. *Pattern Recognition*, Vol. 43, No. 1, pp. 58-68.

Rothe, I., Susse, H. & Voss, K. (1996). The method of normalization to determine invariants. *IEEE Transactions on Pattern Analysis and Machine Intelligence*, Vol. 18, No. 4, pp. 366-376.

Samaria, F. & Harter, A.C. (1994). Parameterisation of a stochastic model for human face identification. Proceedings of the 2nd IEEE Workshop on Applications of Computer Vision (pp. 138 – 142). Sarasota, FL, USA.

Shen, D & Ip Horace H.S. (1999). Discriminative wavelet shape descriptors for recognition of 2-D patterns. *Pattern Recognition*, Vol. 32, No. 2, pp. 151-165.

Sim, D.G.; Kim, H.K. & Park, R.H. (2004). Invariant texture retrieval using modified Zernike moments. *Image and Vision Computing*, Vol. 22, No. 4, pp. 331-342.

Strang, G. & Nguyen, T. (1997). *Wavelets and Filter Banks*. Wellesley-Cambridge Press.

Teague, M. (1980). Image analysis via the general theory of moments. *J. Optical Soc. Am.*, Vol. 70, pp. 920-930.

Triesch, J. & von der Malsburg, C. (1996). Robust classification of hand postures against complex backgrounds. Proceedings of the 2nd International Conference on Automatic Face and Gesture Recognition (pp. 170-175). Killington, Vermont, USA.

Wee, C.Y. & Paramesran, R. (2007). On the computational aspects of Zernike moments. *Image and Vision Computing*, Vol. 25, No. 6, pp. 967–980.

Yap, P.T.; Paramesran, R. & Ong, S.H. (2003). Image analysis by Krawtchouk moments. *IEEE Trans. on Image Processing*, Vol. 12, No. 11, pp. 1367-1377.

Zhu, H., Shu, H., Xia, T., Luo, L., Coatrieux, J.L. (2007). Translation and scale invariants of Tchebichef moments. *Pattern Recognition*, Vol. 40, No. 9, pp. 2530-2542.

3

A Design for Stochastic Texture Classification Methods in Mammography Calcification Detection

Hong Choon Ong and Hee Kooi Khoo
Universiti Sains Malaysia,
Malaysia

1. Introduction

A texture is a pattern represented on a surface or a structure of an object. Classifying a texture involves pattern recognition. Integration of texture classification is a one step ahead for machine vision application. For the past few decades until now, many researchers from various fields have been trying to develop algorithms to do texture discrimination. Alfréd Haar created the first discrete wavelet transform (DWT) in Haar (1911) which led to the development of the fast Fourier transform (FFT) and the other forms of DWT to detect periodic signals. Haralick had developed grey level co-occurrence probabilities (GLCP) with statistical features to describe textures (Haralick et al., 1973). The hidden Markov model (HMM) is another statistical method used for pattern recognition (Rabiner, 1989).

The classification process starts with image acquisition to retrieve the partial information carried by the test image. The general framework of texture classification is divided into two important stages, which are feature extraction and feature selection. Feature extraction is a process of transforming a texture into a feature domain based on the intensity distribution on a digital image. On the other hand, feature selection is a process of integrating a set of conditional statements and routines, so that the computing system can logically decide which pixels belong to which texture.

The texture classification methods are the tools which have been used to assist in medical imaging. For example, to classify the breast cancer tumour in Karahaliou et al. (2007) based on mammography imagery, to detect abnormalities in patients using Magnetic Resonance Imaging (MRI) imagery (Zhang et al., 2008), and precisely segmenting human brain images on Computed Tomography (CT) imagery for visualization during surgery (Tong et al., 2008).

In food science, texture classification techniques aid on improving the quality of food and decrease the rate of food poisoning cases. For instance, a non-supervised method of texture classification is proposed to estimate the content of Intramuscular Fat (IMF) in beef on Du et al. (2008) and thus improving the meat quality.

In remote sensing, texture classification is used to analyze satellite Synthetic Aperture Radar (SAR) imagery for multiple purposes. The analyzed satellite imagery might be used to monitor flood situations (Seiler et al., 2008), large scale construction planning, archeological research, weather forecasting, geological study etc. Texture segmentation is also applied in the study of global warming by detecting and estimating the size of the icebergs at the North Pole from time to time (Clausi, 2002a).

Another breakthrough in the advancement of security is in biometric authentication. One of the biometric measures is in using the human eye as an identity of a person. The human iris contains texture patterns which are unique in nature and thus texture classification techniques can be applied on this iris imagery (Bachoo & Tapamo, 2005).

The first section has briefly introduced the texture classification and its applications. We highlighted the importance of texture classification in science. A literature review on the current existing methods is discussed in Section 2 and 3. The main challenge of texture classification is pointed out. Section 4 explains the theories behind our research methodologies. The non-parametric statistics are developed and used to generate statistical features from a given textured image. In the feature extraction section, we will provide a general formulation for our proposed method called cluster coding and explain briefly the parameters being used for texture classification purposes. Furthermore, the solution to solve the misclassification problem is also provided. A practical analysis on the digital mammogram using our proposed method is shown in Section 5. We will conclude with a summary of our contributions in Section 6.

There are four goals in this chapter which are as follows: -

a. To show how statistical texture descriptions can be used for image segmentation.
b. To develop algorithms for feature extraction based on texture images.
c. To develop algorithms for texture segmentation based on texture features analyzed.
d. To illustrate the above objectives using an application on a mammogram image.

2. Feature extraction

There are several mathematical models which are used to extract texture features from an image. This section briefly discusses the five main feature extraction methods, namely autocorrelation function (ACF), Gabor filter, DWT, HMM, and GLCP. Besides, some combination of methods using different models are also developed to increase the robustness of texture segmentation system. We will briefly discuss two hybrid methods; these are Gabor wavelet and wavelet-domain HMM.

Gabor filter is one of the texture descriptors based on the Fourier transform (FT). A discrete FT is first taken from the test image to generate a two dimensional (2D) sinusoidal signal. For texture recognition, the Gabor filter bank contains a list of sub-bands of different signals generated by different textures. After the sub-bands are determined, the 2D signal of test image will multiply one of the chosen sub-bands and yield only the frequencies that match the sub-band. The product is then transformed back by taking the inverse FT and this leaves only the location of the texture feature which matches the signal. The process continues with each possible sub-band and produces the locations where the same signals occur (Petrou & Sevilla, 2006).

Gabor filter is useful in adapting sinusoidal signals whereby it can be decomposed into a weighted sum of sinusoidal signals. Thus Gabor filter is suitable to decompose textural information. Experiments done by Clausi & Deng (2005) stated that the Gabor filter can well recognize low and medium frequencies, but it produces inconsistent measurements for high frequencies due to the noise in the signal. The feature domain generated by Gabor filters are not distinctive enough for high frequencies and thus could affect the segmentation result (Hammouda & Jernigan, 2000).

Texture pattern can also be modeled as a transitional system using HMM. A Markov model assumes a texture pattern have a finite number of states and times. Each probability of a state is determined by the previous probability of the state. Three issues can arise from HMM observations; these are evaluation, decoding, and learning. HMM evaluation is to compare the probabilities of different models which best describe the texture feature. HMM decoding is to decompose and provide an estimated basis of texture patterns based on the HMM observations. The HMM learning searches for which model parameters best describe the texture pattern (Sonka et al., 2007).

The HMM can generate a consistent measurement for texture patterns based on the best probabilities. However, one or more observations which produce undesired probabilities could generate disorderly sequences due to the noisy pattern in the test image (Sonka et al., 2007).

ACF is another method to describe texture patterns. The function helps to search for repeated patterns in a periodic signal. The function also identifies the missing basis of texture patterns hidden under the noisy patterns. In using the ACF, the mean of each image is adjusted before applying the general formula. Thus we are actually computing the normalized auto-covariance function. One can characterize a texture pattern by inferring the periodicity of the pattern (Petrou & Sevilla, 2006).

The ACF feature is well demonstrated and distinctive between textures on a three dimensional (3D) graph. In feature selection, inferring the periodicity of a texture feature is done by observing several threshold points of the auto-covariance function and then counting the number of peaks for each threshold in a fixed variation. This may result in a random fluctuation and texture segmentation may fail because of two issues; there is not enough information by taking only one dimensional (1D) threshold to compare and an appropriate set of standard deviation of the distances between peaks are needed to know when the periodicity end. For example, the lagged product estimator and time series estimator are proposed to select ACF feature in Broerson (2005). But to appropriately characterize the texture pattern by its periodicity is still an active area of research.

Instead of using the Gabor filter for feature extraction, wavelet is well known today as a flexible tool to analyze texture. Wavelet is a function whereby the basic function, namely the mother wavelet is being scaled and translated in order to span the spatial frequency domain. The DWT is done by the product of a corresponding signal generated by a pattern and the complex conjugate of the wavelet, and then integrating over all the distance points conveyed by the signal. In texture analysis, a tree data structure namely a packet wavelet expansion is used to split the signal into smaller packets and expand a chosen band at each level of resolution (Petrou & Sevilla, 2006).

The DWT can become rotation invariant in texture analysis by taking the logarithm of the frequency sub-band. However this will damage the frequency components of the corresponding signal generated by a texture pattern and thus may obtain inaccurate result (Khouzani & Zadeh, 2005).

GLCP method is a non-parametric solution whereby the textures are described in a discrete domain (Petrou & Sevilla, 2006). GLCP statistics are used to preserve the spatial characteristics of a texture. The selection of certain texture is possible as it is based on the statistical features. The best statistical features that are used for analysis are entropy, contrast, and correlation (Clausi, 2002a). However, further analysis in Jobanputra & Clausi (2006) shows that correlation is not suitable for texture segmentation. GLCP statistics can also be used to discriminate between two different textures. Boundaries can be created from the shift on statistical feature while moving from one texture to another (Jobanputra & Clausi, 2006). Clausi & Zhao (2002) also proposed grey level co-occurrence linked-list (GLCLL) structure and grey level co-occurrence hybrid histogram (GLCHH) structure in Clausi & Zhao (2003) to this non-parametric solution for storing purpose in order to speed up the computational time for GLCP feature extraction.

Wavelet-domain HMM can be described as a finite state machine in the wavelet domain. The hidden Markov tree (HMT) can identify the characteristics of the joint probabilities of DWT by capturing the scale dependencies of wavelet co-efficient via Markov chains (Fan & Xia, 2003). Since this method is based on the wavelet domain, the disorder sequence of signal generated by the noise in the texture patterns may weaken the cross-correlation between DWT sub-bands (Fan & Xia, 2003). Ming et al. (2008) proposed the wavelet hidden-class-label Markov random field to suppress the specks of noise, but there are some small blobs of noises still appearing in the results of the segmented imagery.

3. Feature selection

The texture feature selection stage is the most important part of the texture segmentation process because it determines which pixels belong to which texture of an image. The use of parameters of a chosen method is crucial to the output of the result.

K-means algorithm has become a popular clustering method which is used for pattern recognition. Given the number of clusters, K, the algorithm will start at a random K number of centres. Then, each of the centres will group the features using the closest distances or Euclidean distance measures. The locations of the features with the same cluster will determine the new centre for each cluster. The process will then repeat until the centre of each texture class remains the same.

K-means algorithm assumes that all clusters are in spherical shape, but it may return inappropriate result for non-spherical clusters (Clausi, 2002b). In the real life 2D feature set is not always in spherical shape and normally the number of classes is unknown.

Support vector machines (SVM) algorithm is a slow but highly accurate clustering method. The SVM training algorithm was introduced by Boser et al. (1992). The purpose of SVM is to map feature vectors into a higher dimensional feature space, and then creating a separating hyperplane with maximum margin to group the features. Support vectors (SVs) contain highlighted pixels that help to create the margins or boundaries in an image. The higher dimensional space is defined by a kernel function. Some of the popular kernels are shown in Schölkopf & Smola (2002). A combined GLCP and SVM technique has been proposed for two class segmentation with significant result in Khoo et al. (2008).

Expectation-maximization (EM) algorithm is a statistical estimation algorithm used for finding maximum likelihood and estimates of parameters in probabilistic models. The parameters involve means, variances, and weights (Tong et al., 2008). The EM algorithm starts by initializing the parameters to compute the joint probability for each cluster. The algorithm then iterates to re-estimate the parameters and maximize the probability for each cluster until the set of convergence values of probabilities are obtained (Bishop, 2006). The convergence probabilities are only dependent upon the statistical parameters, so we must carefully choose these parameters, especially the parameters for texture patterns (Diplaros et al., 2007).

The self-organizing map (SOM) is an unsupervised single layer artificial neural network (ANN). In the SOM training environment, a digital image is mapped as a grid. A set of neurons will be placed at random grid points where each neuron is stored as a cluster centre (Chen & Wang, 2005). SOM clusters regions which have similar pattern and separates the dissimilar patterns based on a general distance function (Martens et al., 2008). The SOM learning process is similar to the K-means clustering where it iterates until each of the cluster centre converges to the centre of the possible texture patterns.

The advantage of SOM is that the more number of neurons are placed in the grid, the higher classification result will be obtained. However, if the numbers of neurons are too large, SOM may end up with over classification (Martens et al., 2008). On the other hand, the numbers of neurons required is unknown. Furthermore, the classification using SOM may fail at the local minimum in training (Abe, 2005).

4. Methodology

A texure pattern can be identified by

a. Counting the number of repetition of its primitive,
b. Average brightness of the primitive, and
c. The structural distribution of its primitive.

In a stochastic texture, it is not possible to determine (a), (b), and (c). To classify this texture, a measure of its density has to be computed. Therefore, the statistical modelling of GLCP is used to extract textural features. A general classification approach, namely the cluster coding is proposed. This approach preserves the textural information of a given textured image.

4.1 Enhanced two-dimensional statistical features

Given a textured image, the grey level intensities of the pixel set can be retrieved. A grid with equal sized cells is fitted onto the image. For each cell, the grey level intensities of the local neighbourhood pixels are taken into consideration when computing the joint probabilities density function. The Equation 1 shows the statistical feature for a cell, $v(i,j)$ based on the joint probability density function. i and j are the positions of a cell on the image.

$$v(i,j) = \sum_{s,t=0}^{G-1} \left(\frac{F(s,t)}{\sum_{s,t=0}^{G-1} F(s,t)} \right) \tag{1}$$

where $F(s,t)$ represents the frequency of occurrence between grey levels, s and t. G is the quantized grey levels which forms a $G{\times}G$ co-occurrence matrix.

Histogram equalization is applied to achieve higher separability between to different textures in the image. The feature set, v is distributed in a frequency histogram in order to calculate the cumulative distribution function, cdf_k using Equation 2,

$$cdf_k = \begin{cases} f_k & , \quad k = 0 \\ cdf_{k-1} + f_k, & k \in \{1,2,...,G-1\} \end{cases} \tag{2}$$

The general definition for histogram equalization (Gonzalez & Woods, 2006), H_k is

$$H_k = \frac{cdf_k - cdf_{min}}{t - cdf_{min}} \times (G-1), \ k \in \{1,2,...,G-1\} \tag{3}$$

where cdf_k, a cumulative distribution function is the total number of feature sets and min is the minimum for the set of cumulative distribution function. The design process is shown in Figure 1.

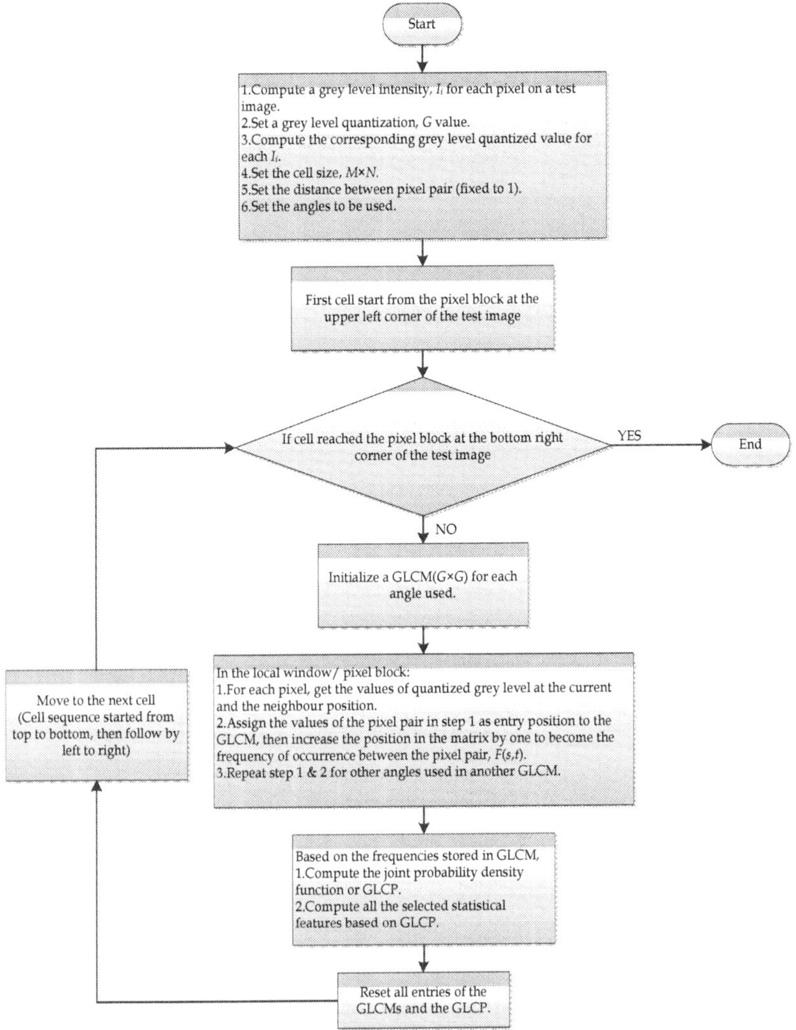

Fig. 1. The flowchart of the GLCP algorithm for feature extraction.

4.2 Cluster coding classification

Figure 2 demonstrates the basic concept of the cluster coding algorithm. The classification process is run on a split-and-merge operation. The splitting part is shown in Figure 2(b) and 2(c), while the merging part is shown in Figure 2(d).

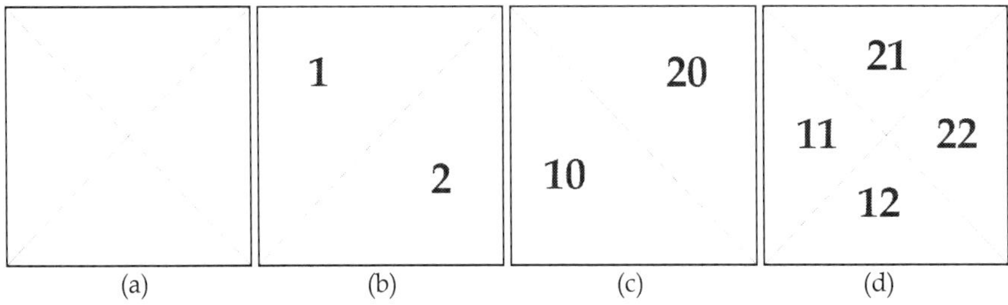

Fig. 2. Cluster coding conceptual diagram. (a) Desired segments. (b) Feature A coded in 2 clusters. (c) Feature B coded in 2 clusters. (c) Summation of codes from (b) and (c).

Each feature set is split up into coded clusters using the mean shift estimator (MSE). Mean shift estimator locate the local maxima of a feature set. The MSE is defined as,

$$MSE(v(i,j)) = \frac{K\left[\,|\,v(i,j)-v(i+\delta_1,j+\delta_2\,|\,)\right]v(i,j)}{K\left[\,|\,v(i,j)-v(i+\delta_1,j+\delta_2)\,|\,\right]} \tag{4}$$

where K is the smoothing kernel function. δ_1 and δ_2 are the shifting parameters of $v(i,j)$. The mode seeking of one-dimensional version of feature set is illustrated in Figure 3. In the figure, the dotted line is the splitting point at the position 3.5. The flowchart for cluster coding is shown in Figure 4.

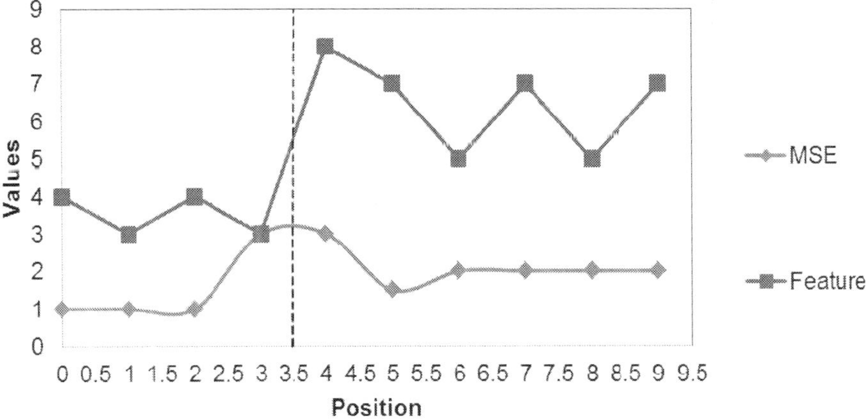

Fig. 3. Line graph of the feature values and the corrresponding MSE.

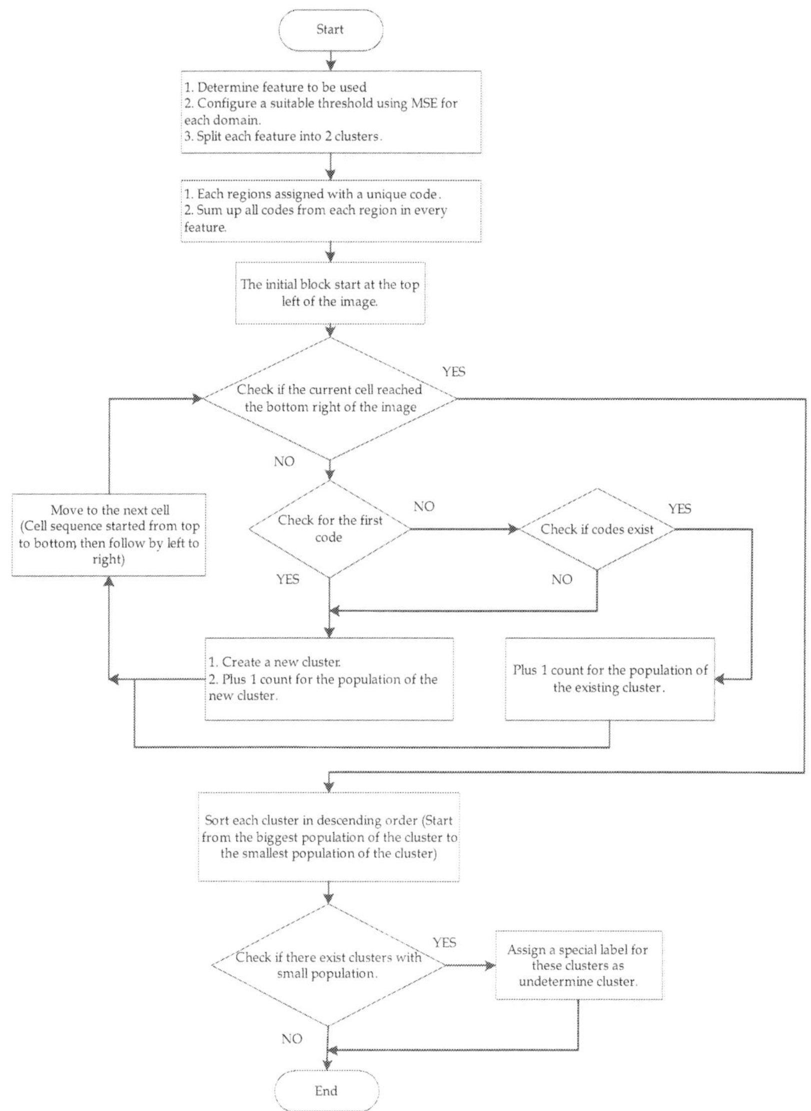

Fig. 4. The flowchart of the cluster coding algorithm.

4.3 Correction for misclassification

Each classified region on the image is identified. Two rules are set, in order to examine the region as to whether it is a misclassified blob or a texture class on the image. If the region is the texture class, then

Rule I: The located region has achieved the minimum population, and
Rule II: There is no dominated population encircled by it's neighbourhood region.

The region reclassifies if there exist a dominated population surrounding its neighbourhood region. Figure 5 provides the detail flowchart for this approach.

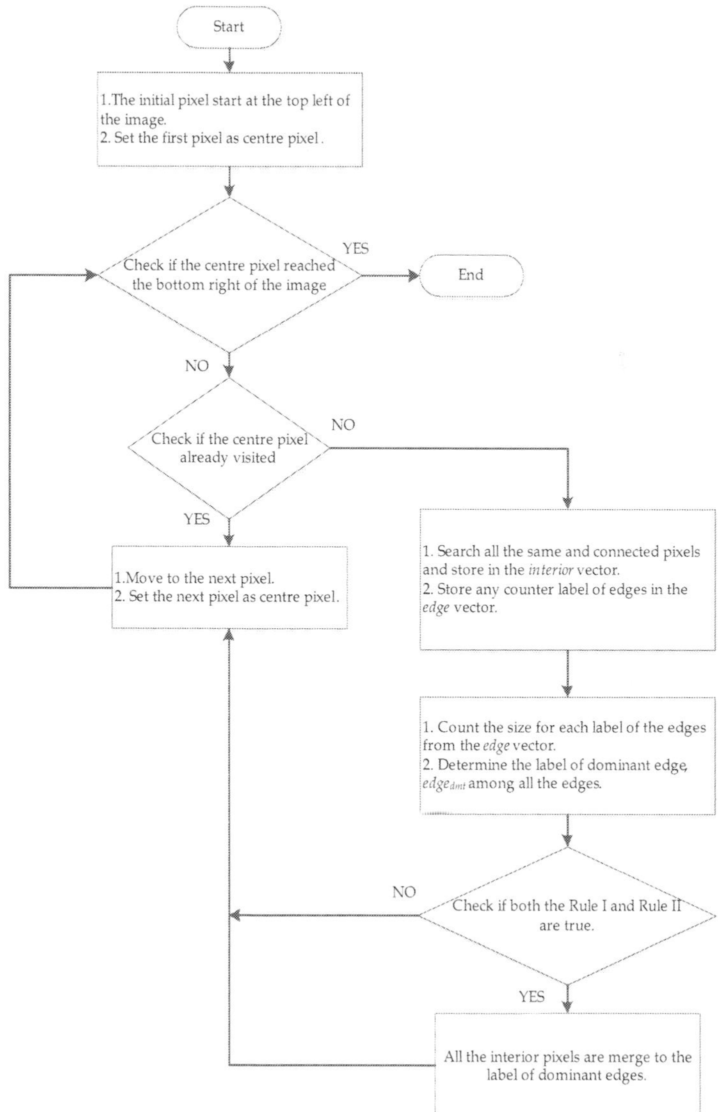

Fig. 5. The flowchart of the modified flood fill algorithm for cluster merged.

5. Results and applications

The design in Section 4 is developed using C++ programming language and implemented on a computer with the specification of 1.66GHz Intel Core 2 Dual processor, 3.37GB DDR2 RAM memory, and 256MB nVidia Quadro FX 1500M GPU for image display. This section is divided into three subsections; the initial tests using artificially created texture images followed by the application background and the application results.

5.1 Initial test

An initial testing procedure is being carried out to verify the design mentioned in Section 4. Three Brodatz's textures are used to fill the regions as can be seen in Figure 6(a). The oriental rattan (D64) is fitted in the Times New Roman font type of the character 'S'. The non-linearity of the 'S' shape in Figure 6(a) is intentionally created to add the complexity of the classification process.

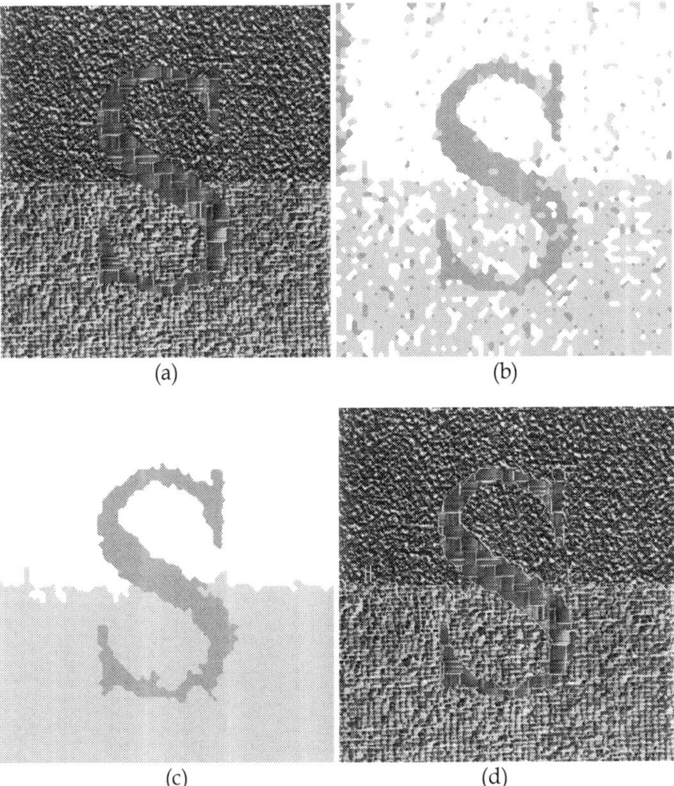

(a)   (b)

(c)   (d)

Fig. 6. Brodatz's textures classification test. (a) Texture mosaic contains handmade paper (D57), oriental-rattan (D64), and raffia (D84). (b) Classification with cluster coding. (c) Blobs correction with Rule I and II in Section 4.3. (d) Edge detection based on (c).

Although there are misclassfied blobs in Figure 6(b), the reclassification has effectively corrected the entire classified image as illustrated on Figure 6(c). Figure 6(d) is the final classification result based on the edge detection in Figure 6(c). The edges in Figure 6(d) is captured by detecting the boundaries between the different classes using both the vertical line and horizontal line scans.

Test Data	Accuracy (%)	
	Euclidean Distance K-means Clustering	Proposed Method
Bi-dimensional data sets, Hammouche, et al. (2006)	78.7178	97.2484

Table 1. Comparative performance with K-means Clustering.

We also perform a quantitative comparison with the Euclidean distance based K-means clustering (EDKMC) using the image data sets from Hammouche, et al. (2006) with a summary of the accuracy shown in Table 1. The proposed method has achieve less classification errors with only 2.7516% as compared to EDKMC errors with 21.2822%.

5.2 Mammographic scanner

Mammographic scanner is a specialized device which is used to detect early stage of breast cancer. The device makes use of a low dose X-ray, which is a safer way to make diagnosis as compared to other vision machines which use higher doses of radiation, such as normal X-ray and Positron Emission Tomography (PET).

Besides, the introduction of digital mammography has made it possible to acquire image data from the electrical signals of the device for analysis. The classification algorithms can be integrated to analyse the image data with the computer.

The device still emits ionizing radiation, which could cause mutations of human cells. Therefore an appropriate design of algorithm is crucial to reduce false positive of diagnosis and at the same time reduces the frequencies of scanning.

5.3 Mammogram results and analysis

Three possible masses can be seen in the mammogram, which are the calcification clusters, cysts, and fibroadenomas. Table 2 explains the details of these masses. The masses need to have a multiple viewing observations because the ductal carcinoma or cancer cells might be hidden beneath them. Figure 7 shows the examples of masses appearance in mammograms. Further diagnosis can be found in Breast cancer - PubMed Health (2011).

Masses	Description
Calcification clusters	Calcium salts crystalized in the breast tissue.
Cysts	Fluid-filled masses.
Fibroadenomas	Movable and rounded lumps.

Table 2. The common masses appearance in mammogram.

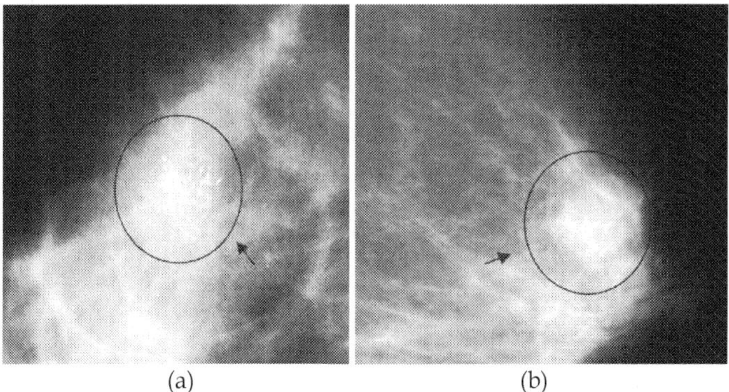

Fig. 7. Masses appearance in mammograms (Ribes, et al., 2008). (a) A sample of microcalcification clusters. (b) A sample of simple cyst.

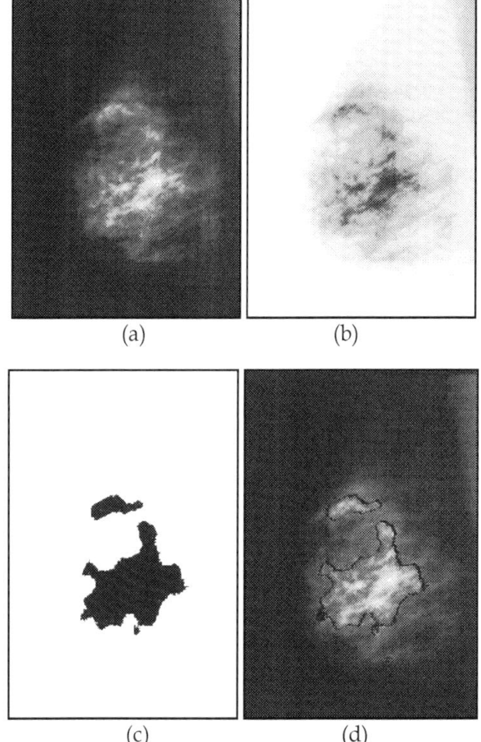

Fig. 8. Mammogram test. (a) A mammogram captured from a woman's left breast (BreastCancer.org, 2011). (b) Image negative. (c) Areas of macrocalcification clusters using the approach in Section 4. (d) Edge detection based on (c).

In Figure 7, doctors may have difficulty to spot cancer cells in these masses, particularly the calcification clusters in a mammogram. This is because the areas contain textural information which are random in nature. Statistical features can be used to measure the correlation between the breast tissues and the masses.

Figure 8(a) shows a women's left breast. Notice that the breast contains calcification clusters scattered around the tissues and there is no sign of cyst or fibroadenomas, as appeared in the mammogram.

Negative image is first obtained to remove the unnecessary dark areas in the mammogram (Gonzalez & Woods, 2006), as shown in Figure 8(b). The $v(i, j)$ of the enhanced-GLCP is then computed to produce 2D feature space for classification. Finally, the classification is carried out using the proposed cluster coding algorithm.

The propose method highlights the areas of calcification which have the potential spread of cancer cells. The end result in Figure 8(d) is optimum since the areas of calcification are in the closed boundaries.

6. Conclusion

The semantic of cluster coding with MSE is easy to understand and program. The enhanced 2D statistical features have obtained separability between different textures using histogram equalization. The design has been successfully applied in the mammogram for calcification clusters detection purpose. This approach can help the doctor or radiologist to focus on the critical areas of the mammogram.

7. Acknowledgment

This work was supported by Universiti Sains Malaysia (USM) Research University (RU) Grant no. 1001/PMATHS/817037.

8. References

Abe, S. (2005). *Support vector machines for pattern classification*, Springer Science+Business Media, LLC, ISBN 978-1849960977, Spring Street, New York

Bachoo, A. K. & Tapamo J. R. (2005). Texture detection for segmentation of iris images, *Proceedings of SAICSIT 2005 annual research conference of the South African institute of computer scientists and information technologists on IT research in developing countries.* pp.236-243, ISBN 1-59593-258-5, South African Institute for Computer Scientists and Information Technologists, Republic of South Africa, 2005

Bishop, C. M. (2006). *Pattern recognition and machine learning*, Springer Science+Business Media, LLC, ISBN 978-0387310732, Spring Street, New York

Boser, B. E.; Guyon, I. M. & Vapnik, V. N. (1992). A training algorithm for optimal margin classifiers, *Proceedings of COLT 1992 5th Annual ACM Workshop on Computational Learning Theory*, pp.144-152, ISBN 0-89791-497-X, New York, United States, 1992

Breast cancer - PubMed Health (July 2011). Available from http://www.ncbi.nlm.nih.gov/pubmedhealth/PMH0001911

BreastCancer.org. (July 2011). Available from
      http://breastcancer.org

Broerson, P.M.T. (2005). The uncertainty of measured autocorrelation functions, *Proceedings
      of IEEE AMUEM 2005 International Workshop on Advanced Methods for Uncertainty
      Estimation in Measurement*, pp.90-95, ISBN 0-7803-8979-4, Niagara Falls, Ontario,
      Canada, May 13, 2005.

Chen, C. H. & Wang, P. S. P. (2005). Handbook of pattern recognition and computer vision,
      In: Statistical Pattern Recognition, (3rd Ed.), pp.17-19, World Scientific Co., ISBN
      981-256-105-6, Danvers, United States

Clausi, D. A. (2002a). An analysis of co-occurrence texture statistics as a function of grey
      level quantization. *Canadian Journal of Remote Sensing*, Vol.28, No.1, (2002), pp.45-62,
      ISSN 0703-8992

Clausi, D. A. (2002b). K-means Iterative Fisher (KIF) unsupervised clustering algorithm
      applied to image texture segmentation. *Pattern Recognition*, Vol.35, (September
      2002), pp.1959-1972, ISSN 0031-3203

Clausi, D. A. & Deng, H. (2005). Design-based texture feature fusion using Gabor filters and
      co-occurrence probabilities. *IEEE Transactions on Image Processing*, Vol.14, No.7,
      (July 2005), pp.925-936, ISSN 1057-7149

Clausi, D. A. & Zhao, Y.P. (2002). Rapid extraction of image texture by co-occurrence using a
      hybrid data structure. *Computers & Geosciences*, Vol.28, No.6, (July 2002), pp.763-
      774, ISSN 0098-3004

Clausi, D. A. & Zhao, Y.P. (2003). Grey Level Co-occurrence Integrated Algorithm (GLCIA):
      a superior computational method to rapidly determine co-occurrence probability
      texture features. *Computers & Geosciences*, Vol.29, No.7, (August 2003), pp.837-850,
      ISSN 0098-3004

Diplaros, A. ; Vlassis, N. & Gevers, T. (2007). A spatially constrained generative model and
      an EM algorithm for image segmentation. *IEEE Transactions on Neural Networks*,
      Vol. 18, No.3, (May 2007), pp.798-808, ISSN 1045-9227

Du, C. J.; Sun, D. W.; Jackman, P. & Allen, P. (2008). Development of a hybrid image
      processing algorithm for automatic evaluation of intramuscular fast content in beef
      M. longissimus dorsi. *Meat Science*, Vol.80, No.4, (December 2008), pp.1231-1237,
      ISSN 0309-1740

Fan, G. L. & Xia, X. G. (2003). Wavelet-based texture analysis and synthesis using hidden
      Markov models. *IEEE Transactions on Circuits and Systems-I: Fundamental Theory and
      Applications*, Vol.50, No.1, (January 2003), pp.106-120, ISSN 1057-7122

Gonzalez, R. C. & Woods, R. E. (2006). *Digital Image Processing*, (3rd ed.), Prentice Hall, Inc.,
      ISBN 978-0131687288, New Jersey, United States

Haar, A. (1911). Zur Theorie der orthogonalen Funktionen-Systeme. *Mathematische Annalen*,
      Vol.71, No.1, (1911), pp.38–53, ISSN 0025-5831

Hammouche, K., Diaf, M. & Postaire J.G. (2006). A clustering method based on
      multidimensional texture analysis, Vol.39, No.7, (July 2006), pp.1265-1277, ISSN
      0031-3203

Hammouda, K. & Jernigan, E. (2000). Texture segmentation using Gabor filters. Department
      of Systems Design Engineering, University of Waterloo, N2L 3G1

Haralick, R.M.; Shanmugam, K. & Dinstein, I. (1973). Textural Features for Image Classification. *IEEE Transactions on Systems, Man, and Cybernetics*, Vol.3, No.6, (November 1973), pp.610-621, ISSN 0018-9472

Jobanputra, R. & Clausi, D. A. (2006). Preserving boundaries for image texture segmentation using grey level co-occurring probabilities. *Pattern Recognition*, Vol.39, No.2, (February 2006), pp.234-245. ISSN 0031-3203

Karahaliou, A.; Boniatis, I.; Sakellaropoulos, P.; Skiadopoulus, S.; Panayiotakis, G. & Costaridou, L. (2007). Can texture of tissue surrounding microcalcifications in mammography be used for breast cancer diagnosis? *Nuclear Instruments and Methods in Physics Research Section A: Accelerators, Spectrometers, Detectors and Associated Equipment*, Vol.580, No.2, (October 2007), pp.1071-1074, ISSN 0168-9002

Khoo, H. K.; Ong, H. C. & Wong, Y. P. (2008). Image texture classification using combined grey level co-occurrence probabilities and support vector machines, *Proceedings of CGIV 2008 5th International Conference on Computer Graphics, Imaging and Visualization*, pp.180-184, ISBN 978-0-7695-3359-9, Penang, Malaysia, August 26-28, 2008

Khouzani, K. J. & Zadeh, H. S. (2005). Rotation-invariant multiresolution texture analysis using radon and wavelet transforms. *IEEE Transactions on Image Processing*, Vol. 14, No.6, (June 2005), pp.783-795, ISSN 1057-7149

Martens, G.; Poppe, C.; Lambert, P. & de Walle, R. V. (2008). Unsupervised texture segmentation and labeling using biologically inspired features. *Proceedings of IEEE 10th Workshop on Multimedia Signal Processing*, pp.159-164, ISBN 978-1-4244-2294-4, Cairns, Queensland, Australia, October 8-10, 2008

Ming, L.; Wu, Y. & Zhang, Q. (2009). SAR image segmentation based on mixture context and wavelet hidden-class-label Markov random field. *Computers and Mathematics with Applications*, Vol.57, No.6, (March 2009), pp.961-969, ISSN 0898-1221

Petrou, M. & Sevilla, P.G. (2006). *Image processing dealing with texture*, John Wiley & Sons Ltd., ISBN 978-0470026281, West Sussex, England

Ribes, R.; Luna, A. & Ros, P.R. (2008). *Learning diagnosis imaging: 100 essential cases*, Springer-Verlag Berlin Heidelberg, ISBN: 978-3-540-71207-7, Berlin, German

Rabiner, L.R. (1989). A tutorial on hidden Markov models and selected applications in speech recognition. *Proceedings of the IEEE*, Vol.77, No.2, pp.257-286, ISSN: 0018-9219, February 1989

Schölkopf, B. & Smola, A J (2002). *Learning with kernels. support vector machines, regularization, optimization, and beyond*, the MIT Press, ISBN 978-0262194754, London, England.

Seiler, R.; Schmidt, J.; Diallo, O. & Csaplovics, E. (2009). Flood monitoring in a semi-arid environment using spatially high resolution radar and optical data. *Journal of Environmental Management*, Vol.90, No.7, (May 2009), pp.2121-2129, ISSN 0301-4797

Sonka, M.; Hlavac, V. & Boyle, R. (2007). *Image processing analysis and Machine Vision*. International Thomson Publishing Inc., ISBN 978-0534953935, Pacific Grove, California

Tong, H. L.; Fauzi, M.F.A. & Komiya, R. (2008). Segmentation of CT brain images using K-means and EM clustering. *Proceedings of CGIV 2008 5th International Conference on Computer Graphics, Imaging and Visualization*, pp.339-344, ISBN 978-0-7695-3359-9, Penang, Malaysia, August 26-28, 2008

Zhang, J.; Tong, L. Z.; Wang, L. & Li, N. (2008). Texture analysis of multiple sclerosis: a comparative study. *Magnetic Resonance Imaging*, Vol.26, No.8, (October 2008), pp.1160-1166, ISSN 0730-725X

4

Optimized Imaging Techniques to Detect and Screen the Stages of Retinopathy of Prematurity

S. Prabakar[1], K. Porkumaran[2], Parag K. Shah[3] and V. Narendran[4]
[1]Department of Electrical and Electronics Engineering,
[2]Institute of Technology, Coimbatore,
[3,4]Department of Paediatric Retina & Ocular Oncology,
Aravind Eye Hospitals, Coimbatore,
India

1. Introduction

Retinopathy of prematurity (ROP) is an ocular disease of premature infants and it can cause blindness on high threshold stages (Early Treatment of Retinopathy of Prematurity [ETROP] study, 2003). It affects immature vasculature in the eyes of premature babies (Wittchow.K, 2003; Mounir Bashour et al., 2008). It can be mild with no visual defects, or it may become aggressive with new blood vessel formation (neovascularization) and progress to retinal detachment and blindness (International Committee for the Classification of Retinopathy of Prematurity [ICCROP], 2005). As smaller and younger babies are surviving, the incidence of ROP has increased (Gwenole Quellec et al., 2008; Benson Shu Yan Lam & Hong Yan, 2008). All babies who less than 1800g birth weight or younger than 32 weeks gestational age at birth are at risk of developing ROP.

In any neonatal intensive care unit (NICU), the timing of the first evaluation must be based on the gestational age at birth. (a) If the baby is born at 23-24 weeks' gestational age, the first eye examination should be performed at 27-28 weeks gestational age. (b) If the baby is born at or beyond 25-28 weeks' gestational age, the first examination should occur at the fourth to fifth week of life. (c) Beyond 29 weeks, the first eye examination should probably occur by fourth week life time of baby.

It is essential that those caring for premature infants know who is at risk of retinopathy of prematurity, when screening must begin and how often these infants need to be examined. It is also important to know when to treat those infants who develop severe retinopathy of prematurity and what long term follow-up is needed to manage other complications of retinopathy of prematurity (Shankar, P. M. 1986). The discrimination between normal retinal vessels and diseased vessels plays a vital role to detect the ROP as shown in Fig. 1. The ROP occurs when abnormal blood vessels develop at the edge of normal retinal blood vessel. The ophthalmologists who are trained in ROP have to study and analyze the Retcam images.

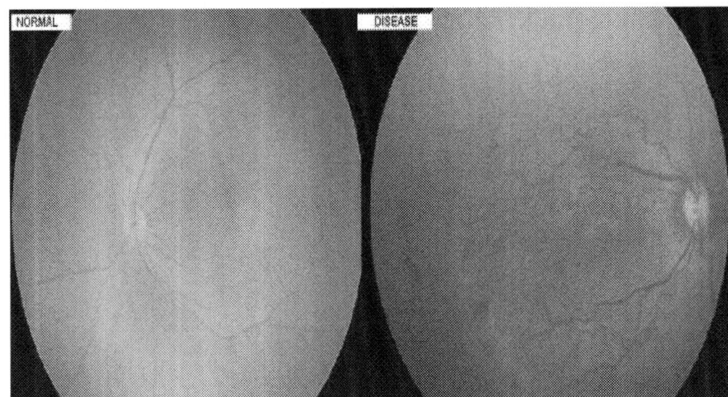

Fig. 1. Normal and Diseased Retinal Blood Vessels image of premature babies.

ROP is an ideal disease for applications and research in medical imaging for several reasons: (a) Clinical diagnosis is based solely on the appearance of disease in the retina. (b) There is a universally-accepted, evidence-based, diagnostic classification standard for ROP (ICCROP,2005). This ordinal system is used by ophthalmologists to define severe cases of ROP that require treatment, as well as cases with high-risk features that warrant particularly careful observation. (c) If severe ROP is diagnosed and treated early enough, blinding complications may be prevented. (d) ROP continues to be a leading cause of childhood blindness throughout the world. (e) Current ROP examination methods are time-intensive, frequently impractical, and physiologically stressful to premature infants. (f) Adequate ophthalmic expertise is often limited to larger ophthalmic centers, and therefore unavailable at the point of care. (g) Pilot studies have suggested that ROP diagnosis using simple interpretation of images captured using wide-angle digital retinal cameras may be feasible (Attar MA et al., 2005; Ells AL, Holmes JM, Astle WF, et al., 2003; Fierson WM, Palmer EA, Petersen RA, et al., 2001 ; Kaiser RS et al., 2001).

Indirect ophthalmoscope is the goal standard for ROP screening. But in a big way the indirect ophthalmoscope has been replaced with Retcam in ROP telescreening. Even though Retcam images can be taken by non ophthalmologist, it is difficult for them to interpret the stages of ROP. So, the proposed method giving a retinal image processing algorithm through which even a non ophthalmologist can give the various stages of ROP. This will provide the effective time utilization for the ophthalmologists. They can concentrate on infants who suffered with high risk threshold ROP and threshold ROP instead of analyzing all ROP images.

In this work, an automatic method is proposed to detect various stages of Retinopathy of prematurity (ROP) in premature infants and low birth weight infants. It is essential that those caring for premature infants should know who is at risk of ROP, when screening must begin and how often these infants need to be examined otherwise it can cause blindness. So, ROP detection is necessary for both screening the pathology and progression measurement. Computerizing this task, which is currently executed manually, would bring more subjectivity and reproducibility. The proposed image processing algorithms for predicting the presence and stages of ROP are histogram equalization methods, feature extraction, measuring curvature by changes in intensity and template matching. The retinal vessels are segmented using simple and standard 2-D Gaussian Matched Filter. Segmented vessels are thinned, smoothened and filtered based on local intensity of the vessels. The classification of ROP stages has been implemented by trained and tested neural network's algorithms such as Back Propagation Feed Forward network (BPN), Radial Basis Function (RBF) network and the combination of both (Kai Chuan Chu & Dzulkifli Mohamad, 2003; Li Min Fu, 1994 ; Laurene Fausett, 1999 ; Meng Joo Er, shiqan wu, et al., 2002).   The effectiveness of the proposed methods has been verified through machine vision techniques and the trained networks have been tested and validated with appropriate ROP input images. The results obtained are encouraged by experts and the data have been clearly discriminating the severity of ROP. Automatic ROP staging system comprises several advantages, like a substantial time reduction of ophthalmologists in diagnosis, a non ophthalmologist can provide stage of ROP, improving the sensitivity of the test and a better accuracy in diagnosis.

The following is the outline of the dissertation work presented in this paper:

Chapter 2 is devoted to the analysis and classification of ROP based on its severity. The common clinical procedure and diagnostic technique to detect the stage of ROP development in an infant has been discussed. Different images are provided for the illustration of the ROP localization and the feature extraction.

Chapter 3 deals with the development of generalized design of ROP classification and screening system. The design of proposed system model has been extended and a new combined model consists of Back Propagation Network (BPN) and Radial Basis Network (RBF).

In Chapter 4 and Chapter 5, various ROP image processing schemes such as image enhancement, fine classification, feature extraction, representation and ROP classification have been explained by different algorithms such as histogram equalisation technique, thresholding, averaging filter, median filter, edge detection and feature extraction. In the proposed neural network model, BPN network is combined with RBF network and the model outcomes have been compared and the computational details such as classification rate, and the time consumed by them have been evaluated and the results have been tabulated.

Chapter 6 is proposed to express the results and outcomes of various imaging techniques and neural network algorithms. The graphical representation and the tabulated values of extracted data provided the scope for the ROP screening. The results have been validated with experts and compared with common manual techniques for enhancement and future development and modifications

In chapter 7 proposed ROP image screening schemes and neural network classifiers are summarized together with suggestions for further research.

The acknowledgement and list of references which have been based on this work are given at the end chapters of this dissertation.

2. Retinopathy of prematurity (ROP)

Retinopathy of Prematurity (ROP) is a fibrovascular proliferative disorder, which affects the developing peripheral retinal vasculature of premature infants. It is an avoidable cause of blindness in children. The initial signs of ROP are detectable by a few weeks after birth, and the condition progresses rapidly thereafter. This means that screening has to be timely, and there is only a very narrow window of opportunity for treating. If not treated, the condition progresses rapidly to Stage 4 or 5 in approximately 50% of babies (Shah PK, Narendran V, et al., 2009). The visual prognosis for babies with Stage 5 disease (total retinal detachment) is very poor, even after complex vitreoretinal surgery. The primary goal of screening is to detect all babies with treatable disease in time for treatment to be effective.

2.1 Classification of ROP

Blood vessel development in the retina occurs from the optic nerve out towards the periphery, that is, from the back of the eye towards the front. The location of the disease is referred by the ICROP (International Classification of Retinopathy of Prematurity) classification and is a measure of how far this normal progression of blood vessel development has progressed before the disease takes over (Mounir Bashour et al., 2008). Generally Zone II disease is more severe than Zone III disease and Zone I disease is the most dangerous of all since progression to extensive scar tissue formation and total retinal detachment is most likely in this location.

From the "flattened" retina shown in Fig. 2, we can see that:

* Zone I is a small area around the optic nerve and macula at the very back of the eye.
* Zone II extends from the edge of Zone I to the front of the retina on the nasal side of the eye (i.e. nose side) and part way to the front of the retina on the temporal side of the eye (i.e. temple side, or side of the head).
* Zone III is the remaining crescent of retina in front of Zone II on the temporal side of the eye.

Think of the eye as in time sections of a twelve hour clock to classify the stages of ROP. The extent of ROP is defined by how many clock hours of the eye's circumference are diseased. The numbers around the "flattened" retina in the Fig.2 shows the hours of the clock for each eye. For example, 3 o'clock is to the right, which is on the nasal side for the right eye and temporal side for the left eye. Often the disease is not present around all twelve clock hours, so a description may often refer to "x" number of clock hours of disease (e.g. nine clock hours would mean that three quarters of the circumference of the retina is involved).

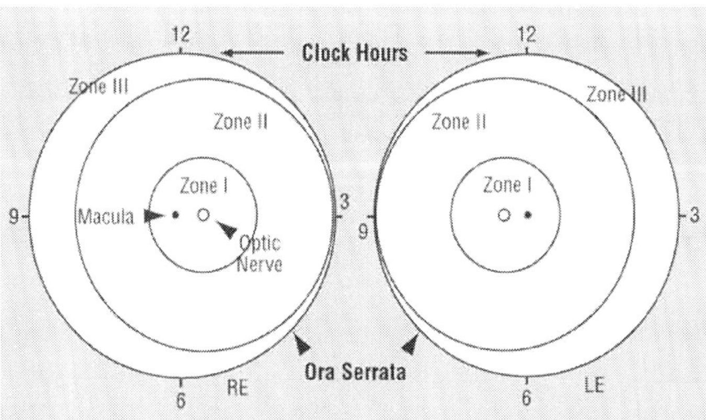

Fig. 2. Zone 1 is the most posterior retina that contains the optic nerve and the macula (zone of acute vision). Zone 2 is the intermediate zone where blood vessels often stop in ROP. Zone 3 is the peripheral zone of the retina, where vessels are absent in ROP, but present in normal eyes.

2.2 Stages of ROP based on ICROP

ROP is a rapidly progressive disease. It starts slowly, usually anywhere from the fourth to the tenth week of life, and may progress through successive stages, from Stage 1 to Stage 5, or it may stop at Stage 1 or Stage 2 or mild Stage 3 and disappear completely. The common ROP stage classification is shown in Table 1.

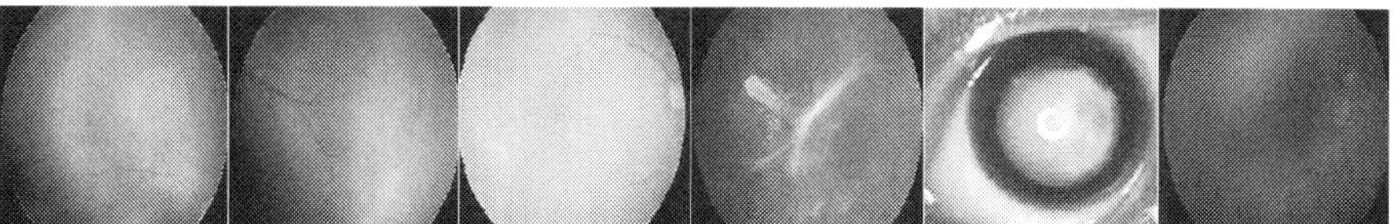

Fig. 3. Sequence of ROP Images visualizes Stage 1, Stage 2, Stage 3, Stage 4, Stage 5 and Plus Disease.

Stage 1. Demarcation line: a flat, white, thin line that separates the avascular retina anteriorly (toward the retinal periphery) from the vascularized retina posteriorly.

Stage 2. Ridge the flat line from stage 1 has grown in height, width, and volume and has become a pink-white ridge.

Stage 3. Ridge with extraretinal fibrovascular proliferation: proliferating tissue can be continuous with the posterior aspect of the ridge; immediately posterior to the ridge, or extending directly into the vitreous.

Stage 4. Subtotal retinal detachment: dragging vessels and subtotal traction retinal detachment can be seen. Stage 4A disease does not affect the macula and has a relatively good prognosis for vision; stage 4B disease affects the fovea and usually has a poor prognosis for vision.

Stage 5. Total retinal detachment: funnel-shaped retinal detachment. Anterior and posterior portions appear open or narrowed on ultrasonographic scans.

Plus Disease. The designation "+" is placed after the stage when dilated posterior veins, tortuous retinal arteries, vitreous haze, and pupillary rigidity are observed. If plus disease is observed in the posterior portion of the retina, patients must be monitored closely, as there is high risk of ROP progressing rapidly within a few days and lead to retinal detachment and may cause blindness with high risk ROP.

Category	Definitions
Stage 1	Demarcation line separating the avascular retina anteriorly from the vascularized retina posteriorly, with abnormal branching of small vessels immediately posterior.
Stage 2	Intra retinal ridge; the demarcation line has increased in volume, but this proliferative tissue remains intraretinal.
Stage 3	Ridge with extra retinal fibrovascular proliferation.
Stage 4	Partial retinal detachment.
Stage 5	Total retinal detachment.
Plus Disease	Two or more quadrants of vessel tortuosity and fullness at the optic nerve

Table 1. Definitions of ROP Severity Categories

2.3 Diagnosis of ROP

ROP is diagnosed from dilated ophthalmoscopic examination by an experienced ophthalmologist, and there are accepted guidelines for identifying high-risk premature infants who need serial screening examinations. Each image set consisted of 1 to 7 photographs from a single eye. Because imaging was performed at the bedside under typical working conditions, it was not possible to capture a standard set of photographs on each infant. The images have captured by Retcam for stage 1, stage 2, stage3, stage 4, stage 5 and Plus Disease as shown in Fig. 3.

Each infant underwent two examinations, which are sequentially performed under topical anaesthesia at the neonatal intensive care unit bedside: (a) Dilated ophthalmoscopy by an experienced ophthalmologist, based on well-known protocols (Kaiser RS et al., 2001; Fetus and Newborn Committee, Canadian Paediatric Society, 1998; Siatkowski RM & Flynn JT, 1998; Schaffer DB, Palmer EA, et al. 1993). The presence or absence of ROP disease, and its characteristics when present, were documented according to the international classification standard. (b) Wide-angle retinal imaging by an experienced ophthalmic photographer using a digital camera system (RetCam-120; MLI Inc., Pleasanton, California), based on guidelines established by the manufacturer.

The examinations are usually performed in the neonatal intensive care nursery where the neonatal staff can continue to monitor the baby. The infant will continue to be examined every 1 to 2 weeks until one of the following occurs:

- Development of the normal blood supply to the retina is complete.
- Two successive 2-week exams show Stage 2 in Zone III. Infants will then be examined every 4 to 6 weeks until the blood supply to the retina is fully developed.
- ROP is at "low risk prethreshold", just prior to requiring treatment. Follow-up exams will then occur every week until either "high risk prethreshold ROP or Threshold ROP" occurs, which requires treatment, or the retinopathy of prematurity disappears.
- The ROP is disappearing.

After two successive 2-week exams have shown regression, examinations should be continued every 4 to 6 weeks. Once the normal blood supply to the retina is completely developed, the infant will continue to be examined every 6 to 12 months by a pediatric ophthalmologist to ensure that no further complications of ROP occur.

3. Materials and methods

3.1 General design

Screening for ROP usually begins when the infant is about 4 to 6 weeks of age. An eye doctor (ophthalmologist), who specializes in either retinal disorders (retinal specialist) or children's eye diseases (pediatric ophthalmologist), uses a special instrument (an indirect ophthalmoscope) which allows a view through its optic lens into the back of the eye to examine the retina and determine whether development of the blood vessels is occurring normally or not. Before acquiring the retina images through Retcam, the infant is usually given some eye drops to make the pupil dilate so that the viewing field is as wide as possible. A light anaesthetic, in the form of numbing eye drops, may also be administered.

The general ROP screening system's flow diagram of the overall process as shown in Fig. 4, beginning with retinal image acquisition from the patient through Retcam. This image has been enhanced and removes the unwanted noise to obtain the object of interest. The required ROP features have been extracted by segmentation techniques and represent the image to train the machine to display that the severity of ROP. The error eradication system has been developed to obtain the better result. The decision making and classification modules used to provide the ROP presence and its stage. Normally the Stage 4 and Stage 5 ROP could not be treated. So, the present developed scheme has concentrated only on first three stages of the disease and Plus disease prognosis of ROP. Automatic ROP stage screening system will entail several advantages, like a substantial reduction in the labour workload of clinicians, improving the sensitivity of the test and a better accuracy in diagnosis by increasing the number of images.

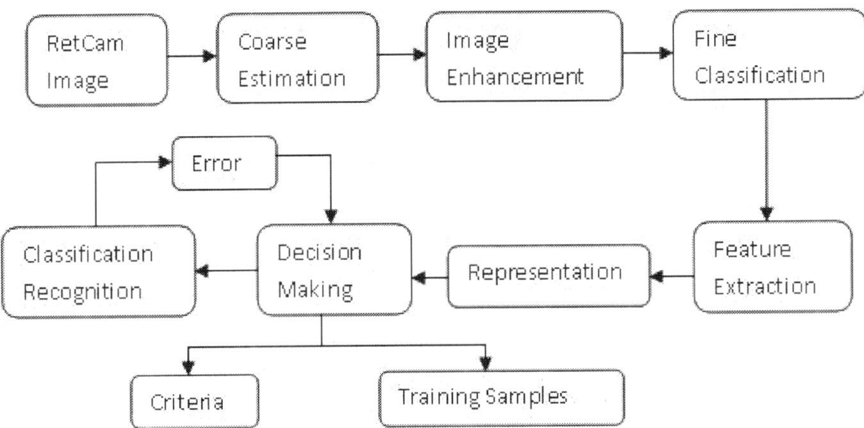

Fig. 4. Block diagram of the ROP detection and screening system.

The aim of this dissertation work is to design and develop an efficient ROP stage screening system. The main objectives of this work are as given below.

a. To design a ROP image localizer to localize the region of interest from the image. ROP image localizer is used for segmenting the required blood vessels region from the input image.
b. To develop a feature extractor for extracting the required classification features. Feature extractor is applied for getting the local features such as dilated vessels.
c. To design a proper recognizer for recognizing the given image, Back Propagation network, Combination of BPN and RBF are to be developed for screening and recognition.

3.2 Proposed system model

Based on the general block diagram, the proposed system is designed. The model of the proposed system is given in Fig. 5.

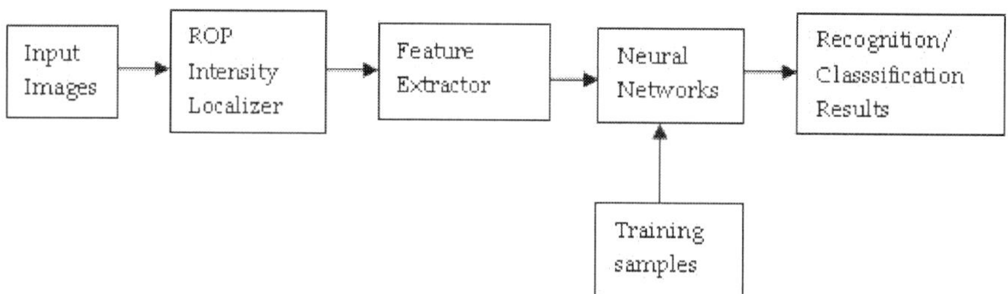

Fig. 5. Architecture of the proposed ROP classification and recognition system.

First, various pre-processing activities have been performed on the image for improving the quality of the image. These activities include image resizing, contrast stretching, histogram equalization and so on. The method of locating region of interest and dilated blood vessels are known as ROP image localization. Then, the local features such as abnormal branching of small vessels, Intra retinal ridge, ridge with extra retinal fibrovascular proliferation and partial and total retinal detachments are extracted from the region of interest. These values are given as the inputs to the neural networks for classification and recognition. Neural networks are trained with a set of training samples (Li Min Fu, 1994 ; Laurene Fausett, 1999 ; Meng Joo Er, shiqan wu, et al., 2002). The input images are compared with the trained samples and the similarity measures have been given as the classification and screening result. In this paper, Back Propagation Network (BPN), BPN + Radial Basis Function network (RBF) are used for classifying the ROP input images.

In the next section, we discover the appropriate machine vision techniques to detect the various stages ROP and the efficient neural network to classify and recognize the various ROP stages. The discussion begins with ideal model and to train the machine to identify the problem based on the requirements of the clinicians.

4. ROP image processing schemes

4.1 Proposed ROP image localization technique

ROP image localizer is designed to serve as a pre-processor of ROP stage classification and recognition systems for detecting the stage of ROP. The first step in this ROP image processing system is detecting the locations of blood vessels in the Retcam images. ROP image localization aims to localize the region of interest from the input image where blood vessels have been presented. Here the regions of interests are segmented and the regions that contain dilated, twisted and tortuosity of blood vessels. Various pre-processing activities are done in this stage to make the raw data into usable format.

A new algorithm is proposed in this proposal for localizing the ROP images, which consists of the following steps.

1.   The input image is converted into the gray scale image.
2.   The gray scale image is converted into its binary form.
3.   The dilation operation is performed on the binary image. The dilation process removes the noise encountered in the binary image.

4.   The dilated image is mapped on to the gray scale image.

Let I_m denotes the intensity of mapped image

I_d denotes the intensity of the dilated image and

I_g denotes the intensity of the gray scale image.

$$I_m (i, j) = \begin{cases} I_g (i, j) & \text{if } I_d (i, j) = 1 \\ \\ \text{Otherwise} \end{cases}$$

5.   The mapped image has been converted into its binary form.
6.   The required ROP region has been cropped from the binary image.

For developing a reliable ROP stage screening system, several ROP image processing activities have to be done. In this paper, the region on interest has been localized i.e., the required tortuosity and dilated vessels have been selected from the given input image using the proposed ROP localization technique. Instead of giving the whole image as input, the localized ROP image alone be given as input to the feature extractor and it diminishes the computational burden. A new algorithm is proposed in this work for extracting the local features and these features alone given as inputs to the neural network recognizer and classifier. This algorithm reduces the number of inputs to the recognizer as well as the training time.

4.2 Histogram equalization approach

First, it is necessary to describe the brightness variation in an image using its histogram. Then look at operations which manipulate the image so as to change the histogram, processes that shift and scale the result by making the image brighter or dimmer, in different ways. The intensity histogram shows how individual brightness levels are occupied in an image; the image contrast is measured by the range of brightness levels.

Histogram equalization is a non-linear process aimed to highlight image brightness in a way particularly suited to human visual analysis (Russ J. C., 1995; Jia X. & Nixon M. S. 1995; Baxes G. A., 1994; Parker J. R., 1994). Histogram equalization aims to change a picture in such a way as to produce a picture with a flatter histogram, where all levels are equiprobable. In order to develop the operator, it is important to inspect the histograms as shown in Fig. 6.

For a range of M levels, the histogram plots the points per level against level. For the input (old) and the output (new) image, the number of points per level is denoted as $O(1)$ and $N(1)$ (for $0 < 1 < M$), respectively. For square images, there are N^2 points in the input and the output image, so the sum of points per level in each should be equal:

$$\sum_{1=0}^{M} O(1) = \sum_{1=0}^{M} N(1) \tag{1}$$

Also, this should be the same for an arbitrarily chosen level p, since the aim is for an output picture with a uniformly flat histogram. So the cumulative histogram up to level p should be transformed to cover up to the level q in the new histogram:

$$\Sigma_{1=0}^{p} O(1) = \Sigma_{1=0}^{p} N(1) \qquad (2)$$

Since the output histogram is uniformly flat, the cumulative histogram up to level p should be a fraction of the overall sum. So the number of points per level in the output picture is the ratio of the number of points to the range of levels in the output image:

$$N(1) = \frac{N^2}{N_{max} - N_{min}} \qquad (3)$$

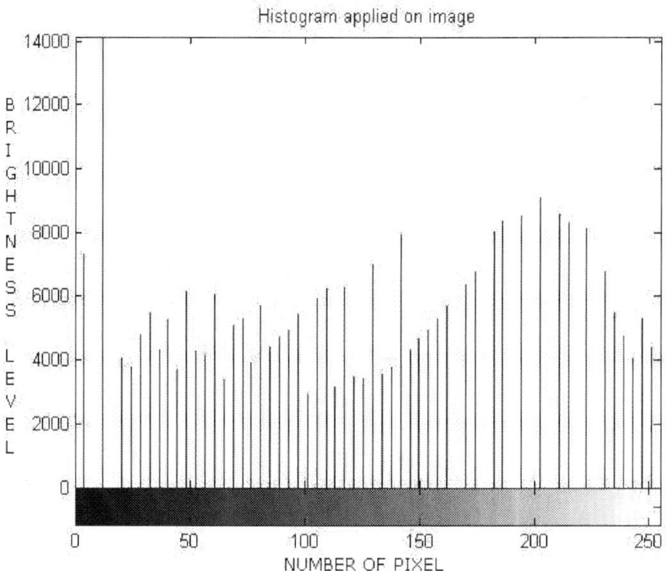

Fig. 6. Resulting Histogram applied on ROP image for enhancement.

So the cumulative histogram of the output picture is:

$$\Sigma_{1=0}^{p} N(1) = q \times \frac{N^2}{N_{max} - N_{min}} \qquad (4)$$

Equation (2) shows that it is equal to the cumulative histogram of the input image, so:

$$q \times \frac{N^2}{N_{max} - N_{min}} = \Sigma_{1=0}^{p} O(1) \qquad (5)$$

This gives a mapping for the output pixels at level q, from the input pixels at level p as:

$$q = \frac{N_{max} - N_{min}}{N^2} \times \Sigma_{1=0}^{p} O(1) \qquad (6)$$

This gives a mapping function that provides an output image that has an approximately flat histogram. The mapping function is given by phrasing (6) as an equalizing function i.e., E of the level (q) and the image (O) as

$$E(q,O) = \sum_{l=0}^{P} O(l) = \sum_{l=0}^{P} N(l) \tag{7}$$

The output image is then

$$N_{x,y} = E(O_{x,y}, O) \tag{8}$$

The intensity equalized image has much better defined features than in the original version. The histogram reveals the non-linear mapping process whereby white and black are not assigned equal weight. Accordingly, more pixels are mapped into the darker region and the brighter intensities become better spread, consistent with the aims of histogram equalization. Its performance can be very convincing for ROP image, since it is well mapped to the properties of human vision.

4.3 Thresholding

There are more advanced techniques, known as optimal thresholding. These usually seek to select a value for the threshold that separates an object from its background. This suggests that the object has a different range of intensities to the background, in order that an appropriate threshold can be chosen.

Otsu's method (Sahoo P. K., Soltani S., Wong, A. K. C. et al., 1988) is one of the most popular techniques of optimal thresholding; applied for fine classification of ROP. Essentially, this technique maximizes the likelihood that the threshold is chosen so as to split the image between an object and its background. This is achieved by selecting a threshold that gives the best separation of classes, for all pixels in an image.

4.4 Averaging filter

For an averaging operator, the template weighting functions are unity. The template for an 7×7 averaging operator is implemented for the image. The result of averaging the ROP image with an 7×7 operator shows much of the details of the broad image structure.

The effect of averaging is to reduce noise, this is its advantage. An associated disadvantage is that averaging causes blurring which reduces detail in an image. It is also a low-pass filter since its effect is to allow low spatial frequencies to be retained, and to suppress high frequency components (Parker J. R., 1994; A.C. Bovik, T.S.Huang, & D.C.Munson, 1983). The size of an averaging operator is then equivalent to the reciprocal of the bandwidth of a low-pass filter it implements.

The averaging process is actually a statistical operator since it aims to estimate the mean of a local neighbourhood. The error in the process is naturally high, for a population of N samples; the statistical error is of the order of:

$$error = \frac{mean}{\sqrt{N}} \tag{9}$$

Increasing the averaging operator's size improves the error in the estimate of the mean, but at the expense of fine detail in the image. The average is of course an estimate optimal for a signal corrupted by additive Gaussian noise. The estimate of the mean maximized the probability that the noise has its mean value, namely zero.

According to the central limit theorem, the result of adding many noise sources together are a Gaussian distributed noise source. By the central limit theorem, the image noise can be assumed to be Gaussian. In fact, image noise is not necessarily Gaussian-distributed, giving rise to more statistical operators. It provides better pre-processing in ROP images and offers coarse estimation for the features.

4.5 Gaussian averaging filter

The Gaussian averaging operator has been considered to be optimal for image smoothing. The template for the Gaussian operator has values set by the Gaussian relationship. Let the x, y are the ROP image intensity values measured in both the (x, y) coordinates. The Gaussian functions 'g' at co-ordinates (x, y) is controlled by the variance 'σ^2' according to:

$$g(x, y) = e^{-\left(\frac{x^2 + y^2}{2\sigma^2} \right)} \tag{10}$$

Where, $g(x, y)$ gives a way to calculate coefficients for a Gaussian template which is then convolved with an image. It is clear that the Gaussian filter can offer improved performance compared with direct averaging: more features are retained whilst the noise is removed. This can lead to better performance in ROP images, since the contributions of the frequency components reduce in a controlled manner.

4.6 Median filter

The median is another frequently used statistic; the median is the centre of a rank-ordered distribution. The median is usually taken from a template centered on the point of interest. The median is the central component of the sorted vector (A.C. Bovik, T.S.Huang, & D.C. Munson, 1983).

The median operator is usually implemented using a template; here a 7×7 template is considered for ROP images. Accordingly, the system process the forty nine pixels in a template centered on a point with co-ordinates (x, y). The median is the central component of the sorted vector; this is the twenty fifth component since we have forty nine values.

The median can of course be taken from larger template sizes. It is available as the median operator in Mathcad, but only for square matrices. The rank ordering process is computationally demanding slow and this has been motivated the use of template shapes other than a square. Common alternative shapes include a cross or a line (horizontal or vertical), centered on the point of interest, which can afford much faster operation since they cover fewer pixels.

The median filter has a well-known ability to remove salt and pepper noise. This form of noise, arising from, say, decoding errors in picture transmission systems, can cause isolated white and black points to appear within an image shown in Fig.6. When a median operator is applied, the salt and pepper noise points will appear at either end of the rank ordered list and are removed by the median process. The median operator has practical advantage, due to its ability to retain edges i.e. the boundaries of shapes in images whilst suppressing the noise contamination.

4.7 Edge detection and feature extraction

The edges and required features of the ROP image have been detected by the Marr–Hildreth approach and Spacek operator (Petrou M. & Kittler J., 1991).

4.7.1 Marr–Hildreth approach

This method uses Gaussian filtering. In principle, we require an image which is the second differential ∇^2 of a Gaussian operator $g(x,y)$ convolved with an image P. This convolution process can be separated as:

$$\nabla g(x,y) = \frac{\partial g(x,y)}{\partial x} U_x + \frac{\partial g(x,y)}{\partial y} U_y$$

$$= -\frac{x}{\sigma^2} e^{\frac{-(x^2+y^2)}{2\sigma^2}} U_x - \frac{y}{\sigma^2} e^{\frac{-(x^2+y^2)}{2\sigma^2}} U_y \tag{11}$$

$$\nabla^2 \left(g(x,y) * P \right) = \nabla^2 g\left((x,y) \right) * P \tag{12}$$

Accordingly, we need to compute a template for $\nabla^2(g(x,y))$ and convolve this with the image. By further differentiation of (11), we achieve a Laplacian of Gaussian (LoG) operator:

$$\nabla^2 g(x,y) = \frac{\partial^2 g(x,y)}{\partial x^2} U_x + \frac{\partial^2 g(x,y)}{\partial y^2} U_y$$

$$= \frac{\partial \nabla g(x,y)}{\partial x} U_x + \frac{\partial \nabla g(x,y)}{\partial y} U_y$$

$$= \left(\frac{x^2}{\sigma^2} - 1 \right) \frac{e^{\frac{-(x^2+y^2)}{2\sigma^2}}}{\sigma^2} + \left(\frac{y^2}{\sigma^2} - 1 \right) \frac{e^{\frac{-(x^2+y^2)}{2\sigma^2}}}{\sigma^2} \tag{13}$$

$$= \frac{1}{\sigma^2} \left(\frac{x^2+y^2}{\sigma^2} - 2 \right) e^{\frac{-(x^2+y^2)}{2\sigma^2}}$$

This is the basis of the Marr–Hildreth operator. Equation (13) can be used to calculate the coefficients of a template which, when convolved with an image, combines Gaussian smoothing with second-order differentiation. It has been implemented to calculate template coefficients for the LoG operator, the function includes a normalization function, which ensures that the sum of the template coefficients is unity, so that the edges in the images are not clearly detected in area of uniform brightness. This is in contrast with the Laplacian operator (where the template coefficients summed to zero) since the LoG operator includes smoothing within the differencing action, whereas the Laplacian is pure differencing. The Gaussian operator again suppresses the influence of points away from the centre of the template, basing differentiation on those points nearer the centre; the standard deviation, σ is chosen to ensure this action. Again, it is isotropic consistent with Gaussian smoothing. Determining the zero-crossing points is a major difficulty with this approach.

4.7.2 Spacek operator

Canny derived an operator to satisfy performance measures describing maximum signal to noise ratio and with good localization and chose a filter functional which maximized a composite measure of these parameters, whilst maintaining the suppression of false maxima (Trichili H et al., 2002). Essentially, whilst Canny maximized the ratio of the signal to noise ratio with the localization, Spacek maximized the ratio of the product of the signal to noise ratio and the peak separation with the localization. In Spacek's work, since the edge was again modeled as a step function, the ideal filter appeared to be of the same form as Canny's (Petrou M. & Kittler J, 1991). After simplification, this resulted in a one-dimensional optimal noise smoothing filter given by:

$$f(r) = (c_1 \sin(r) + c_2 \cos(r))e^r + (c_3 \sin(r) + c_4 \cos(r))e^{-r} + 1 \qquad (14)$$

By numerical solution, Spacek determined optimal values for the constants as: c1 = 13.3816, c2 = 2.7953, c3 = 0.0542 and c4 = -3.7953. Spacek also showed how it was possible to derive operators which optimize filter performance for different combinations of the performance factors. In particular, an operator with the best possible noise suppression formulated by optimizing the noise suppression performance alone, without the other two measures, is given by:

$$f_c(r) = \frac{2\sin(\pi r)}{\pi} - \cos(\pi r) + 2r + 1 \qquad (15)$$

Spacek then showed how these operators could give better performance than Canny's formulation, as such challenging the optimality of the Gaussian operator for noise smoothing (in step edge detection) (Petrou M. & Kittler J, 1988). In application, such an advantage has been produced better output of ROP image. This is the vital feature used to detect the plus disease of ROP.

One difficulty with optimal smoothing functional expressed in one-dimensional form is their extension to become a two-dimensional image operator. For the Spacek operator, one approach is to consider (14) as a circularly symmetric functional expressed in terms of radius 'r' and to generate the coefficients of a template smoothing operator in this manner.

4.8 Image curvature detection

Edges are perhaps the low-level image features that are most obvious to human vision. They preserve significant features, so they can be usually recognized what an image contains from its edge-detected version. However, there are other low-level features that can be used in computer vision. One important feature is curvature. Intuitively, it is important to consider curvature as the rate of change in edge direction (Mokhtarian F. & Mackworth A. K., 1986). This rate of change characterizes the points in a curve; points where the edge direction changes rapidly are corners, whereas points where there is little change in edge direction correspond to straight lines. Such extreme points are very useful for shape description and matching in ROP severity prediction, since they represent significant information with reduced data.

The main problem with this approach is that it depends on the extraction of sequences of pixels. In ROP images, it is very difficult to trace a digital curve in the image. This is because noise in the data can cause edges to be missed or to be found inaccurately. This problem may be handled by using a robust fitting technique. However, the implementation is not evident. By using this robust fitting for each image pixel, then the curvature could be computed as the inverse ratio of a circle.

5. Proposed ROP classification using neural networks

5.1 Proposed BPN and RBF classifier and recognizer model

After extracting the required ROP features from the Retcam images, a classifier and recognizer is needed to screen the severity of ROP. Neural Networks can be applied for such problems to classify and recognize through the training and testing of samples. In this chapter Back Propagation Network (BPN) and a combined model of BPN and Radial Basis Function (RBF) network are proposed as classifiers and recognizers.

5.2 Back propagation network (BPN)

Back Propagation Network (BPN) can train multi layer feed-forward networks with differentiable transfer functions to perform function approximation, pattern association, and pattern classification (Laurene Fausett et al., 1999; Li Min Fu, 1994).

The BPN is designed in this work with one input layer, one hidden layer and one output layer. The input layer consists of six neurons. The inputs to this network are feature vectors derived by applying the image processing calculations and algorithms. The network is trained using the features extracted from processed Retcam ROP images.

The Back propagation training takes place in three stages:

1. Feed forward of input training pattern
2. Back Propagation of the associated error and
3. Weight adjustment

During feed forward, each input neuron receives an input value and broadcasts it to each hidden neuron, which in turn computes the activation and passes it on to each output unit, which again computes the activation to obtain the net output. During training, the net output is compared with the target value and the appropriate error is calculated. From this, the error factor is obtained which is used to distribute the error back to the hidden layer. The weights are updated accordingly. In a similar manner, the error factor is calculated for hidden units. After the error factors are obtained, the weights are updated simultaneously. The output layer contains one neuron. The result from the output layer is considered as the recognition result. The gradient descent algorithm which ahs been utilized in BPN is generally very slow because it requires small learning rates for stable learning. In order to avoid this, BPN is combined with Radial Basis Function Network.

5.3 Combined framework of BPN and RBF

Radial Basis Function (RBF) neural networks have recently attracted extensive research works because of their best approximation property, very compact topology and universal approximators and also their learning speed is very fast because of local-tuned neurons. RBF networks are used for function approximation (Meng Joo Er, shiqan wu, Juwei Lu, et al., 2002). In this paper, a RBF neural network is used as classifier and recognizer in the ROP screening system and the inputs to this network are the results obtained from the BPN. So, the result obtained from the output layer of BPN is given as the input to the RBF. RBF uses the gaussian function for approximation. For approximating the output of BPN, it is connected with RBF.

The RBF neural network has a feed forward architecture with an input layer, a hidden layer and an output layer. Fig. 7 shows the combined framework of BPN and RBF.

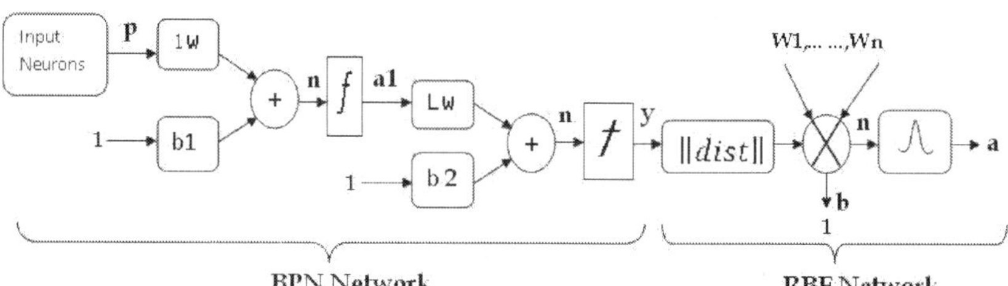

Fig. 7. Combined Framework of BPN and RBF.

a1=tansig(IW*p +b)   y=purelin(LW*a+b)a=radbas(||w-p||b)

where

a1   =   tansig(IW*p+LW+b1)
y   =   purelin(LW*a1+b2)
a   =   radbas(||w-p||b)
p   =   Set of input neurons
b1   =   bias to the input layer
b2   =   bias to the hidden layer
b   =   bias to the RBF neuron
IW   =   Weight between Input and hidden layers
LW   =   Weight between hidden and Output layers
y   =   Output of BPN
Wi   =   Weight vector to RBF
a   =   RBF output

The RBF network is simulated by giving the output of BPN as input to RBF.

6. Results and discussion

The automatic ROP severity identification methodologies have been developed and implemented to analyze the various infant's ROP images with different stages such as stage1, stage 2, and stage 3. Since, the stage 4 and stage 5 are highly critical and almost the retina has been detached as shown in Fig. 2, the images of theses stages have not been considered for our present analysis and prediction and also these stages will not provide fruitful improvement in the vision system on treatment. All the images have been taken by Retcam and are available either in .bmp or .jpeg format with 640X480 sizes. The specific image enhancement and smoothening are obtained by the histogram approach and various filtering techniques such as averaging and median filter methods. The ROP image localizer and other image processing techniques have been implemented and the corresponding results for every stage have been obtained as shown in Fig. 8. The feature extraction and segmentation of the ROP images have been estimated by applying various operators and the exact stage could be identified by the curvature detection approach as shown in Fig. 9.

Detecting pathological retina images in premature infants is a challenging problem. In the proposed methods, the various ROP severities have been identified properly by providing the images to the neural network classifier and recognizer. The results in Table 2 show that our method is able to yield an accurate result and is appreciated by experts. The ROP intensity levels have been extracted in the images taken from various patients with appropriate time interval in terms of prognosis weeks. The ROP diagnosis and treatment are the continuous procedure and will extend minimum for a period of six months. Table 2 shows the four weeks diagnosis of ROP images with various severities in various cases.

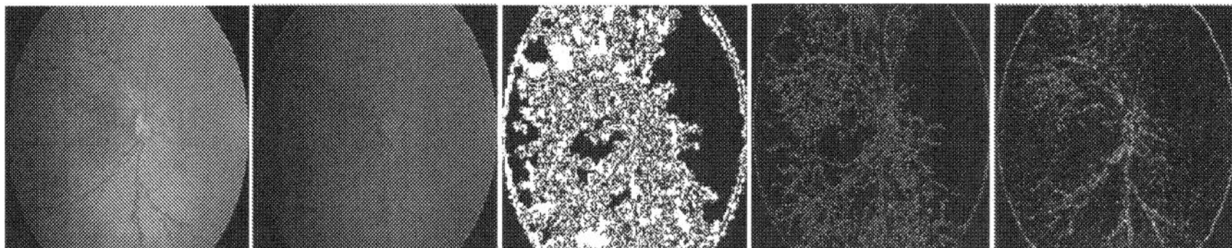

Fig. 8. Processed gray scale images of stage 3 and plus diseased ROP, Image smoothened by Median filter, Binary filled holes, Canny Filtered Image, Dilated Gradient Mask

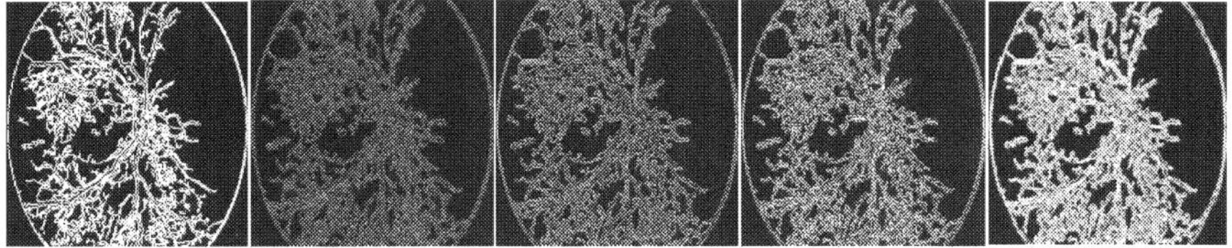

Fig. 9. Processed ROP images such as Dilated Image, Eroded Image, Average Filtered Image, Median Filtered Image, and Segmented Image

For the methodologies application, from each case we have considered 10 to 15 images of various locations of retinal portion and blood vessels development. Initial four weeks of ROP images have been deemed and the averaged ROP intensity level has been calculated by a mixture of image processing algorithms. The ROP images have been acquired for every case with corresponding time interval. Follow-up exams will then occur every week until either high risk prethreshold ROP or threshold ROP occurs, which requires treatment, or procedure continues till the ROP disappears.

The severity of ROP prognosis in various cases with appropriate time duration has been shown in Fig. 10. The proposed method detects the stage 1, Stage 2, stage 3 and plus disease ROP intensity levels and the result has been appraised by the ophthalmologists. Based on the analysis the treatment could be started and further follow-up examinations could be taken place in every week.

The effectiveness of the proposed ROP localization technique and the ROP severity screening algorithm are demonstrated using the computer simulations. The processed ROP image database consists of 130 images for 13 different cases of infants. Out of 130 images, 65 images have been taken for training the BPN and RBF networks. The training database has been stored for feature reference and further differentiation. The fine classification of various stages of ROP based on the severity could be acquired by modifying the stored features of various stages of ROP images. This is the very useful feature of automatic stage screening system using neural network. The number of epochs versus the squared error graph is shown in the Fig. 11.

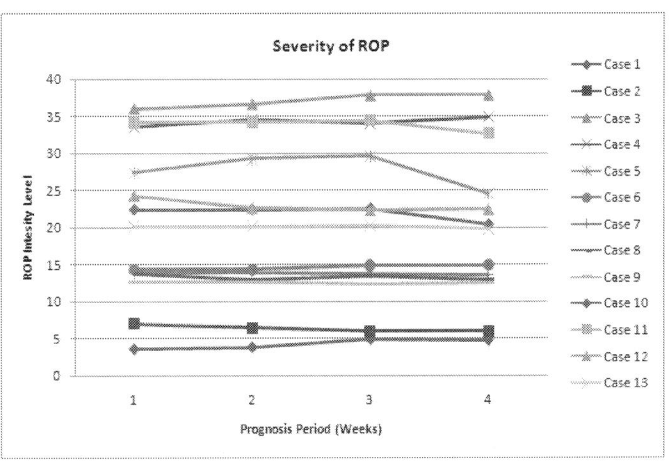

Fig. 10. Severity of ROP intensity distribution for different cases

Severity of ROP	Case	Prognosis Period in Weeks			
		1	2	3	4
Stage 1	1	3.58587	3.81205	4.82632	4.72649
	2	6.97861	6.39284	5.93572	5.92018
Stage 2	3	36.03182	36.61781	37.76183	37.82493
	4	33.52674	34.56846	34.01264	34.92073
	5	27.42039	29.21654	29.56214	24.54281
Stage 3	6	14.33021	14.3312	14.87012	14.88023
	7	13.86317	13.86245	13.78453	13.65245
	8	13.78317	12.89521	13.35481	12.8729
	9	12.62624	12.62434	12.34675	12.4392
	10	22.36995	22.33591	22.45786	20.38219
Plus Disease	11	34.22109	34.22109	34.45215	32.69103
	12	24.28109	22.62306	22.26518	22.35671
	13	20.10566	20.10566	20.24308	19.73859

Table 2. Severity of ROP for various cases in proper time interval.

Then the Neural Networks are tested with the remaining various stages of ROP images. The BPN network predicts 3 cases indistinctly and provides erroneous classification for Stage2, Stage 4 and Stage 5. The combined model of BPN+RBF classifies and recognizes all the ROP images with proper stage classification except stage 2. The time consumption and the classification and recognition rate are tabulated in Table 3.

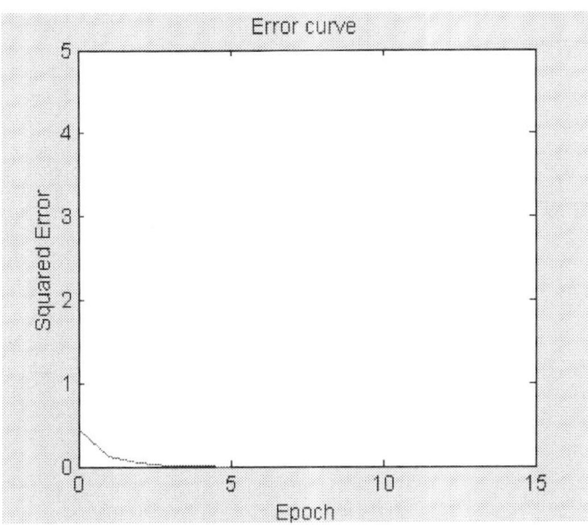

Fig. 11. Error rate versus number of Epochs (BPN Training)

Network	Training+ Testing time (in seconds)	Recognition Rate (in %)
BPN	15.5490	98.4
BPN+RBF	15.5640	99.2

Table 3. Comparison of BPN+RBF framework over BPN.

The false positive and the false negative rates of BPN and BPN+RBF networks are listed in Table 4.

Network	Number of Images	False Classification	False Dismissal
BPN	130	3	0
BPN+RBF	130	1	0

Table 4. Results of the proposed method over the whole test set (BPN and BPN+RBF).

From this result, the proposed model of combined BPN and RBF network has delivered better ROP classifiers and recognizers. The outcomes of this hybrid model have been evaluated by the experts and which may provide the best analysis of ROP severity. ROP severity screening depicts that some stages have rapid difference in its intensity levels in time duration and some have negligible levels of variation in its prognosis. Any how based on the intensity level, classification and recognition the physician could reach up a solution of the necessary method and time period to treat the disease. Then the treatment will reduce the prognosis of the disease and has to be verified every time.

7. Conclusion

In this work, proper ROP screening system has been designed to carry out the classification and recognition of various severity and stages of ROP. Initially, Back Propagation Network (BPN) is used as the recognizer. The features extracted from the different image processing algorithms in Chapter 4 are given as the input to BPN. The implementation of zone fitting and further enhancement of ROP intensity level will produce predominant result. The method introduced here utilizes the well-known framework of commonly using imaging techniques which have provided the best ROP database for further processing such as classification and recognition. BPN is trained with a set of images and the weights are updated. After training, the features of the image has to be tested are given as input. The network is simulated using these input values and the result is obtained. The proposed method shows a good performance for stage 3 and plus disease images. The ratio of the number of images correctly identified the stage of ROP to the total number of images gives the recognition result.

To enhance the performance of BPN, it is combined with RBF. RBF network can approximate any type of function. The output obtained from BPN is given as the input to RBF. RBF is simulated using this input and the output is acquired which is considered to be the Classification and recognition result. From the simulation results, it can be observed that the recognition rate of the combined BPN and RBF model is considerably high. The effectiveness of the proposed method has been demonstrated through experimentation using various ROP diseased cases.

Still further improvement may be required for the precise classification and identification of stage 1 and stage 2. Since, it might be that the exact shape is unknown or it might be that the perturbation of that shape is impossible to parameterize (Huertas A. & Medioni G. 1986; Mokhtarian F. & Mackworth A. K. 1986; Committee for the Classification of Retinopathy of Prematurity, 1984 ; Cryotherapy for Retinopathy of Prematurity Cooperative Group, 1988). In these cases, we seek techniques that can evolve to the target solution, or adapt their result to the data. This implies the use of flexible shape formulations. The snake model could be used to identify the flexible formulations and the results of the same could be delivered to the neural network classifiers.

In future we can combine the proposed methods and different implementations of the snake model to detect the flexible patterns. The wavelet based image fusion technique may also be utilized to produce better result in stage 1 and stage 2 classes of images. The ROP concentration will further be categorized and identified with image registration and fusion techniques. The artificial neural network algorithms may also be enhanced by Adaptive Resonance Theory (ART1) network and the Learning Vector Quantization (LVQ) network to train the system to produce better result and automation of ROP diagnosis in a successful manner. This ROP stage classification recognition system will also satisfy the prediction of stage 4 and stage 5 with better accuracy. The Graphical User Interface (GUI) based menu options will provide user friendly environment for non ophthalmologist so that the time consumption of ophthalmologists can be considerably reduced i.e. instead of analyzing all Retcam images they provide prominent diagnosis on the infants who have suffered with severe stage ROP.

8. Acknowledgment

The authors would like to thank Dr. N.G.P. Institute of Technology, Kovai Medical Center Hospital, Coimbatore and Aravind eye hospital, Coimbatore for providing necessary facilities to carry out this work. The suggestions and comments of anonymous reviewers, which have greatly helped to improve the quality of this paper, are acknowledged.

9. References

A.C. Bovik, T.S. Huang, and D.C. Munson, (1983) "A Generalization of Median Filtering using Linear Combinations of Order Statistics, "*IEEE Transaction on Acoustics, Speech and Signal Processing*, vol. ASSp-31, no.6, pp.1342-1350

Attar MA, Gates MR, Iatrow AM, Lang SW, Bratton SL. (2005) "Barriers to screening infants for retinopathy of prematurity after discharge or transfer from a neonatal intensive care unit," [PubMed: 15496873] *J Perinatol*, 25:36-40

Baxes, G. A. (1994), *"Digital Image Processing, Principles and Applications, "* Wiley & Sons Inc., NY USA

Benson Shu Yan Lam and Hong Yan (2008) "A novel vessel segmentation algorithm for pathological retina images based on the divergence of vector fields," *IEEE Trans. Med. Imag.*, Vol.27, No.2, pp237-246

Committee for the Classification of Retinopathy of Prematurity (1984) "An international classification of retinopathy of prematurity," *Arch Opthalmol*; 102: 1130-4

Cryotherapy for Retinopathy of Prematurity Cooperative Group (1988) "Multicenter trial of cryotherapy for retinopathy of prematurity. Preliminary results," *Arch Ophthalmol*; 106:471-9

Early Treatment of Retinopathy of Prematurity Cooperative Group (2003). "Revised indications for the treatment of retinopathy of prematurity," Arch Ophthalmol; 121: 1684-96.

Ells AL, Holmes JM, Astle WF, et al. (2003) Telemedicine approach to screening for severe retinopathy of prematurity: a pilot study. *Ophthalmology*; 110: 2113-7

Fetus and Newborn Committee, Canadian Paediatric Society. (1998) "Retinopathy of prematurity: recommendations for screening," *Pediatric Child Health*; 3:197-8

Fierson WM, Palmer EA, Petersen RA, et al. (2001) "Screening examination of premature infants for retinopathy of prematurity," *Pediatrics*; 108:809-11

Gwenole Quellec, Mathieu Lamard, Pierre Marie Josselin & Guy Cazuguel (2008) "Optimal Wavelet transform for the Detection of Microaneurysms in Retina Photographs," *IEEE Trans. Med. Imag.*, vol.27, No.9, pp.1230-1241

Huertas, A. and Medioni, G. (1986) "Detection of Intensity Changes with Subpixel Accuracy using Laplacian–Gaussian Masks," *IEEE Trans. on PAMI*, 8(1), pp. 651–664

International Committee for the Classification of Retinopathy of Prematurity (2005) "The international classification of retinopathy of prematurity revisited," *Arch Ophthalmol*; 123:991-9

Jia, X. and Nixon, M. S. (1995) "Extending the Feature Vector for Automatic Face Recognition," *IEEE Trans. on PAMI*, 17(12), pp. 1167–1176

Kai Chuan Chu, and Dzulkifli Mohamad, (August 3-5, 2003) " Development of a Face Recognition System using Artificial Intelligent Techniques based on Hybrid

Feature Selection, " Proc. Of the second Intl. Conference on Artificial Intelligence in Engineering and Technology, Malaysia, pp. 365-370

Kaiser RS, Trese MT, Williams GA, Cox MS Jr. (2001) "Adult retinopathy of prematurity: outcomes of rhegmatogenous retinal detachments and retinal tears," *Ophthalmology* ; 108:1647-53

Lamdan, Y., Schawatz, J. and Wolfon, H. (1988) "Object Recognition by Affine Invariant Matching," *Proc. IEEE Conf. on Computer Vision and Pattern Recognition*, pp. 335–344.

Laurene Fausett, (1999) *"Fundamentals of Neural Networks, "* Prentice Hall, New Jersey

Li Min Fu, (1994) *"Neural Networks in Computer Intelligence,"* McGraw-Hill Inc., Singapore

Loupas, T. and McDicken, W. N. (1987) "Noise Reduction in Ultrasound Images by Digital Filtering," *British Journal of Radiology*, 60, pp. 389–392

Meng Joo Er, shiqan wu, Juwei Lu, and Hock Lye Toh, (May 2002)" Face Recognition with Radial Basis Function (RBF) Neural Networks," *IEEE Transactions on Neural Networks*, vol.13, No.3, pp.697-710

Mokhtarian, F. and Mackworth, A. K. (1986) "A Theory of Multi-Scale, Curvature-Based Shape Representation for Planar Curves," *IEEE Trans. on PAMI*, 14(8), pp. 789–805

Mounir Bashour, Johanne Menassa & C Cornia Gerontis (2008) *"Retinopathy of Prematurity,"* Nov, [Online] Available: http://www.emedicine.medscape.com/article/1225022

Palmer EA, Flynn JT, Hardy R. (1991) Incidence and early course of retinopathy of prematurity. *Ophthalmology*; 98:1628-40

Parker, J. R. (1994), *"Practical Computer Vision using C, "* Wiley & Sons Inc., NY USA

Petrou, M. and Kittler, J.(1991) Optimal Edge Detectors for Ramp Edges, *IEEE Trans. on PAMI*, 13(5), pp. 483–491

Petrou.M and Kittler.J (1988) "On the optimal edge detector," Proc. of The british Machine Vision Conference (BMVC) by BMVA, Alvey Vision Conference, pp 191- 196

Russ, J. C. (1995) *"The Image Processing Handbook,"* 2nd Edition, CRC Press (IEEE Press), Boca Raton, FL USA

Sahoo, P. K., Soltani, S., Wong, A. K. C. and Chen, Y. C. (1988) "Survey of Thresholding Techniques," *CVGIP*, 41(2), pp. 233–260

Schaffer DB, Palmer EA, Plotsky DF, Metz HS, Flynn JT, Tung B, et al. (1993) "Prognostic factors in the natural course of retinopathy of prematurity," *Ophthalmology*;100:230-7

Shah PK, Narendran V, Kalpana N, Tawansy KA. (2009), "Anatomical and visual outcome of stages 4 and 5 retinopathy of prematurity," Eye 2009, 23:176-180

Shankar, P. M. (1986) "Speckle Reduction in Ultrasound B Scans using Weighted Averaging in Spatial Compounding," *IEEE Trans. on Ultrasonics, Ferroelectrics and Frequency Control*, 33(6), pp. 754–758

Siatkowski RM, Flynn JT. (1998) *"Retinopathy of Prematurity. In Nelson L,ed. Harely's Pediatric Ophthalmology,"* 4th ed. Philadelphia: WB Saunders& Co.

Trichili, H.; Bouhlel, M.-S.; Derbel, N.; Kamoun, L.; (6-9 Oct. 2002), "A survey and evaluation of edge detection operators application to medical images," Systems, Man and Cybernetics, 2002 IEEE International Conference on, vol.4, no., pp. 4

Wittchow.K (2003) "Shared liability for ROP screening," *OMIC Journal.P.3* http://www.omic.com/new/digest/ DigestFall03.pdf accessed November 20, (2009)

5

Automatic Scratching Analyzing System for Laboratory Mice: SCLABA-Real

Yuman Nie[1], Idaku Ishii[1], Akane Tanaka[2] and Hiroshi Matsuda[2]
[1]*Robotics Laboratory, Department of Artificial Complex Systems Engineering,*
Hiroshima University
[2]*Division of Animal Life Science, Institute of Symbiotic Science and Technology,*
Tokyo University of Agriculture and Technology
Japan

1. Introduction

Small laboratory animals such as mice, rats and rabbits play important roles in the news drugs development for human beings and in disease pathophysiology. Some examples include the NC mouse used as the model of atopic dermatitis, and the WISTAR rats used as the model of clinic depression in the forced swim test. However, the behaviors of small animals are usually very fast and repetitive, and sometimes very difficult to observe by the naked eyes by other common methods.

Laboratory mice are widely used as the model of human beings' atopic dermatitis, whose scratching behavior could be induced by itching. For the itching evaluation experiments in animal models, automatic quantification system is needed for objective and accurate results. Mouse scratching is the behavior of rapidly scratches its head or other parts by using its hind leg. It is also known to be a model behavior of disorders as a major symptom of skin disease such as atopic dermatitis and other types of dermatitis.

Mice's scratching is also a periodic behavior inhibited at a frequency of more than 10 times/s, and it is extremely difficult to detect such rapid movement accurately with the naked eye or conventional video tracking system. Furthermore, scratching behavior also has to be distinguished from other behaviors, such as grooming and rearing. Grooming is the mice groom themselves with their teeth and claws. The usual grooming routine may involve a mouse scratching itself with the hind feet, then perhaps washing its face or fur with its hands (spreading saliva on the hands, and rubbing them over the fur), and grooming with the teeth. Rearing is the mice standing up with hind legs and sometimes with exploration. Frequencies of grooming and rearing are lower than scratching but also difficult for manual distinguishing and duration time quantification.

Therefore, for an objective evaluation, it is important to perform the automatic quantification of mice, thereby enabling drug developers to assess the grade of dermatitis and the efficacy of new anti-pruritic drugs in laboratory animal experiments.

In this chapter, we describe a real-time mice scratching detection and quantification system based on a specially designed high-speed vision system. Its recording and processing frame rate is much higher than the video signal rate (NTSC 30 fps/PAL 25 fps). The developed system can discriminate the scratching behavior from other behaviors, such as rearing and grooming.

For evaluation, we show the performance of our developed system by experimental results for several laboratory mice in long-time observation. The results also show the objectiveness and accuracy. We estimated the detection correction ratio and compared the scratching times of these mice.

2. State of the art

Laboratory mice scratching can be artificial induced by administering factors triggering itching K. Kuraishi (1995). For scientific purpose, many experiments have been conducted to evaluate mice scratching. These experiments involve the administration of the compound 48/80 R. C. Benyon (1986), histamine N. Inagaki (1999), and serotonin J. S. Thomsen (2002) and acetone or ether painting on animals to induce a dry skin T. Miyamoto (2002). However, all of these experiments have not been evaluated objectively because many of them relied on manual detection which use naked-eye for observations.

In recent years, some automatic systems are also developed for the objective detection and quantification of scratching. Inagaki et al. planted a metal marker under the skin of a laboratory animal N. Inagaki (2003) and reported the benefits of MicroAct. It is a quantitative scratching analysis system that utilizes magnetic field fluctuations when the metal marker vibrates violently as a result of scratching. The marker methods are very invasive to animals, and make it very difficult to obtain an objective result.

It is worth noting that we can consider similarity with human motion, since the vision based human motion analysis has also been studied by many researchers T. B. Moeslund (2006). To solve the inherent complexities in general activity recognition and classification, hierarchical models, spatio-temporal features, temporally aligned pyramid matching and many other advanced methods have been utilized Y. KYan (2007); J. C. Niebles (2007); D. Xu (2008); S. Savarese (2008); L. Wang (2008).

However, there are inherent differences in small laboratory animals' behaviors and primate's behaviors. The primate's behaviors such as human activities are usually contain multiple patterns and the motion is slow. For purpose, the human behavior recognition may be used in surveillance, control, and analysis. However, small laboratory animals such as mice or rats, are observed under constructed environments whose behaviors are usually simplex, but sometimes high frequency and repetitive. Furthermore, small laboratory animal behavior detection and quantification are mainly used for new drugs effect evaluation, and the detection and quantification accuracy and high-throughput are mostly required. Thus the analysis method should be different from human behaviors'.

To detect some periodic human motions, such as gaits characteristics extraction, quite a few researches have been conducted A. Sundaresan (2003); X. Yang (2008); M. H. Cheng (2008). These studies mainly focus on behavior recognition and classification, but all of them based on 30 fps video images.

Real-time automatic visual inspection (AVI) systems have also become widely used in industries. Typical systems such as E. Guerra (2001); L. Zhang (2005) used the methods of color space transform and three-dimensional techniques, respectively.

However, these systems are characterized by slow frame rates and low resolutions. A high-speed inspection system presented in I. Ishii (2007) used the coded structured light projection method, but it could not be a solution for behavior detection.

Elliott et al. have applied frequency analysis to a mouse's motion data with a magnetic sensor to extract scratching data G. R. Elliott (2000). However, one of the serious problems associated with these systems is that a magnetic marker needs to be embedded under the skin of the animal, thereby inducing stress.

Brash et al. have developed a quantifying system based on a sensitive force transducer positioned below a recording platform, but it cannot distinguish the individual movements in one series H. M. Brash (2005).

Umeda et al. have reported on an acoustic scratching counting system K. Umeda (2006). The acoustic system eliminates the necessity of planting markers in animals; it requires a special setting to eliminate sound noise because acoustic information is extremely sensitive.

Finally, SCLABA K. Orito (2004) is a vision-based automated scratching detection system. In the SCLABA method, colored markers are painted on a mouse's head and toe. Their positions are extracted from offline 30 fps video images that are not sufficiently fast for accurate recording of mice scratching. Hence, this system often inaccurately identifies non-scratching movements as scratching; these include grooming and rearing that are slower than scratching.

3. Mice scratching detection algorithm based on frame-to-frame difference feature

3.1 Frame-to-frame difference feature

Mice scratching, at 10 times per second or more, is a very fast movement for the commonly available 30 fps video cameras recording. Fig. 1 shows the sample images recorded at 30 fps in 167 ms, and 240 fps in 21 ms.

Moreover, it is desirable for accurate quantification of mice scratching to detect scratching patterns by image analysis without any markers on a mouse, because the plant or paint markers on a mouse is difficult, and the markers themselves can affect the mouse's behavior and cause serious problems.

To solve these problems, a non-marker image analysis method has been proposed for scratching detectionI. Ishii (2008). It is based on the fact that mice scratching involves periodic movements of the motor components with a frequency higher than that observed for movements associated with behaviors.

It's assumed that the video camera employed had a frame rate that was sufficiently fast to accurately capture the scratching movements. Then the mice scratching could be detected by extracting high frequency motion components in frame-to-frame difference images. The evaluation experiments of the proposed method demonstrated that the scratching detection accuracy was considerably better than conventional analysis methods.

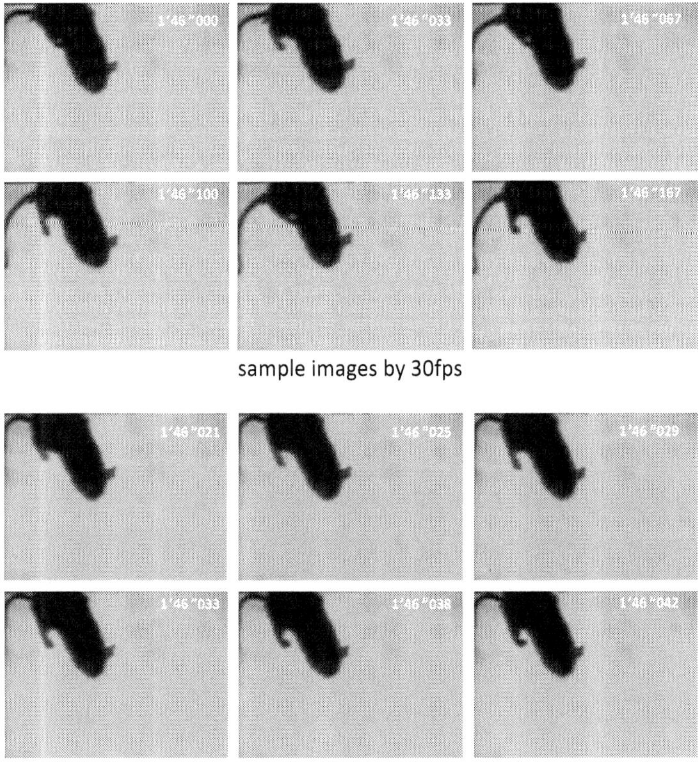

Fig. 1. Mice scratching sample images.

However, several areas of improvement need to be investigated by laboratory mice experiments. One of concern is that non-scratching behaviors that involves movements of the entire body, such as rearing, is occasionally mistaken for scratching because whole body movements generate high-frequency motion components. Further, the method has not been implemented as a real-time and long-time detection system. The employed high-speed camera is offline which can only record a short interval of 6.0 s. This is far from the requirement of real application.

3.2 Mice scratching detection algorithm

In this chapter, we introduce an improved mice scratching detection algorithm for more accurate quantification based on a high-speed vision system for calculating frame-to-frame difference feature at real-time.

Especially we pay attention to the fact that when a mouse scratches, repetitive short-term pulses are generated in frame-to-frame difference feature. A short-term pulses detection method is adopted for extracting scratching behaviors instead of frequency filtering. The flowchart of our method is shown in Fig. 2 and it can be described as in the following.

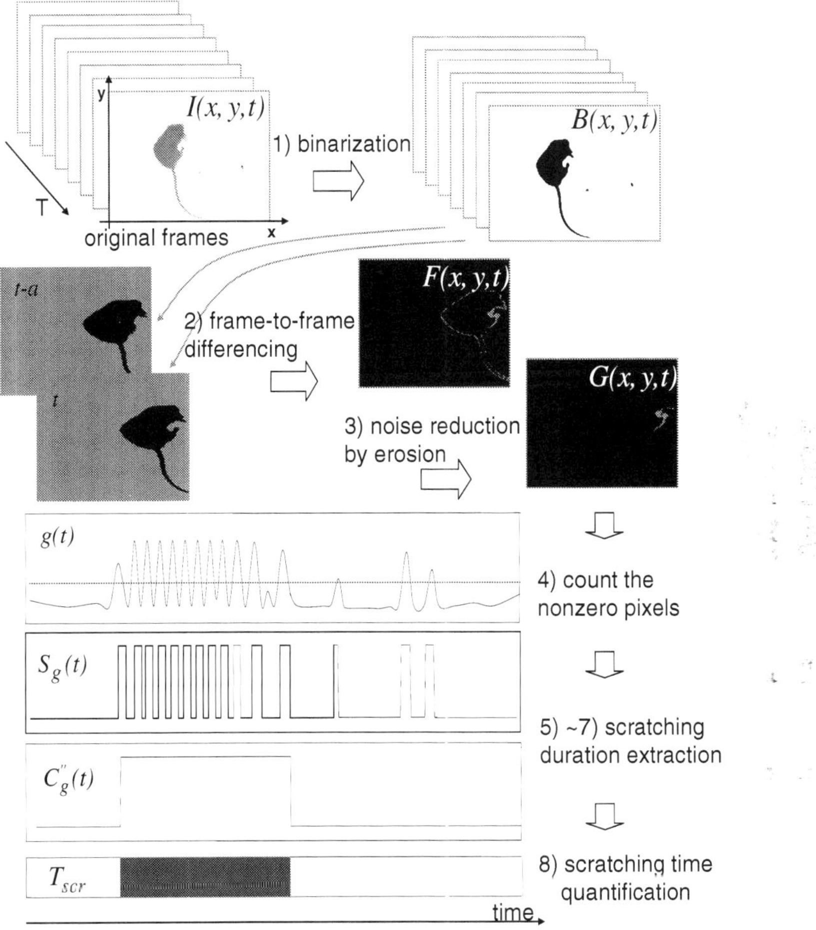

Fig. 2. Mice scratching detection algorithm.

1) binarization

The input image $I(x, y, t)$ at time t is binarized to segment a silhouette image of a mouse from background. Here θ_b is a threshold for binarization.

$$B(x, y, t) = \begin{cases} 1 & (I(x, y, t) > \theta_b) \\ 0 & (\text{otherwise}) \end{cases}. \tag{1}$$

2) frame-to-frame difference

$F(x,y,t)$ is calculated as the absolute value of the frame-to-frame differential images between time $t-a$ and t to extract the motion in the silhouette image. Here a is the time difference in the differential images. If the mouse moves, the motion area could be observed in $F(x,y,t)$.

$$F(x,y,t) = |B(x,y,t) - B(x,y,t-a)|. \tag{2}$$

3) noise reduction by erosion

$G(x,y,t)$ is calculated as a erosion image of $F(x,y,t)$ to reduce edge or isolated noises. The noise will appear in $F(x,y,t)$ by fluctuated illumination even if there is no motion.

$$G(x,y,t) = F(x,y,t) \cap F(x-1,y,t) \cap F(x,y-1,t). \tag{3}$$

4) count the nonzero pixels

By counting the number of nonzero pixels in $G(x,y,t)$ as a frame-to-frame difference feature, the area of movement $g(t)$ is quantified. The $G(x,y,t)$ means whether there is motion or not at each pixel.

$$g(t) = \sum_x \sum_y G(x,y,t). \tag{4}$$

5) pulse threshold

By thresholding $g(t)$, $S_g(t)$ are calculated as pulses. It shows whether there is motion or not at time t. Here θ_c is a threshold to remove small-scale movements. Here, Fig.3 shows the detail of pulse processing in 5)~8).

$$S_g(t) = \begin{cases} 1 & (g(t) > \theta_c) \\ 0 & (\text{otherwise}) \end{cases}. \tag{5}$$

6) short-term pulses detection

$C_g(t)$ are extracted short-term pulses from $S_g(t)$, which contain repetitive short-term pulses generated in mice scratching and reject other large-scale or long-term pulses generated in other mice movements. Here $d(t)$ is a duration time of $C_g(t) = 1$ involving time t, and τ_0 is a threshold to reject long-term pulses.

$$C_g(t) = \begin{cases} 1 & (d(t) < \tau_0) \\ 0 & (\text{otherwise}) \end{cases}. \tag{6}$$

7) long-term duration detection Duration time is calculated to detect repetitive short pulses. First, short intervals are compensated to make the repetitive pulses as a whole one. Here duration time is a threshold interval to decide whether the repetitive pulses are compensated as one pulse or not.

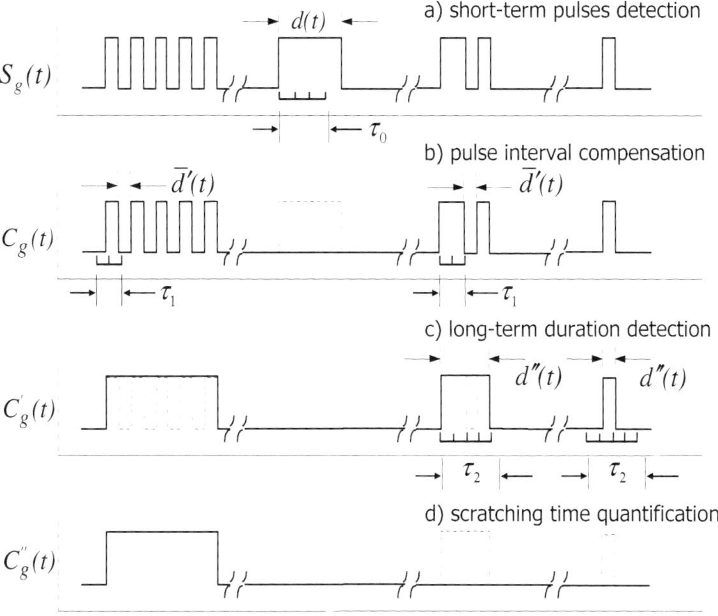

Fig. 3. Pulse processing for scratching quantification.

$$C1_g(t) = \begin{cases} 1 & (\overline{d}(t) < \tau_1) \\ 0 & (\text{otherwise}) \end{cases}. \tag{7}$$

Here the scratching is judged when duration time is over than a threshold interval, supposing that multiple short-term pulses exist in a certain interval when a mouse scratches. Then, scratching time is extracted by reducing pulses with short duration times.

$$C2_g(t) = \begin{cases} 1 & (d2(t) > \tau_2) \\ 0 & (\text{otherwise}) \end{cases}. \tag{8}$$

8) scratching time quantification The total scratching time $T_{scr}(t_1; t_2)$ between $t = t_1$ and t_2 is counted by integrating the time of $C2_g(t) = 1$, because we can suppose $C2_g(t)$ contain only repetitive short-term pulses related to mice scratching.

$$T_{scr}(t_1; t_2) = \int_{t_1}^{t_2} C2_g(t)dt. \tag{9}$$

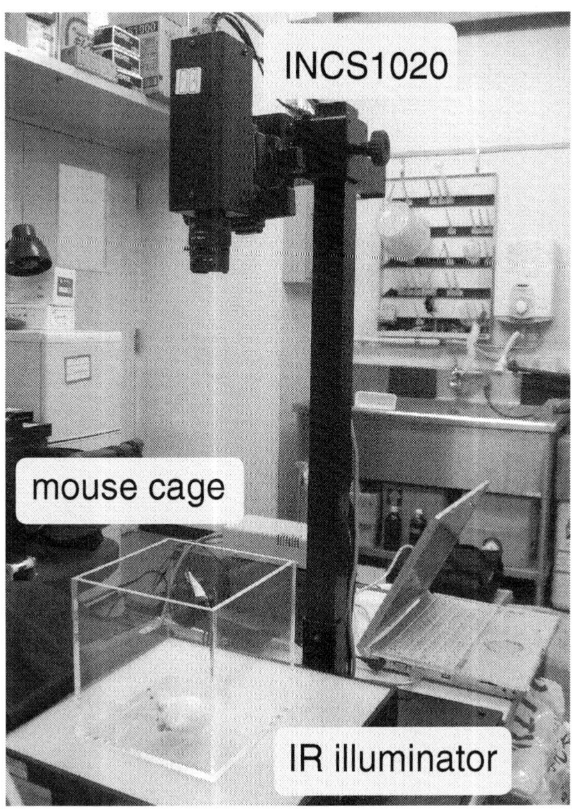

Fig. 4. An overview of real-time scratching quantification system.

4. Real-time scratching quantification system

Based on the scratching detection algorithm, a mice scratching quantification system for real-time and long-time observation is developed. It can quantify the behaviors of a mouse in a cage without painting markers on it by calculating frame-to-frame differential feature on a specially designed high-speed vision system INCS1020.

Fig. 4 shows the measurement set-up: the mouse is enclosed in a transparent acrylic cage with dimensions of 12 cm × 12 cm. The high-speed vision system INCS1020 is installed at a height of 50 cm from the bottom of the cage. On the background of the transparent cage, we set an IR flat illuminator IR95-DF from CCS Corporation from Japan, and the dimensions of 30 cm × 30 cm are larger than those of the bottom of the cage. The peak wavelength in the illuminator is 950 nm. By introducing the background illuminator, the clear silhouette images of a mouse can be captured regardless of the kind of mouse. This system also has a feature that adopt to dark night experimental condition as well as day light condition for scratching quantification, because a mouse has no vision to the IR light.

Fig. 5. An overview of INCS1020.

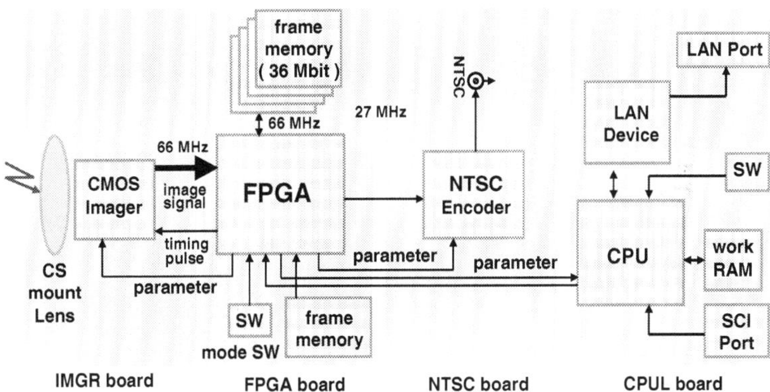

Fig. 6. Internal configuration of INCS1020.

Size	60 mm × 60 mm × 160 mm
Weight	450 g
Imager	Micron MT9V403
Imager Size	659 × 494 pixels
FPGA LSI	Xilinx XC2VP100
Processing rate/Resolution	640 × 480 pixels @120 fps 640 × 400 pixels @240 fps
Processed image feature	frame-to-frame difference feature
Video signal	NTSC 1ch
Lens mount	1/2 inch, C/CS mount
Network	100Base-TX

Table 1. Specification of INCS1020.

INCS(Intelligent Network Camera System)1020 is a high-speed vision system. It is specially designed for calculating frame-to-frame difference feature for mice scratching.

Fig. 5 shows the images of INCS1020. INCS1020 is configured by four internal functional boards, i) image sensor board (IMGR board), ii) main processing board(FPGA board), iii) Image Output board(NTSC board), and iv) Interface board(CPUL board) as shown in Fig. 6.

The IMGR board has a CMOS imager MT9V403 from Micron Technology Inc., and the size is 659×494 pixels.10 bit gray-level video images of 640×480 pixels at 240 fps or 640×480 pixels at 120 fps can be transmitted from the IMGR board to the FPGA board.

The FPGA board has a FPGA LSI XC2VP100 of Xilinx and frame memories for image processing that requires image size computation as hardware logics. The processing results are transmitted to the NTSC board and the CPUL board.

The FPGA board can calculate frame-to-frame difference feature as described subprocessings Eqs. (1)~(4) for 640×400 pixels image at 240 fps or 640×480 pixels at 120 fps.

The NTSC board outputs monitor images to a NTSC video signal output, which can be selected from an original 10 bit image, a binarized image, or a frame differential image. The CPUL board has a LAN device and CPU for network communication between external personal computers(PCs), which can send frame-to-frame difference features to external PC and control the FPGA board by using setting parameters sent from the external PC.

Then, an external PC can obtain frame-to-frame difference features and send several setting parameters of INCS1020 by using network connection. Here API functions library is available for parameter settings and data transmission to control INCS1020, which works on Windows XP/Vista and Windows 7 both 32 bit and 64 bit.

The specification of INCS1020 are listed in Table 1.

5. Experimental results

We quantified scratching in the behavior of 4 laboratory mice, namely, ICR1, ICR2, ICR3, and ICR4. The laboratory mouse we used was the ICR mouse which is a Swiss mouse that is widely used in oncological and pharmaceutical research as well as in studies associated with atopic dermatitis.

All the 4 ICR mice were administered with 100 mg of compound 48/80 in the heads to induce frequent scratching. Then they were placed the cage without any further treatment. Then the frame-to-frame difference was calculated on INCS1020 for 20 min for each ICR mouse, and the processed images had 640×400 pixels recorded at a frame rate of 240 fps. Duration time of each experiment is 20 min.

In these experiments, parameters were set as follows: the threshold for gray-level video image binarization, θ_b, was adjusted for each mouse; the maximum value is 255, and the threshold value range is 150 ± 30. The frame rate is set at 240 fps, thus the time difference a in the frame differencing of two consecutive frames is 4.2 ms.

For scratching behavior detection, parameters are suggested by experienced experts: the threshold for removing small scale movements, θ_c, was 55 pixels; the threshold for rejecting long-term pulse, τ_0, was 21 ms; the threshold interval for combined pulses, τ_1, was 83 ms; and the threshold for reducing short duration pulses, τ_2, was 208 ms. All the parameters except θ_b were applied to all the 4 experimental ICR mice.

No.	sc→no	gr→sc	re→sc	oth→sc	scr	corr
1	0.0	10.3	5.3	0.0	205.3	0.92
2	16.7	0.0	16.8	3.4	461.5	0.92
3	30.4	0.0	5.3	0.0	734.0	0.95
4	0.0	3.0	0.0	0.0	377.0	0.99

Table 2. Evaluation for scratching quantification (unit: s).

Fig. 7 shows the 1-min analysis result from $t = 2$ to 3 during the 20-min observation for ICR1: (a) shows the frame-to-frame difference $g(t)$; (b) shows the pulse $S_g(t)$ that determines the presence or absence of motion; (c) shows the pulse $C_g(t)$ that indicates the automated detection result for scratching; and (d), shows the manual naked-eye observation results for scratching, grooming, and rearing.

The start time of this experiment was set to $t = 0$. The data in 1 min contained 5 periods of scratching, 1 period of grooming, and several periods of rearing, as shown in Fig. 7(d).

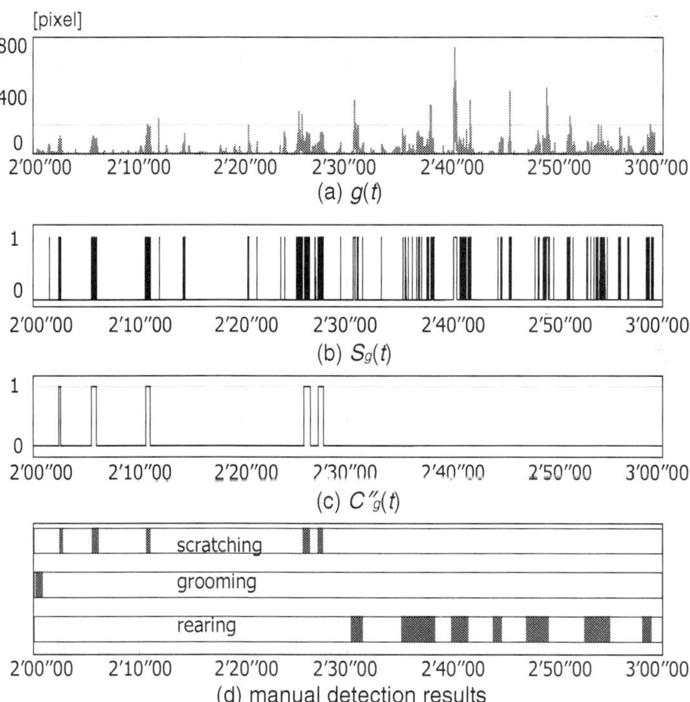

Fig. 7. Scratching detection result (ICR1, 1 min).

Fig. 8. Typical behaviors of an ICR mouse.

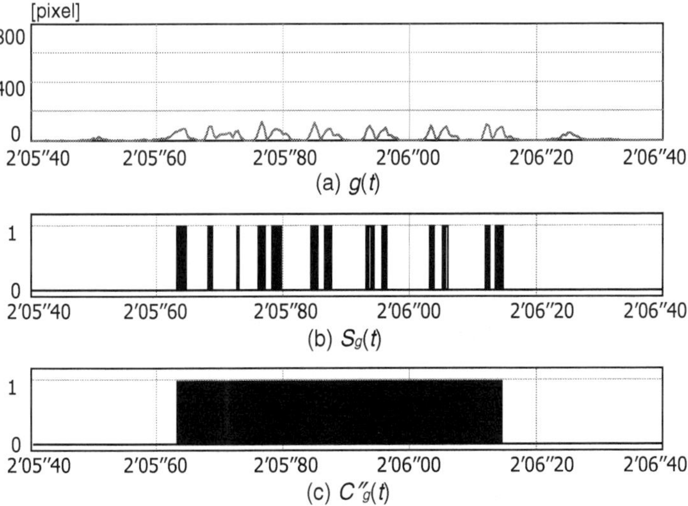

Fig. 9. Detection results for scratching (ICR1, 1 s).

Here, "grooming" refers to the actions of licking the fore and hind legs, back, belly, groin, etc. "Rearing" refers to the mouse action of standing on the hind legs with the forefeet touching a wall. The snapshots of these typical behaviors are displayed in Fig. 8.

To understand the principle underlying the working of our scratching detection algorithm, we also show a magnified graph in 1 s with regard to scratching, grooming, and rearing. Fig. 9 shows the detection result for scratching for the duration $t = 2m05s40$ to $2m06s40$, Fig. 10 exhibits the result for grooming for the duration $t = 2m00s30$ to $2m01s30$, and Fig. 11 exhibits the results for rearing for the duration $t = 2m39s60$ to $2m40s60$. In all the graphs, (a), (b), and (c) indicate $g(t)$, $S_g(t)$, and $C_g(t)$, respectively.

In Fig. 9, scratching 6 times or more within 1 s generates repetitive short-term pulses in $S_g(t)$, and the scratching duration in $C_g(t)$ is detected as the pulse from $t = 2m05s64$ to $2m06s15$. In Fig. 10, no pulse is detected in $S_g(t)$ and no scratching duration is revealed in $C_g(t)$, although there are repetitive movements.This is because the value of $g(t)$ is not greater than θ_c. In Fig. 11, $g(t)$ values are higher than those for θ_c due to the whole body movement of the mouse

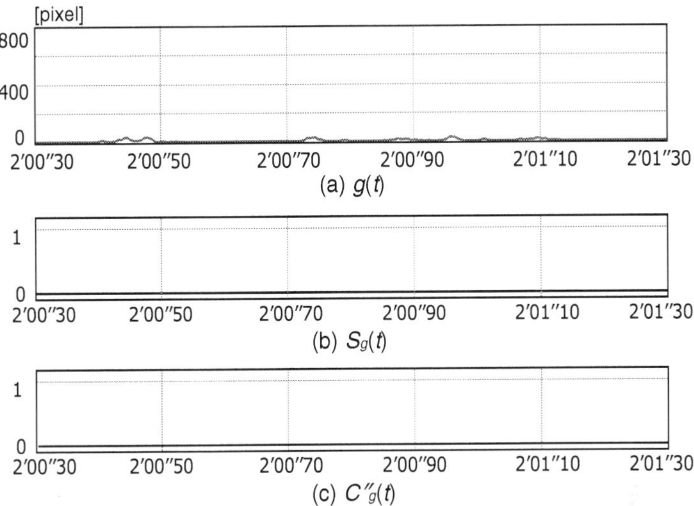

Fig. 10. Detection results for grooming (ICR1, 1 s).

during rearing. The pulses generated in $S_g(t)$ are mostly long term. However, no scratching duration is discovered in $C_g(t)$ because most of the pulses are rejected during short-term pulse detection.

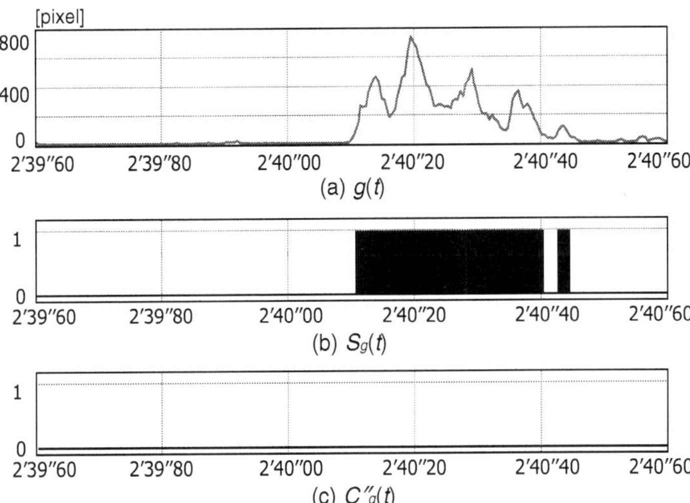

Fig. 11. Detection results for rearing (ICR1, 1 s).

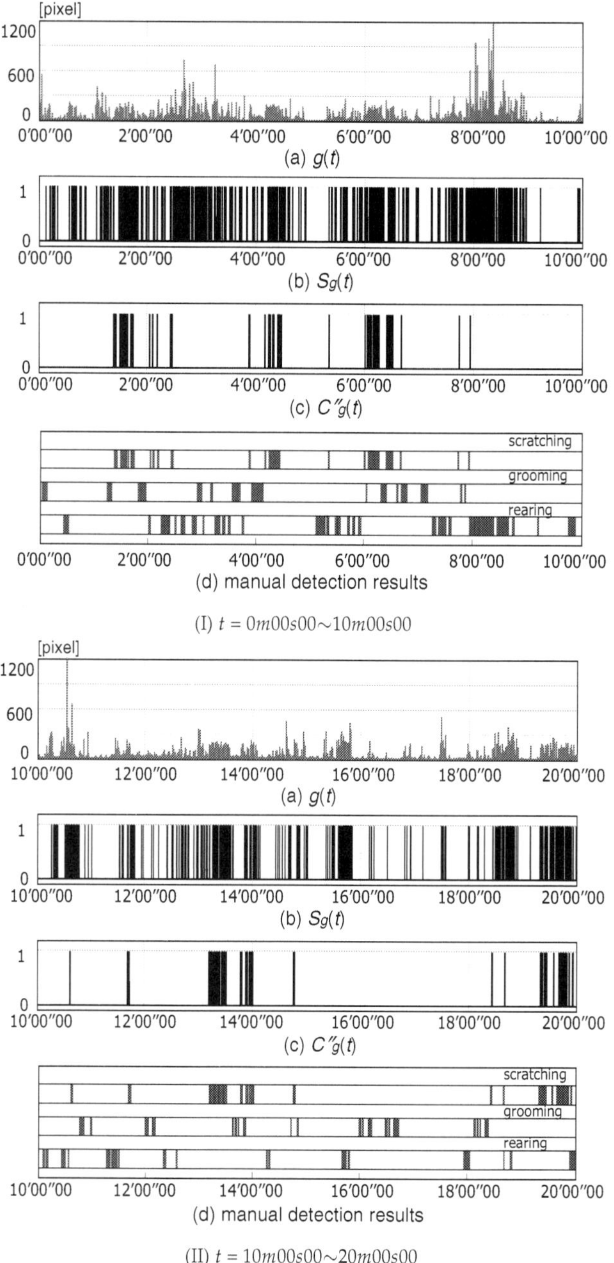

Fig. 12. Scratching detection results (ICR1, 20 min).

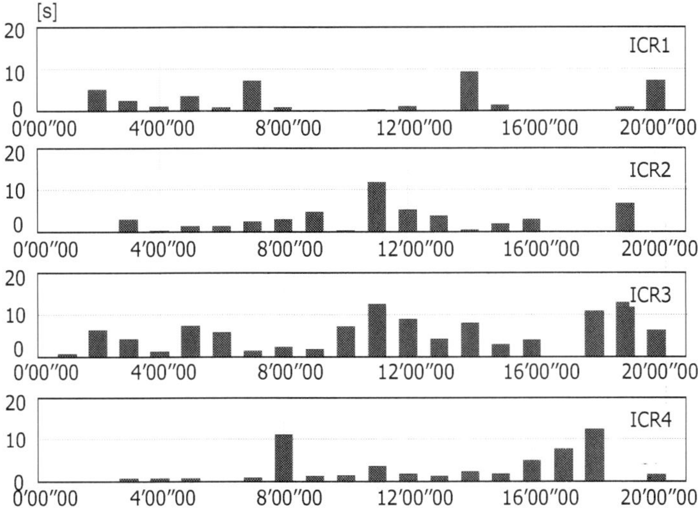

Fig. 13. Quantified scratching times.

Fig. 12 displays the result for the entire duration of the analysis from $t = 0m00s00$ to $20m00s00$ for ICR1. For clear exhibition, part (I) and part (II) show the result for each 10 min. Here, (a), (b), and (c) indicate $g(t)$, $S_g(t)$, and $C_g(t)$, respectively; (d) shows the manual naked-eye observation results for scratching, grooming and rearing.

The accuracy of scratching detection is evident on comparing Fig. 7 (c), Fig. 12 (c) with Fig. 7 (d), Fig. 12 (d) . The automated scratching detection result $C_g(t)$ in (c) corresponds to the manual scratching detection result in (d).

The manual detection results contain other behaviors such as grooming and rearing. These non-scratching behaviors can interfere with the detection of scratching. However, in the automatic detection results $C_g(t)$, only scratching are abstracted by the proposed algorithm.

Table 2 shows the evaluation for scratching quantification in the behaviors of 4 laboratory mice. No.1, 2, 3, 4 correspond to ICR1, 2, 3, 4, respectively. The abbreviations used in the tables are listed in the following: (1) sc→no: the time when scratching motion is detected as non-scratching motion, (2) gr→sc: the time when grooming is misdetected as scratching, (3) re→sc: the time when rearing is misdetected as scratching, (4) oth→sc: the time when other behaviors are misdetected as scratching, (5) scr: manually observed result of total scratching duration time, we considered as the actual scratching time. (6) corr: correctness ratio of the scratching detection.

From Table 2, we could compare the behavior difference of each mouse and calculate the correctness ratio of scratching detection. The ICR1 mouse is active at grooming and rearing, and for duration of 15.6 s of these behaviors was misdetected as scratching. Thus, the correctness ratio of ICR1 experiment is 92.4%. The ICR2 and ICR3 mice are particularly active moving and scratching. Their total scratching times are up to 461.5 s and 734.0 s, while their total misdetection times are 39.1 s and 35.7 s, respectively. The correctness ratio of ICR2 and ICR3 are 92.0% and 95.1%, respectively. Here, we ignore the counteraction of sc→no with other misdetections, which may help to increase the correctness ratio. The ICR4 mouse likes grooming and scratching, and the scratching motion is more "standard" than that of the other 3 mice. Thus, misdetection occurred for only 3.0 s from grooming to scratching during the total 377.0 s scratching time. Thus, the correctness ratio of ICR4 is as high as 99.2%.

In our experiments, the correctness ratios vary from 92.0% to 99.2%, and the mean is 94.7%. We consider it is sufficiently high for most quantification requirements.

The scratching times for all 4 ICR mice are quantified in Fig. 13, where the bar graphs indicate scratching times T_{scr}/min. It confirmed that the mice scratching duration times are quantified as numerical values, even in real-time and long-time observation.

Results of these experiments also demonstrate that the proposed method is objective and accurate. The developed system has the ability to automatically detect mice scratching, even in long periods of observation such as 20 min or even longer.

6. Conclusions

In this chapter, we have developed a real-time scratching behavior quantification system for laboratory mice; for this purpose, we introduced a specially designed high-speed vision system that can calculate the frame-to-frame difference for a 640×400 pixel image at a rate of 240 fps. An improved scratching quantification algorithm is implemented in the system and demonstrated experiment for detecting scratching behavior for 20 min in 4 ICR mice. The analysis results demonstrate the system's effectiveness with regard to accurate mice scratching quantification for real-time and long-time observation.

For next step, the current method will be improved and an automated system will be developed for objective and quantitative evaluations of laboratory animal behaviors for practical use such as the development of new drugs for various diseases including atopic dermatitis.

7. References

Y. Kuraishi, T. Nagasawa, K. Hayashi, and M. Satoh, "Scratching behavior induced by pruritogenic but not algesiogenic agents in mice," *Eur J Pharmacol* vol.275, pp.229–233, Mar.1995.

R. C. Benyon, M. K. Church, L. S. Clegg, and S. T. Holgate, "Dispersion and characterization of mast cells from human skin," *International Archives of Allergy and Immunology*, vol. 79, pp. 332–334, 1986.

N. Inagaki, N. Nakamura, M. Nagao, K. Musoh, H. Kawasaki, and H. Nagai, "Participation of histamine H1 and H2 receptors in passive cutaneous anaphylaxis-induced scratching behavior in ICR mice," *European Journal of Pharmacology*, vol. 367, pp. 361–371, Feb. 1999.

J. S. Thomsen, L. Simonsen, E. Benfeldt, S. B. Jensen, and J. Serup, "The effect of topically applied salicylic compounds on serotonin-induced scratching behaviour in hairless rats," *Clin Exp Dermatol*, vol. 11, pp. 370–375, Aug. 2002.

T. Miyamoto, H. Nojima, T. Shinkado, T. Nakahashi, and Y. Kuraishi, "Itch-associated response induced by experimental dry skin in mice," *The Japanese Journal of Pharmcology*, vol. 88, pp. 285–292, Mar. 2002.

N. Inagaki, K. Igeta, N. Shiraishi, J. F. Kim, M. Nagao, N. Nakamura, and H. Nagai, "Evaluation and characterization of mouse scratching behavior by a new apparatus, MicroAct," *Skin Pharmacology and Applied Skin Physiology*, vol. 16, no. 3, pp. 165–175, May 2003.

T. B. Moeslund, A. Hilton, and V. Krüger, "A survey of advances in vision-based human motion capture and analysis," *Computer Vision and Image Understanding*, vol. 104, no. 2-3, pp. 90–126, Nov. 2006.

Y. Ke, R. Sukthankar, and M. Hebert, "Spatio-temporal Shape and Flow Correlation for Action Recognition," *IEEE Conference on Computer Vision and Pattern Recognition*, pp. 1-8, July, 2007.

J. C. Niebles and L. Fei-Fei. "A hierarchical model of shape and appearance for human action classification," *IEEE Computer Vision and Pattern Recognition*, no.17-22, pp. 1–8, June. 2007.

D. Xu and S. F. Chang. "Video Event Recognition Using Kernel Methods with Multilevel Temporal Alignment," *IEEE Transactions on Pattern Analysis and Machine Intelligence archive*, vol. 30, no. 11, pp. 1985–1997, November. 2008.

S. Savarese, A. D. Pozo, J. C. Niebles and L. Fei-Fei, "Spatial-temporal correlations for unsupervised action classification," *IEEE Workshop on Motion and Video Computing*, Copper Mountain, Colorado, 2008.

L. Wang and D. Suter, "Visual learning and recognition of sequential data manifolds with applications to human movement analysis," *Computer Vision and Image Understanding*, vol. 110, no. 2, pp. 153–172, May. 2008.

A. Sundaresan, A. R. Chodhury, and R. Chellappa, "A hidden markov model based framework for recognition of humans from gait sequences," *International Conference on Image Processing*, vol. 2, 2003, pp. 93–96.

X. Yang, Y. Zhou, T. Zhang, G. Shu and J. Yang, "Gait recognition based on dynamic region analysis," *Signal Processing*, vol. 88, no. 9, pp. 2350–2356, Sept. 2008.

M. H. Cheng, M. F. Ho, and C. L Huang, "Gait analysis for human identification through manifold learning and HMM," *Pattern Recognition*, vol. 41, no. 8, pp. 2541–2553, Aug. 2008.

E. Guerra, J. R. Villalobos, "A three-dimensional automated visual inspection system for SMT assembly," *Computer and Industrial Engineering*, vol. 40, pp. 175–190, 2001.

L. Zhang, A. Dehghani, Z. Su, T. King, B. Greenwood, M. Levesley, "Real-time automated visual inspection system for contaminant removal from wool," *Real-Time Imaging*, vol. 11, pp. 257–269, June. 2005.

I. Ishii, K. Yamamoto, K. Doi, and T. Tsuji, "High-Speed 3D Image Acquisition Using Coded Structured Light Projection," *IEEE/RSJ International Conference on Intelligent Robots and Systems*, pp. 925–930, 2007.

G. R. Elliott, R. A. Vanwersch, and P. L. Bruijnzeel, "An automated method for registering and quantifying scratching activity in mice: use for drug evaluation," *Journal of Pharmacological and Toxicological Methods*, vol. 44, pp. 453–459, Nov. 2000.

H. M. Brash, D. S. McQueen, D. Christie, J. K. Bell, S. M. Bond, and J. L. Rees, "A repetitive movement detector used for automatic monitoring and quantification of scratching in mice," *Journal of Neuroscience Methods*, vol. 142, no. 1, pp. 107-114, Mar. 2005.

K. Umeda, Y. Noro, T. Murakami, K. Tokime, H. Sugisaki, K. Yamanaka, I. Kurokawa, K. Kuno, H. Tsutsui, K. Nakanishi, and H. Mizutani, "A novel acoustic evaluation system of scratching in mouse dermatitis: rapid and specific detection of invisibly rapid scratch in an atopic dermatitis model mouse." *Life Sciences*, vol. 79, pp. 2144–2150, 2006.

K. Orito, Y. Chida, C. Fujisawa, P. D. Arkwright, and H. Matsuda, "A new analytical system for quantification scratching behaviour in mice," *British Journal of Dermatology*, vol. 150, pp. 33–38, Jan. 2004.

I. Ishii, S. Kurozumi, K. Orito, and H. Matsuda, "Automatic scratching pattern detection for laboratory mice using high-speed video images," *IEEE Transactions on Automation Science and Engineering*, vol.5, no.1, pp. 176-182, Jan. 2008.

6

Machine Vision Application to Automatic Detection of Living Cells/Objects

Hernando Fernández-Canque
*Glasgow Caledonian University, Scotland,
UK*

1. Introduction

The concept of Machine Vision (MV) originates in the early 1950's and practical MV applications appeared in the early 1980's. Early theoretical work suggested serious limitations in computational abilities as the main reason for inefficient use of MV. MV is a 'simple' processing system which receives and combines signals from cameras by manipulating images at the pixel level to extract information that can be used in a decision making activity to produce the output required. MV has several advantages over systems utilising conventional technologies. The attention span of human operators is relatively short (Butler, 1980). Camera images are detailed and therefore contain a large amount of information. This combined with the computer power available provides a huge potential for MV applications. The chapter will provide an overview on the developments and historical evolution of the concept of MV applications. This chapter will concentrate on MV application to automatic detection of objects with ill defined shape, size, and colour with high variability. Objects that change with time have no fixed structure; can present extra problems on application of automatic detection using MV. For this type of application, current manual detection requires highly specialised and highly trained operators. The application of MV will facilitate the detection of these objects with the advantage of fast response. It is easy to use, cost effective with consistent and reliable results. The detection of micro-organisms and the detection of suspicious activity in humans fall into this category. The first example examines development of an automatic system for microscopic examination of the recovered deposit for the detection and enumeration of the microorganism Cryptosporidium. The second example addresses the application of MV to the task of intruder monitoring within the context of visual security systems. The chapter will present these two applications to illustrate problems encountered in this type of detection.

In section 2, the chapter presents a general overview of MV applications and discusses some problems associated with the application of MV to objects of high variability. Section 3 will present software architecture of a MV application and its characteristics. Section4 will discuss MV application to variable objects. Section 5 concentrates on two problems associated with this type of application: focus control and error due to changes in illumination conditions. In section 6 AI implementation is discussed and in section 7 Two MV application examples of detection of highly variable objects as are presented.

2. An overview of MV applications

Computer-based vision and automation tools are used in a wide variety of industrial and scientific applications, including electronics, automotive, semiconductor, pharmaceutical, and research applications. These systems perform process monitoring, information gathering, and "on-the-fly" feedback/control to correct manufacturing problems. Research and development into machine vision can be traced back for more than 30 years. The impact of new technologies in machine vision, as well as the historical evolution of this concept can be extracted from published papers in journal, conferences and industrial applications. This field is highly explored at the moment. Table 1 include a list where the generic terms identifying MV applications of more than 10 applications have been implemented; there is a vast potential for applications in variety of topics. A search in BIDS (BIDS 2011) database, using "MACHINE VISION" as keywords revealed 73,773 published articles covering the period 1952 to 2011. Of those 73,773 publications found not all present relevance to application of MV and most of them cover image processing in general term.

Acoustics	Food science	Oceanography	Robotics	Dermatology
Agriculture	Forestry	Oncology	Sociology	Education
Anatomy	Internal medicine	Ophthalmology	Spectroscopy	Engineering
Astronomy	Genetics	Optics	Surgery	Media studies
Biochemistry	Geography	Pathology	Telecommunications	Gastroenterology
Business	Geology	Pharmacy	Toxicology	Geochemistry
Cardiology	Gerontology	Physiology	Transportation	Health care
Chemistry	Immunology	Plant science	Veterinary	Photography
Communication	Infections	Polymers	Zoology	Material science
Biology	Instrumentation	Psychology	Control systems	Mathematics
Education	Mechanics	Nuclear medicine	Behavioural science	Microscopy
Electrochemistry	Metallurgy	Rehabilitation	Biophysics	Management
Energy & fuels	Mining	Remote sensing	Microbiology	Evolutionary biology
Entomology	Neurology	Reproduction	Economics	Surgery
environment	dietetics	Respiratory system	Cell biology	Library science

Table 1. Subject areas with more than 10 MV applications

The early papers refer in general to the idea of image processing and pattern recognition in general terms. A more refined search in BIDS database, using "MACHINE VISION APPLICATIONS" as keywords revealed 1,042 published articles covering the period 1984 to 2010. Figure 1 shows a graph of the number of applications over a 5 years period between 1980 and 2010.

The graph shows a steady increase in the number of applications. In the first 5 years there was an increase from 12 applications in late 1980's to 83 applications in the early 1990's indicating a 7 fold increase. Since its introduction MV has seen an explosion in the number of applications. In the first 10 years the number of application had increased of about 30 times. In general the steady increase in the number of application is due to the increase in computing power, new and better image processing algorithms, better quality in acquisition of images (hardware) and reliability of Artificial Intelligent (AI) tools. To illustrate the problems of the detection of living/variable objects from the search in BIDS database the articles were classified according to the type of application algorithms/technology. This classification is presented in table 2. By sorting these articles according to the different algorithms/technology used, a general impression on the technology achievements can be approximated. This also provides information of expected development on the MV application.

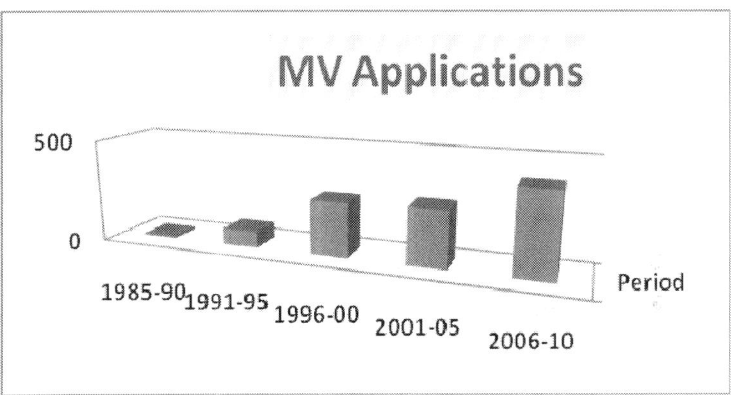

Fig. 1. Number of MV applications between 1980 and 2010.

Field	MV Applications	%
General (theoretical) algorithms or technologies	158	15.16%
Industry related applications	259	24.85%
Control, Instrumentation	124	11.90%
Optics, Robotics, computer science	159	15.26%
Microorganisms, Living cells, variable shape objects	54	5.18%
Agriculture, Food Industry	135	12.96%
Flight Control, Car Control, Automatic Tracking, Traffic Safety	87	8.35%
Textile, Leather, Jewellery	66	6.33%

Table 2. Research Statistics MV applications period 1980-2010

The vast majority of the research and application in the field of Machine Vision is found in the development of general algorithms. The needs of industry strongly influence the type of algorithms developed. The industry generally demands algorithms specialised in pattern recognition, especially algorithms tolerant to lighting variance and partial (dust) occlusion, and occasionally to changes in size (scaling). The industry's demand for gauging application encourages also the development of sophisticated edge detection algorithms, using sub-pixel accuracy (Hanks, 1998). This is also the main reason why powerful Vision Software development platforms such as IMAQ from National Instruments, Visilog from Norpix or PatMAX from Cognex Corporation, (these being just a few examples) appear on the market. The main benefit that these development environments have provided is that it is no longer necessary to spend long time developing routine algorithms for image processing. Algorithms such as threshold, image manipulation, spatial filtering, Binary Large Object (BLOB) analysing, edge detection, etc. are ready available. A vision engineer can concentrate on the development of the specific algorithms for each application. Also the management of Operating System related tasks are easier to handle and thus time saving. The movement of computer vision from the "experimental technology" category into industry-strength mainstream applications provides another benefit: the amount of research undertaken in the development of more powerful equipment for image acquisition is increasing, colour cameras with mega-pixel resolutions being widely available this days. The lighting system for machine vision is continuously evolving, different solutions being available with respect to the application demand (Braggins, 2000) e.g. Reflective Surfaces, Undulating Surfaces, Moving Parts. The fourth place in Machine Vision development of algorithms is taken by the agriculture and food industry (13%). The vast majority of these algorithms involve particle sorting e.g. Grain, Olives, Apples, etc or quality tests. This sorting is usually done using BLOB analysis, but advanced algorithms such as combining specific morphological and colour characteristics (Luo et al., 1999) can be found in this field and used for other applications. The algorithms involved in Flight Control, Car Control, Automatic Tracking, and Traffic Safety are usually highly specialized for these fields and are appearing with more frequency. This also applies for algorithms involving texture analysing, developed for textile and leather industry.

The research undertaken in the field of living cells/variable objects represents a total of only 5.18% of the total machine vision applications. The main reason for this low number of applications is the fact that the living cells are not size and shape invariant. On the contrary, the size, shape and sometimes even the colour vary during their life cycle. Hence a really large number of factors have to be taken into consideration when designing a machine vision application in this field. Also in terms of automatic classification the amount of artificial intelligence embedded in these applications is relatively complex and high. The "If-Then, "True-False" logic is usually not suitable, and a different, more advanced approach is needed e.g. Fuzzy Logic, Neural Networks. The intelligence embedded in these applications is relatively high; however the results can be impressive. The application of machine vision to detect this type of objects presents the problems associated with the physical variance of living cells and requires the development of specialized algorithms.

3. Machine vision software architecture

A proposed architecture may include a block to control the camera/microscope and a block to control the image acquisition required to control the hardware. Ideally all controls should be done automatically. The system requires an image processing block with the required image processing algorithms to manipulate and analyse images according to the application. The algorithms will extract information required to provide an output for decision from the system. In many cases the MV should take a decision without human intervention but with the aid of an AI application section. The AI block will add computer capability to the MV system that exceeds human performance in some cases. A MV's software architecture should include all the elements presented in block diagram in figure 2. The MV should provide a way of informing users of the results. The communications block allows information to be provided in various forms/formats including remotely to any place required.

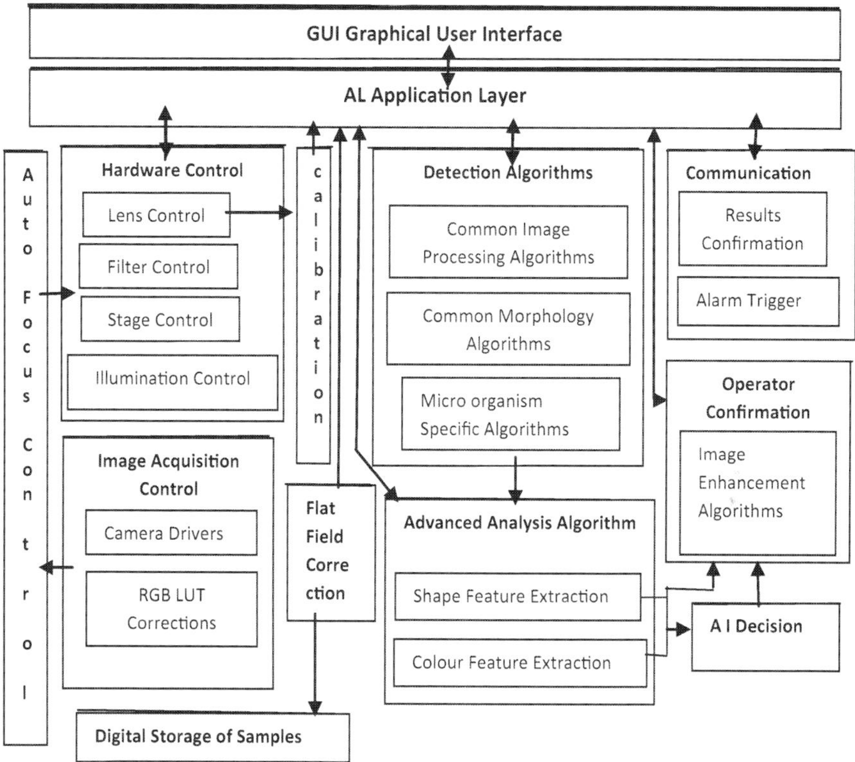

Fig. 2. Machine Vision Software Architecture

All blocks are accessed and organised by the Application Layer (AL), the MV incorporates a Graphical User Interface, providing access to an operator or expert to analyze/confirm results if required.

The MV system presented in figure 2 includes all the features and control algorithms required by a MV application. The AI decision section is tailored to a particular application.

4. MV application to variable objects

To establish a MV application to variable objects it is necessary to consider the general characteristics of the environment in which the MV will operate.

- in which hierarchy the MV will be used (decision making, alarm, identification...).
- application type. It can range from very complex systems with a lot of different information required to be extracted from images to simple applications with easy application.
- frequency of application (mass samples, batch or single analysis).
- level of MV automation (manual, semi automatic, automatic, mixed system).

Depending on the application an MV topology, architecture and algorithms can be planned. Subsequently the relevant outputs variables required for the AI application should be selected. It requires experience to find the best combination of outputs variables. Usually it is required to work with several algorithms at the same time in order to select the ones that perform best. Once the appropriate algorithms are selected they may require to be optimised to increase efficiency of the application.

5. Problems associated with automatic detection of living 'objects'

For both image analysis and image processing, attention has to be paid to errors occurring during the image formation and acquisition, as it is far more difficult if not impossible to eliminate these errors later using image post processing algorithms. There are limitations with respect to the accuracy of the object representation by an acquired image. Both the optics which forms the image of the object on the sensor and the digitisation process introduce errors (Ellenberger & Young, 2000). There are several phenomena which directly influence the acquired image therefore awareness is necessary (Ellenberger & Young, 2000). Living objects have high variability over their life cycle. They can change shape, size, colour or biological structure. In order to detect these objects advance algorithms need to be applied. The success of the advance algorithms application will depend on the elimination or reduction of variability of image due to the acquisition of frames. In this context the variation of image due to change in illumination and change of focus needs to be reduced. Some general problems in image processing affect the detection of objects. In the case of living cells, extraction of information to be input to artificial intelligence for the analysis requires minimizing these problems, in particular the problem with autofocus and problem with illumination. Some solutions are presented in this chapter.

5.1 Problems associated with autofocus control

In order for any image processing algorithms to be effective, the quality of the acquired image must be optimal. In microscopy one of the most important factors is the focus quality, as the even smallest focus deviation produces a blur effect on the acquired image. Therefore the focus control must be automated and performed as often as possible. Under these circumstances an autofocus algorithm must be employed. The autofocus algorithm must be relatively fast, involving the minimum computational effort possible. The image is brought to focus on the camera controlling the tuning of focus lenses stage using a stage controller. Auto-focus could be achieved by developing a feedback focus controller as exemplified in figure 3. This is possible if a measure of the focus quality in a numeric form is extracted (focus score). The hill climbing algorithm (Russell & Norvig, 2002) can be iterated with focus scores until the best focus is found.

The focus quality of an image can be linked with the perceived "sharpness" of the acquired image, therefore the number and the strength of edges in it. The number of edges can be determined using an edge-extraction algorithm. One of the fastest algorithms to extract edges in any direction is the Laplacian Edge Detection as it involves only one convolution. One problem associated with edge detection algorithms is the noise influence; therefore noise reduction algorithms are necessary. A good choice could be a median filter, as it has a minimal influence over continuous edges.

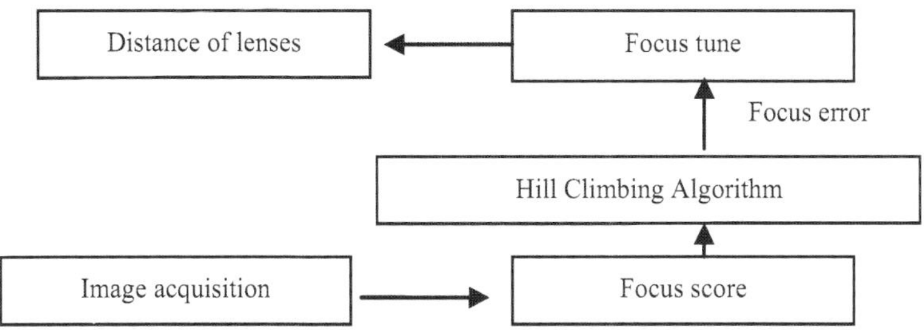

Fig. 3. Autofocus control

5.2 Autofocus control implementation

A series of images of a test pattern are acquired using the minimal resolution possible and greyscale representation to minimise the computational effort. These images are shown in figure 4, in the acquisition order, with the first 2 being completely out of focus, and the other being close to optimal focus:

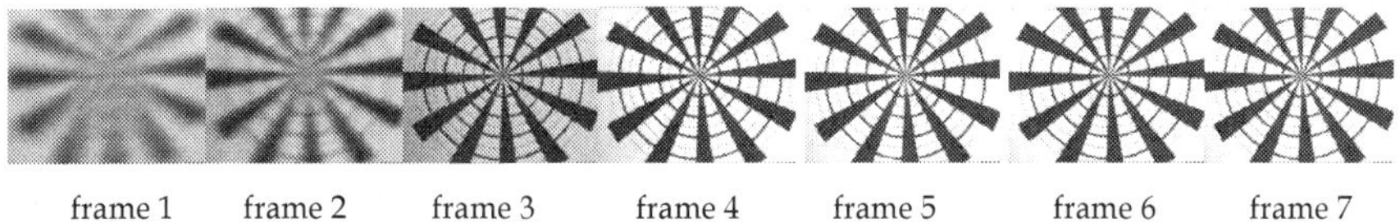

Fig. 4. Focus test frame 1 to 7

From each image the light plane is extracted and a Laplacian Edge Extraction algorithm is applied. The kernel used in this case was

$$\begin{pmatrix} -1 & -1 & -1 \\ -1 & 8 & -1 \\ -1 & -1 & -1 \end{pmatrix}. \tag{1}$$

One of the resulting images is presented in figure 5(a).

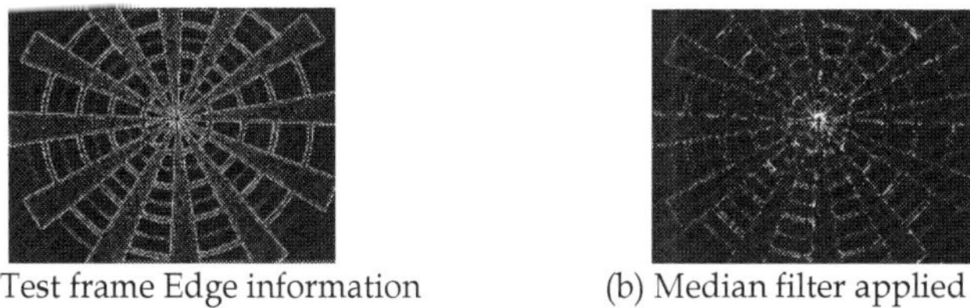

(a) Test frame Edge information   (b) Median filter applied

Fig. 5. Edge extraction

A median filter defined on a small neighbourhood is applied to minimise the noise effect on the final focus score. The result is shown in figure 5(b). Although the extracted edges are slightly affected, all continuous edges are still present while most of the background noise has been eliminated. A larger neighbourhood may be considered to improve accuracy, but a significant increase in computational time has to be expected. A sum of all pixel values is then performed, the result being a single numerical value. By applying this algorithm on 10 test images the results presented in Table 3 are obtained. By comparing the focus score with the test images, it can be seen that they are closely tied up.

Image	*Focus Score*	*Image*	*Focus Score*
Frame 1	1317531	Frame 6	5765586
Frame 2	1374433	Frame 7	5873043
Frame 3	5374843	Frame 8	5879743
Frame 4	5902432	Frame 9	5868048
Frame 5	5756735	Frame 10	5868667

Table 3. Focus Measure Results

On the first two images, the score is relatively low, as they are completely out of focus. On the last seven the focus score is comparable, with the 4th image obtaining the best result. When comparing some of these frames the human eye will have difficulties detecting the optimal focus. The focus score will differentiate the best focus in frames that appear to have the same focus. The algorithms presented here have the advantage of high processing speed in reaching the best focus, in the order of milliseconds in an average PC system. Real time software controlled autofocus is possible.

5.3 Problems associated with illumination

It is possible to combine several light sources that illuminate the specimen in different ways. The monochromatic or narrow band light sources emit light at a single wavelength or a very narrow band (e.g. Laser, which is also coherent). Halogen and mercury lamps are broad band incoherent light sources. Such an incoherent light source can be converted to quasi coherent by closing the aperture to a pinhole (Pawley, 1995). Acquiring images using coherent illumination has some advantages and also some disadvantages: a sharp edge will show ringing effects and the edge will be shifted into the bright area. Also the images look granular (speckle effect), and any aberration or dust on the lens can produce disturbance in the image. However, the most important advantage is that resolution achievable can be better than with incoherent illumination (Goodman, 1996). One of the most important advantages of incoherent illumination is that the image brightness is not changed with modifications of the focal position, a very important consideration when auto-focus algorithms are employed. Another significant aspect for a Machine Vision System is the Image Representation. Colour images can be represented in several different formats (also called Colour Spaces).

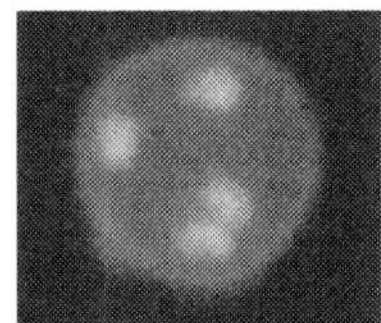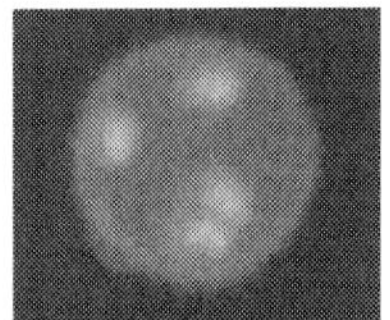

(a) Oocyst under normal illumination   (b) Same image 10% brighter

Fig. 6. Cryptosporidium oocyst with 10% change in illumination.

The most common representation of colours is the RGB colour space, as most image sensors provide data according to this model. RGB colour plane is suitable for image capture and reproduction, but can be very inconvenient for feature extraction. Problems are noticed when minor changes in the lighting conditions occur. Figure 6 shows a sample of a microorganism oocyst common in drinking water known as cryptosporidium. In figure 6 the illumination has been increased by 10% in capturing the image of this cryptosporidium oocyst. Figure 7 presents the histogram of the same cryptosporidium oocyst image with 10% difference in lighting conditions. The histograms are very different and make it difficult to separate the object of interest and its background.

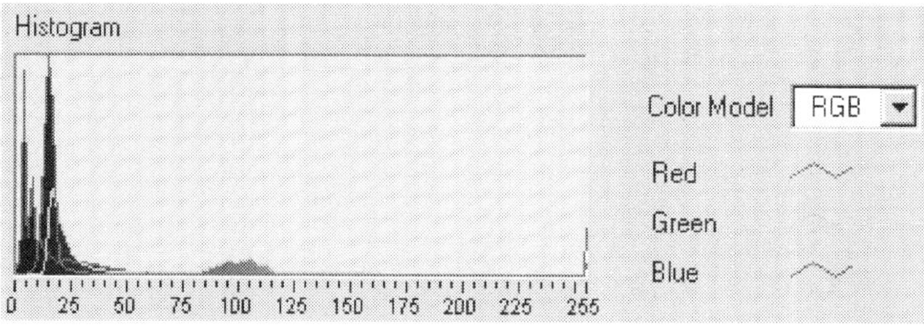

(a) Image normal illumination

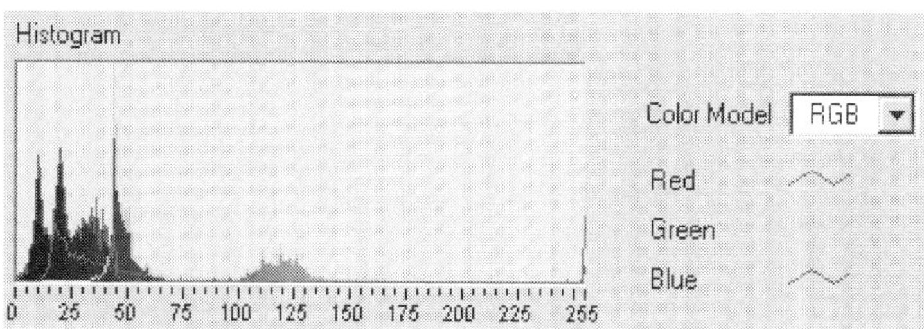

(b) Same image with 10% change in illumination

Fig. 7. RGB histograms

One solution to overcome this problem is the use of a linear transform from the RGB colour space into an alternative model such as HSL – Hue, Saturation and Lightness, or HSI – Hue, Saturation and Intensity. Hue refers to the perceived colour (viewed technically as the dominant wavelength), saturation refers to the dilution of the colour by white light, and the lightness (or value) refers to the sensation of brightness relative to a white reference. The advantages of HSL over the RGB colour space are illustrated in figure 8 where the same 10% change in lighting condition is applied to the same cryptosporidium oocyst object of the previous histograms.

The results of the histograms indicate that the Saturation plane is slightly affected and the Hue plane is relatively unaffected. The HSL space will make it possible to isolate the object of interest from the background. The RGB-HSL conversions are computational intensive and hardware conversions are preferred.

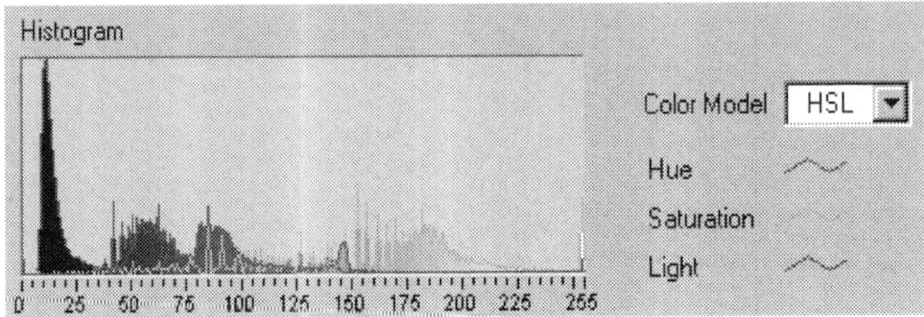

(a) Image normal illumination

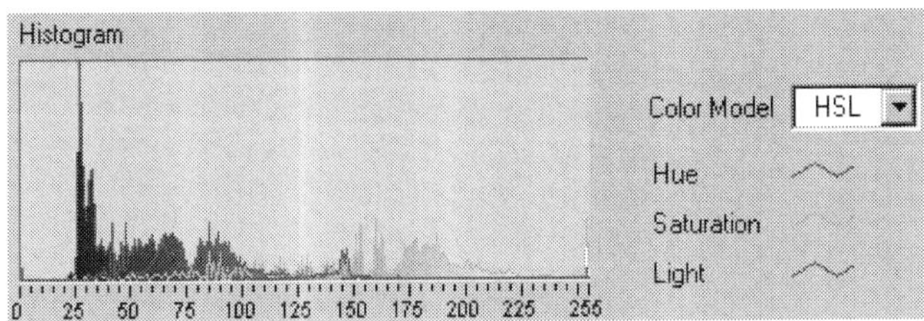

(b) Same image with 10% change in illumination

Fig. 8. HSL histograms

6. Artificial intelligence applied to MV

In many cases the MV should take a decision without human intervention but with the aid of an artificial intelligent (AI) application section. The AI application will depend on:

- the type of application.
- the outputs from the vision algorithms.
- the testing/training samples available.
- availability of training vectors statically independent.

Computers already emulate some of the simpler activities of the human mind. They can perform mathematical calculations, manipulate numbers and letters, make simple decisions, and perform various storage and retrieval functions. In these applications, the computer is exceptional and usually exceeds the human mind in performance. Artificial intelligence gives computers added computing capability, allowing them to exhibit more intelligent behaviour. The most common types of artificial intelligence system are Expert Systems, Fuzzy Logic and Artificial Neural Networks (ANN). Providing a set of parameters that would completely and undoubtedly describe highly variable objects is extremely difficult. Choosing to implement the classification process by means of an ANN seems optimal, as all it should achieve is to provide a suitable training set to a carefully chosen neural network. Because of the variability of the objects in some cases problems are encountered with this type of AI in that there are not sufficient numbers of training samples to train the ANN. Under this circumstance confident training cannot be performed successfully. For this type of application a more flexible approach is needed to take into account different variation of the objects. Fuzzy logic system can in some cases successfully address this issue, as it logically implements degrees of membership based on likelihood. Therefore a fuzzy logic inference engine is in many cases the preferred AI decision tool in this type of applications.

7. Examples of application to variables objects

Two examples of MV application to objects that are highly variable are presented in this section. The first example detects the existence of Cryptosporidium in water and the second example detects suspicious activity of humans using Closed Circuit Television (CCTV).

7.1 Example 1. detection of cryptosporidium in water

Cryptosporidium has been widely recognized as a serious cause for concern, with a very large number of waterborne infections caused by its oocysts. In its transmissive stage – the oocyst - is a frequent inhabitant of raw water sources used for the abstraction of potable water. Its importance is heightened because, coupled with its low infection dose, conventional water treatment process, including chemical disinfection, cannot guarantee to remove or destroy oocysts completely. Waterborne transmission is well documented (Smith & Rose, 1990, 1998), and can affect a large number of individuals. More than an estimated 427,000 have been affected in 19 documented waterborne outbreaks (Smith & Rose, 1998). Transmission is via an environmentally robust oocyst excreted in the faeces of the infected host (Smith & Rose, 1998). At least 21 species of Cryptosporidium have been named (Frazen & Muller, 1999). Cryptosporidium parvum is the major species responsible for clinical disease in human and domestic animals (Current, 1988; Currents & Gracia, 1991).The laboratory diagnosis of Cryptosporidium is dependent upon demonstrating oocysts in the sample by microscopy. Here, oocysts must be distinguished from other, similarly shaped, contaminating bodies present in the sample, and the microscopic identification of oocysts is dependent upon morphometry (the accurate measurement of size) and morphology. The current manual is expensive, labour intensive, time consuming and unreliable. Cryptosporidium is difficult to identify because of its size and morphology. Regulatory bodies from all over the world acknowledge the continuous monitoring of water sources for Cryptosporidium as imperative. Many requirements, rules and regulations are in place to attempt to address the control of Cryptosporidium which threatens the safety of drinking water. As an example the EEC produced a drinking water directive (EEC, 1998). The example presented here complies with this directive. The cryptosporidium structure in a computer generated model is shown in figure 9. Samples are stained and dried onto microscope slides and micro-organisms are detected using fluorescence microscopy. The drying process causes oocysts to collapse which in some cases leads to shape distortion and the physical release of sporozoites. This made the manual detection difficult.

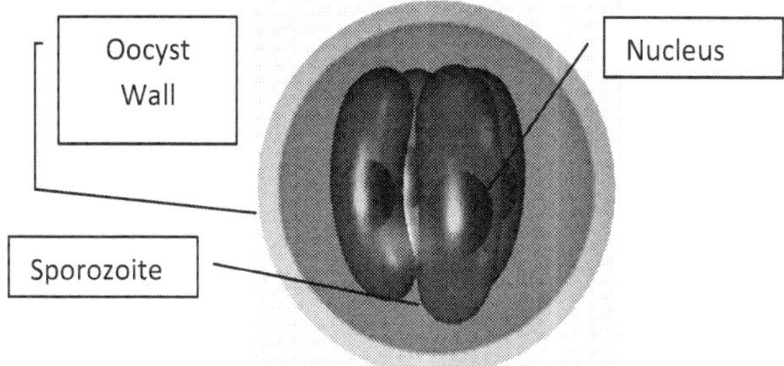

Fig. 9. Computer generated model of Cryptosporidium

The acquired image of a slide containing Cryptosporidium, viewed under Differential Interference Contrast (DIC) is presented in figure 10. Figure 10 shows a sample containing cryptosporidium oocysts.

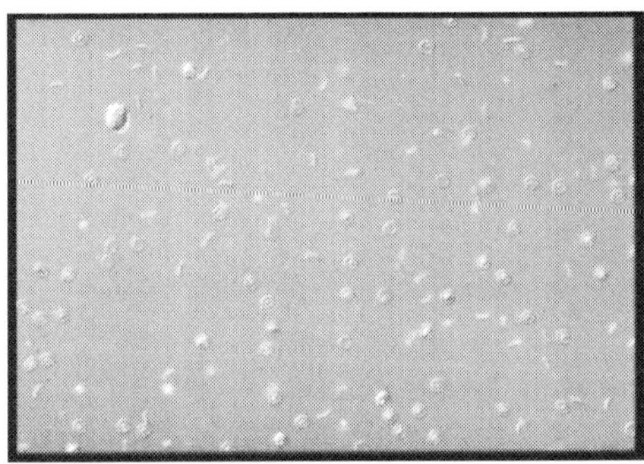

Fig. 10. Water sample containing cryptosporidium oocysts

Significant contrast is achieved using a highlight details filter and elimination or reduction of noise. The binary noise present is efficiently eliminated using the following algorithm: (Fernandez-Canque et al, 2008, 2000).

i.   A buffer copy of the image to be cleaned up is generated.
ii.   Two successive erode functions are applied on the original image.
iii. All pixels from the buffer copy 8-connected to the non-zero pixels from the image are added to the image
iv.   Step (iii) is repeated until no pixel is added.

Figure 11 (a) shows part of the sample with the noise eliminated and with the missing pixel reinserted.

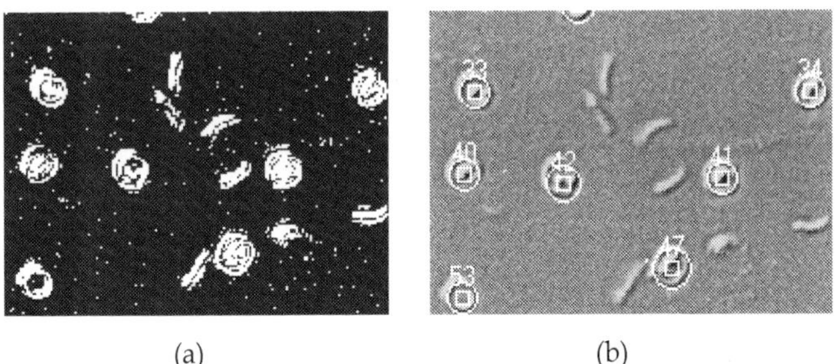

(a)   (b)

Fig. 11. (a) Sample with threshold images combined (b) Sample final result oocysts identified

The next step is to reinsert the missing pixels within the objects boundaries (Fernandez-Canque et al, 2000). A closing algorithm is performed, using a kernel size of 5. A NOT function is performed, followed by a labelling function. The result is an image which has a value of 0 associated with all objects, a value of 1 associated with the background and a value greater than 1 for every hole in the objects. By replacing the values greater than 1 with

0 and negating the image again we achieve holes filling. All objects too small to be a Cryptosporidium are eliminated. This is achieved using the same algorithm as for binary noise removal, but with 7 erosion functions applied. Then a distance function is applied, and a circle detection algorithm (Danielsson, 1980) is used for Cryptosporidium detection. The result is presented in Figure 11(b).An advance analysis algorithm can use different colour planes to allow the determination the existence of the 4 nucleus in an oocyst. On the green plane, both the wall and the nucleons of the Cryptosporidium are detected. Figure 12(a) show the wall and nucleons of a cryptosporidium oocyst after noise is reduced and objects of interest are separated from background.

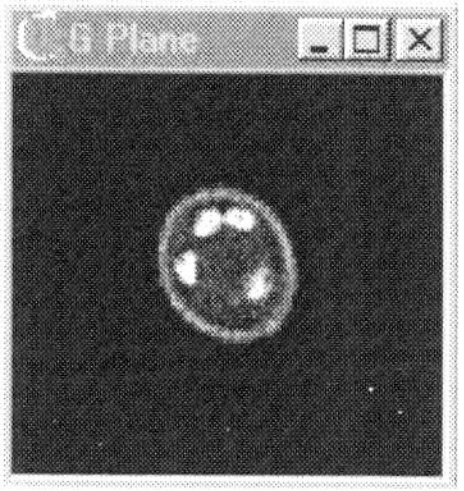

(a) Green Plane wall and nucleons

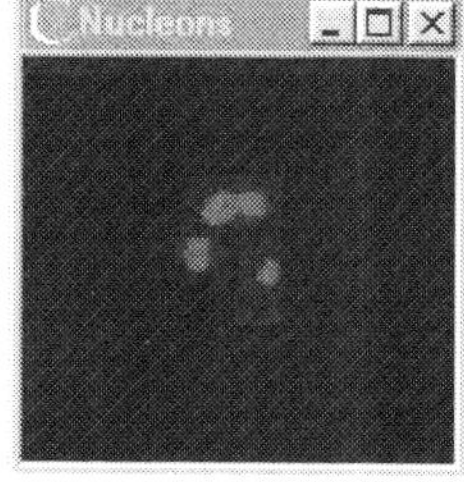

(b) Red plane nucleons

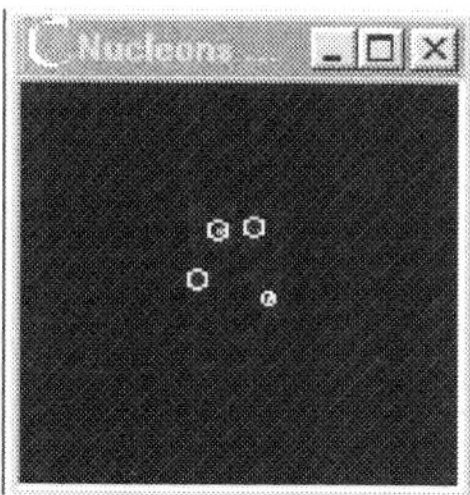

(c) Red Plane noise reduced

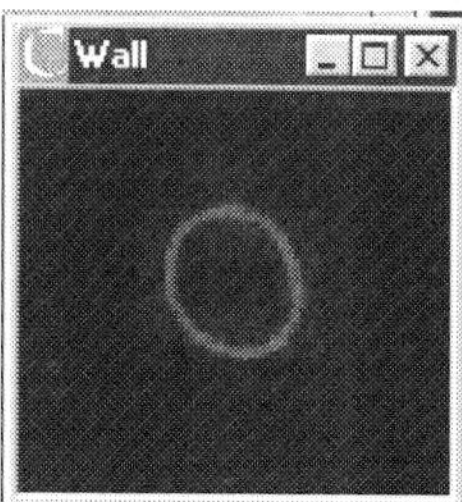

(d) Wall: subtraction of green and red plane

Fig. 12. Green and Red plane

On the red plane, only the nucleons are detected. This gave an easy method of separation. Figure 12(b) shows the red plane after the image is cleaned of noise. On the red plane a look-up table function was applied. Finally, threshold and binarisation was used, followed by noise removal and BLOB closing. Figure 12(c) shows clearly the 4 nucleons to identify cryptosporidium. By subtracting the nucleons from the green plane in binary format the wall was obtained and measurements were done, this is shown in figure 12(d). The morphological characteristics of cryptosporidium can be extracted unequivocally. Image processing allows the manipulation of these figures at the pixel level to analyse details of very small dimensions. As Cryptosporidium have a diameter in the range of 4 to 6 microns, a human operator would find difficult to identify this micro-organism under the microscope. This provides a method of identification of cryptosporidium. After the completion of the Advanced Analysis the system goes into the next stage – A I Decision Making. Expert Systems have problems with flexibility for this application and ANN encounter problems with training. It was found that the use of Fuzzy Logic suits this application by mimicking human knowledge based decision making. The classification is based on the features extracted by the Advanced Analysis Algorithm and a customisable rule base. The proposed approach allows a reliable detection of waterborne micro-organisms in large quantities of water and outperforms the current manual detection in term of cost, time of results, accuracy and reliability (Fernandez-Canque et al., 2009).

7.2 Example 2: Detection of suspicious activity

In recent years, the use of surveillance cameras has increased in popularity. This is partially due to reduction in cost and technological advances. CCTV systems have become very popular in observing public places. Current technology makes provision for an operator to examine live surveillance footage from remote locations as they can be transmitted over the internet, cables or wireless mediums. In this example the MV application detects suspicious activity automatically by studying human posture and observing full trajectories of people (Fernandez-Canque et al., 2009). In this study, work has been carried out with the aim of achieving fully automatic detection of intruders using a static camera and in real time. CCTV has the advantage that relatively large areas can be monitored and intruders can be seen as compared to other detection methods. The main use of CCTV is based on reaction to a past incident by revising image recorded; the aim of this work is to make the use of CCTV more efficient by assessing suspicious activity in an active manner and alert operators to an intrusion. By achieving an automatic detection some problems associated with this type of surveillance can be avoided. It is known that the span of concentration of any operator is very short (Saarinen & Julesz, 1991; Goolkasian, 1991), and there is unreliability due to operator's fatigue and poor detection due to large number of irrelevant images known as Eriksen effect(Eriksen & Murphy, 1982; Eriksen & Hoffman, 1972).

7.2.1 Intruder detection

To detect an intruder, the background with no intruders present is recorded while the camera transmits the video to the computer, and each frame is analyzed. After reduction of noise and distortion, frames are compared to the original image of the plain background with no intruder present. This process results in accruing the pixels of the object of interest. Pixels in this object are counted, large numbers these pixels reflect a significant background change, thus an intruder is likely present. If no intruder is detected, the background image is replaced with the current frame of the video, which is compared against the next video frame as the program repeats this cycle once. A pixel count is then applied to confirm if an object has been detected, and finally the parameters can be computed for a bounding box. This sequence of steps will encapsulate any detected objects in its bounding box, maintaining the original grey-levels of the object. This sequence of actions is illustrated as block diagram in figure 13.

The bounding box contains the coordinates of the intruder. This object of interest within this bounding box can be used for further analysis in the detection of suspicious activity. This simple process will allow the detection of an intruder. The comparison of frames can be efficiently implemented after noise is eliminate or reduced as indicated in the previous section.

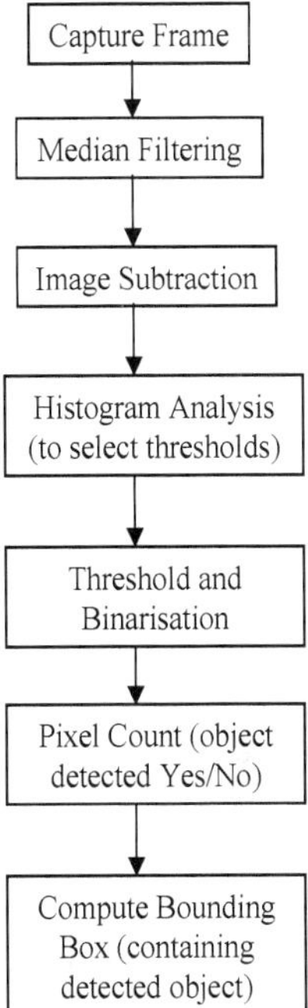

Fig. 13. Block diagram object detection.

7.2.2 Motion analysis

A particle analysis is performed on the binary image produced after thresholding. This analysis calculates two measures for each detected object or pixel cluster within the binary image. A pixel cluster is a grouping of connected pixels. The measures calculated are *pixel area (size)* and *shape factor*.

Pixel area is the number of pixels of intensity value 1 (white) in a given cluster. X is the cluster containing all pixels in the object of interest. The *area* of an object can be calculated as a relative measure with respect to the entire image area. In the discrete case, it is approximated by the number of pixels in the object of interest.

$$A(X) = \sum_{i,j} g(x_i, y_j) \tag{2}$$

Where $A(X)$ is the area of the object X, $g(x_i, y_j)$ = 1 if the pixel lies within the object X *and* $g(x_i, y_j)$ = 0 otherwise

The *area* measure can be used given a binary image to obtain the relative size of the object. This measure can give an indication of whether the object is sufficiently large (in relative terms) to warrant further analysis. It can also be weighted by a size factor which characterises the area of a single pixel. In that case, the measure is physically homogeneous to an area. A shape cannot be characterised by a single measure, or even a simple set of measures. Several quantities have been defined to account for specific shape characteristics.

The *shape factor*, F_C, is defined as:-

$$F_C = \frac{L(X)^2}{4\pi.A(X)}$$ (3)

Where $A(X)$ is the area of the object X *and* $L(X)$ is the perimeter of the object, defined below.

The perimeter designates the length of the object boundary. In the discrete case, the perimeter can be simply estimated as the number of points which lie on the object boundary. The *shape factor* measure is invariant to rotation, reflection and scaling. It has no dimension and is equal to 1 for a disk. It measures the elongation of an object. An elongated set has a higher *shape factor*. This measure, with its ability to distinguish the elongated form of a human figure, is particularly useful in the object detection process. The *area* and *shape factor* for all pixel clusters (which are potential objects of interest) within the binary image is calculated. A fixed threshold for each measure is used to select objects for further analysis. Any small differences in pixel intensity between the captured frame and the previously acquired frame will be effectively removed during the *area* and *shape factor* thresholding operation. Small differences do not indicate the presence of an object in the frame, but can often be attributed to small changes in illumination between successive frame captures. The threshold chosen for each measure is scene dependent. Once the approximate size of objects of interest is known relative to the size of the entire image, thresholds can be calculated to ensure only object *areas* greater than the threshold are retained for further analysis. After thresholding, the resulting binary image will contain the pixel clusters corresponding to objects meeting the selection criteria. The object detection algorithm is performed on each frame acquisition. Detected objects that have met the size, shape and Si factor (as defined in equation (7) Fernandez-Canque et al, 2009) criteria are tracked in terms of their position within camera images. The tracking algorithms require each object to be represented by a single pixel co-ordinate position within the image. The *barycentre* of detected objects is used to provide the single co-ordinate. The *barycentre* of an object is similar to its centre of gravity. The resultant co-ordinate position for each object gives a uniform positional locator between successive frame captures which is independent of object size and shape. The inertia moments define some global characteristics of the object but it is the first order moments of inertia which define the *barycentre*. They are defined in the discrete case as:-

$$M_{1x} = \frac{1}{A(X)}\sum_X x_i$$ (4)

and

$$M_{1y} = \frac{1}{A(X)}\sum_X y_j$$ (5)

Where M_{1x} is the first moment of inertia in the x plane.
        M_{1y} is the first moment of inertia in the y plane
        $A(X)$ is the area of the object X
        (x_i, y_j) is a point in the object

The *barycentre* of each detected object is passed to the tracking algorithm after every frame acquisition. The positional locator of each object is passed to the tracking algorithm. Subsequent frame acquisitions provide a new positional locator for each detected object. The tracking algorithm computes the linear distance from every initially detected object to every object detected in the subsequent frame acquisition. The shortest distance between each initially detected object and subsequently detected objects is selected and the object which lies the shortest distance from the initial object is then determined to be the same object as in the previous frame. The process is repeated for each frame acquisition thus allowing objects to be tracked. The distance, *L*, between 2 co-ordinate positions is calculated as follows:-

$$L = \sqrt{(X_1 - X_0)^2 + (Y_1 - Y_0)^2} \tag{6}$$

Where (X_0, Y_0) is the co-ordinate position of the first point

(X_1, Y_1) is the co-ordinate position of the second point

Objects detected between consecutive frames are selected for *Si factor* analysis. Each object pair cannot always be assumed to be the same object between consecutive frame acquisitions. The *Si factor* provides one method for determining that tracked objects between successive frame captures are the same object within the images. The Si factor can be calculated as follows:-

$$Si = \frac{\dfrac{\left|(A(X_{nl1}) - (A(X_{nl2}) - \right|}{A(X_{nl1})} \times 100 + \dfrac{\left|(F_c(X_{nl1}) - (F_c(X_{nl2})\right|}{F_c(X_{nl1})} \times 100}{2} \tag{7}$$

Where $A(X_{nl1})$ is the *area* of object X_n in Image 1

$A(X_{nl2})$ is the *area* of object X_n in Image 2

$F_c(X_{nl1})$ is the *shape factor* of object X_n in Image 1

$F_c(X_{nl2})$ is the *shape factor* of object X_n in Image 2

The *Si factor* is calculated for all *n* objects detected and provides a confidence measure to determine that objects tracked between images are the same object. The lower the Si factor, the more the object detected in the subsequently acquired frame conforms to the size and shape characteristics of the object in the previously acquired frame. Thresholds may be set for the allowable values of Si factor. The value of such thresholds will vary depending on the scene being viewed and the natural variations of objects in the same class that are to be detected. Objects detected between successive frames that have a Si factor which lies above the threshold can be assumed to be different objects. This provides the capability for the tracking algorithm to detect when an object has been lost rather than tracking the incorrect object. The Barycentre of each detected object is passed to the tracking algorithm after every frame acquisition. Subsequent frame acquisitions provide a new position for each detected object. The tracking algorithm computes the linear distance from every initially detected object to every object detected in the subsequent frame acquisition. For the external scene, a sufficiently large area is covered by the camera to allow object tracking to be verified. The object detection algorithm is applied to capture sequential frames to determine initially if an object has been detected, then to track any such object.

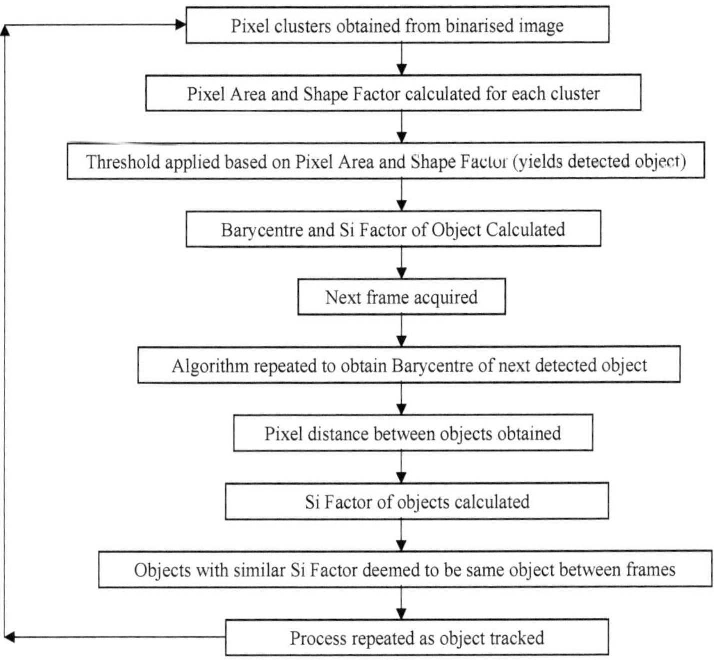

Fig. 14. Block diagram. Object tracking.

Given the small size of objects in the external scene, the additional processing steps are carried out. These steps include the analysis of detected clusters yielding data on object size and shape characteristics. Such analysis is not required for an internal scene because any detected objects would be sufficiently large in comparison to the total area of the scene that errors due to noise could effectively be eliminated by setting large thresholds. However, in the external scene, any detected object will yield a small pixel area so setting high thresholds would likely cause even objects of interest to be thresholded out. The size and shape characteristics can be used to assist in not only detecting objects, but also to subsequently track them. Kalman filter (Kalman, 1960) can provide a good way of tracking an object of interest, in the case of identifying the object the use of the Si factor may be more useful. Especially when objects of similar characteristics are physically close the Si factor can distinguish between objects. A summary in block diagram for the additional series of processing steps for the external scene to track an object of interest are specified in figure 14. The following example details the application of the outlined algorithms to the external scene and also to the task of object tracking.

The captured image in figure 15 is a car park area, and also contained a pedestrian footpath. Figure 15 shows captured frames containing one person.

Fig. 15. Frame car park area containing one object of interest: one person

Figure 16 shows two frames used in the detection of suspicious activity. The example uses a sequence of these frames to track a person in this car park. Cluster will appear for objects of no interest such as birds, movements of branches, etc. After the detection and elimination of unwanted noise, figure 16(c) shows the detected person of the two scenes superimposed.

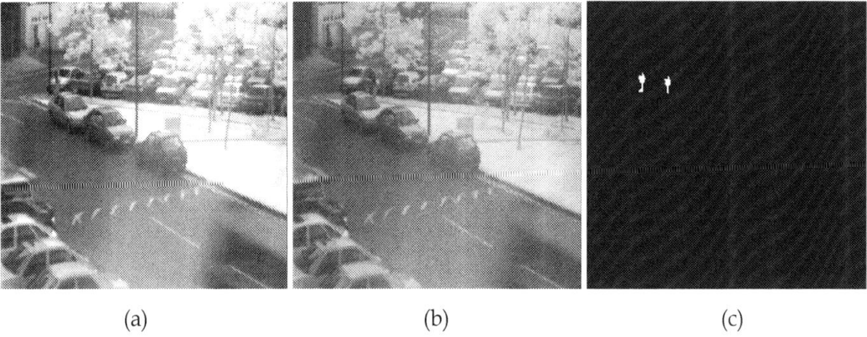

(a)   (b)   (c)

Fig. 16. Two consecutive scenes (a) and (b) of a captured sequence of frames from a car park scene. In (c) the object of interest is shown for the 2 scenes after detection algorithms have been applied.

For the first frame of figure 16 the object detection algorithm is applied to this image producing the thresholded and binarised image for this frame. This frame contains 44 pixel clusters. The *area* and *shape factor* for each cluster is calculated.

Table 4 shows the analysis of the detected clusters. The minimum and maximum values for *area* and *shape factor* show the range of these measures across the 44 detected clusters.

Threshold selection is determined for a given scene based on the pixel size of the object type to be detected.

This thresholding operation yielded one detected object of *area* 211 (the largest cluster *area*), *shape factor* 3.11 and *barycentre* 102,137.

	Area	Shape Factor	Barycentre
Minimum	1	0.47	n/a
Maximum	211	3.21	n/a
Threshold	150	2.5	n/a
Object	211	3.11	102.137

Table 4. Analysis of Clusters detected

The pixel clusters which have been filtered out are caused by changes in the image between subsequent frame acquisitions. These clusters can be attributed to the movement of the tree branches in the wind. The analysis of each detected cluster and subsequent selection operation successfully removes these unwanted particles to leave only the desired object. The modified object detection algorithm can now be applied to 2 consecutive frame acquisitions. The object tracking algorithm is iteratively applied to each detected object in the initially acquired frame. The first order moments of inertia in the x and y plane are calculated for all detected clusters in each frame acquisition, and used as a positional reference by the tracking algorithm. The completion criteria for this algorithm is met when the nearest neighbouring cluster to each object in the initially acquired frame is found in the subsequently acquired frame. The object detection algorithm, when using the *Si factor*, is more immune to noise.

A sequence of images is captured from an external scene, figure 17 shows a test scene used. To determine suspicious activity the car park image is divided into four distinct areas, as shown in figure 17. The scene has four distinct areas: Area 1 pathways, Area 2 car park, Area 3 exit/entrances, Area 4 perimeter area. Risk Index takes values between 0 and 1, where 0 represent the lowest risk. For this exercise the areas were given the following risk indices: Area 1 risk 0.2, area 2 risk 0.6, Area 3 risk 0.7, and area 4 risk 0.8. The risk indices are determined based on the knowledge of the scene and the threat associated with human movement within that area. In the image presented, the Risk Indices have been chosen such that the higher the Risk Index the greater the risk associated with human movement within that area.

In the experiment conducted, human movement is represented by crosshairs within the segmented images. The crosshairs on each segmented image represents the time-series motion of a human walker in the image. Figure 17 shows the movement of a person within the segmented areas of the scene analysed.

The aim of analysing the time series motion is to elucidate the information relevant to the task of ultimately identifying suspicious activity, and present this data in a format which the detection system can use. The aim of this experiment is to automatically determine if a given activity, identified by the time series motion of a human walker in conjunction with the segmented image data, can be interpreted as suspicious. The information used by the detection system should incorporate both the walker's positional data, as well as the Risk Index data.

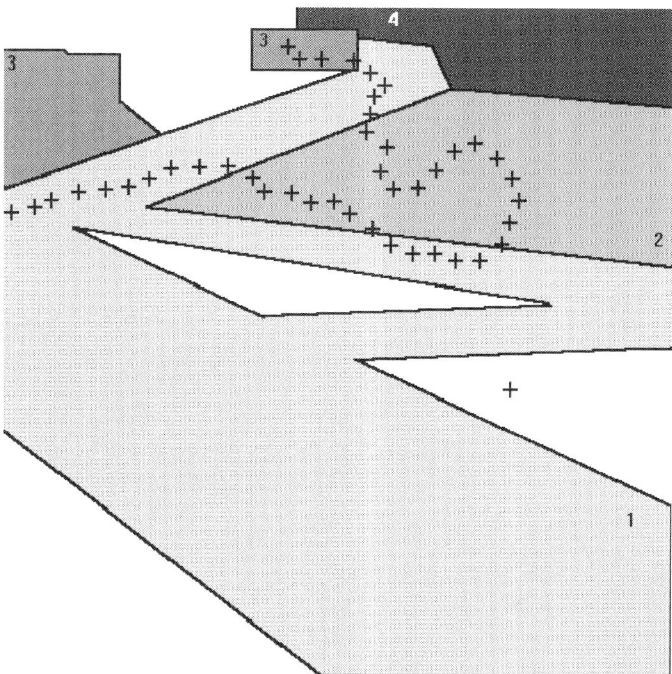

Fig. 17. Trajectory of a human walker within a scene

From this tracking scene information of speed, direction and presence in any zone is extracted and presented to a trained ANN for determination of suspicious activity.

In this experiment, twenty five segmented images are presented, each identifying the path a human walker takes within the scene. Figure 18 shows the response of the ANN to the 25 path samples of people walking patterns in the different areas of the scene analysed indicating the degree of suspicious activity for each pattern.

The ANN results of suspicious activity show a good correlation with the human operator response within scenes. This provides a good forewarning role allowing further investigation by a human operator. The MV application presented here can provide an indication of suspicious activity as the output of the ANN. This ANN response is based on the direction of the intruder, the speed of movement, the position on the different risk areas and the pattern of movement within the scene.

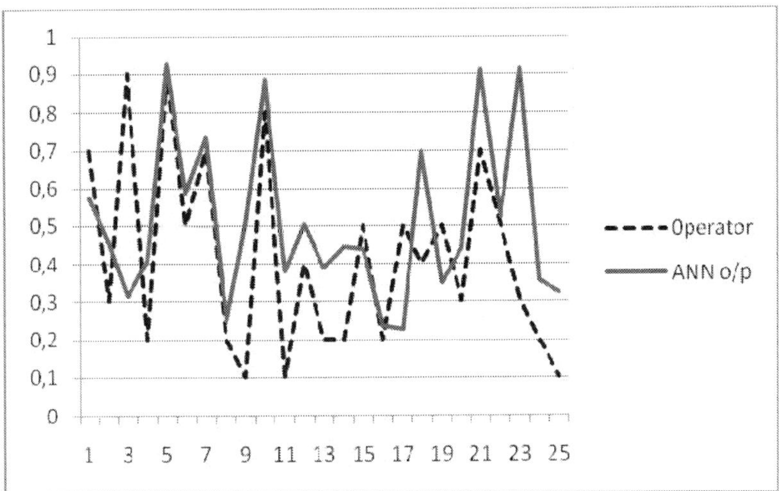

Fig. 18. Response from the ANN and operator to 25 segmented image samples

7.2.3 Posture analysis

If the person is not moving in areas that are considered a risk, his or her posture may indicate suspicious activity. Each image is subjected to a reduction algorithm, producing a quantised image, followed by a 16 by 16 data array to be presented to the ANN.

The ANN used is trained to provide an output for waling, standing and crouching postures. Figures 19-21 shows results from a trained ANN to a set of 26 images containing humans in these positions.

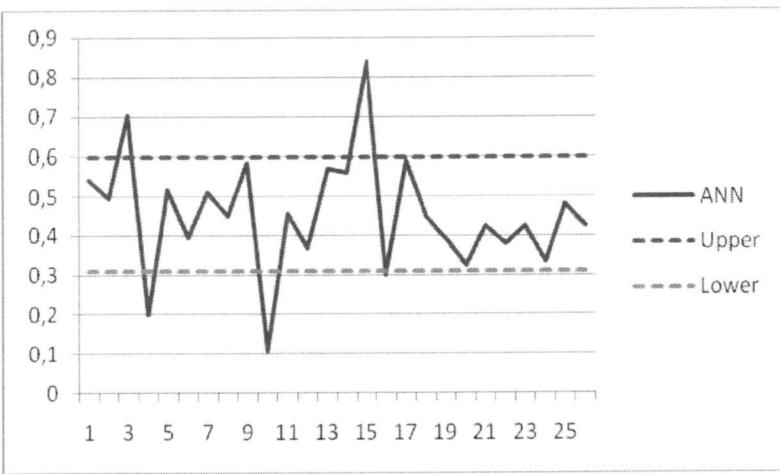

Fig. 19. Classifier results from the ANN for walking postures

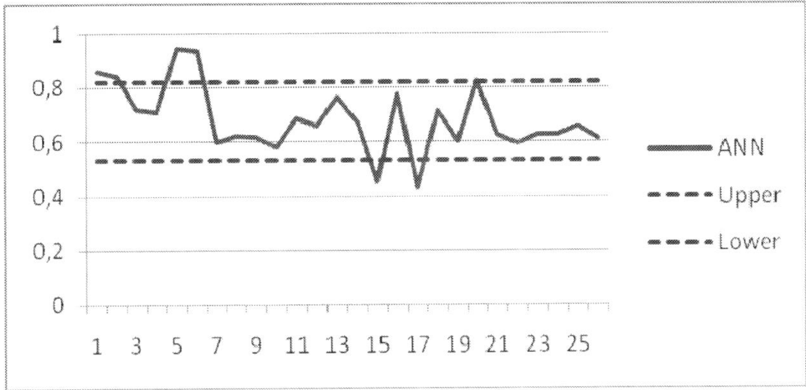

Fig. 20. Classifier results from the ANN for standing postures

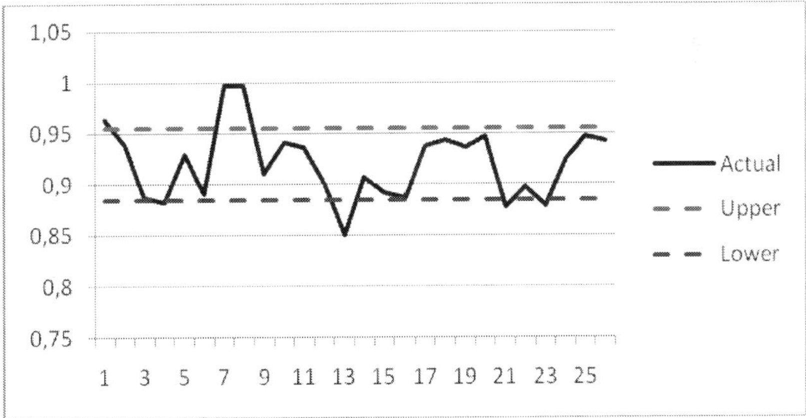

Fig. 21. Neural Network response for crouching postures.

Figure 19 shows results for walking postures, Figure 20 for standing postures and Figures 21 for crouching postures. The ANN has been trained in such way that values on the y-axis between 0.3 and 0.6 indicate that a walking posture has been detected. Values between 0.52 and 0.81 indicate that a standing posture has been detected and values between 0.88 and 0.95 indicate detection of a crouching posture.

On the basis of the results obtained for each newly analysed posture, upper and lower limits (shown by chain lines) have been set which provide a range of values within which lies a high probability that a given posture has been detected. The walking posture test images included various viewing orientations. In the case of a person walking directly towards or away from the camera, difficulties are encountered in determining if the person is standing or walking. These walking postures are very similar in appearance to standing postures when presented as a two-dimensional camera image. This similarity, and consequent classification difficulty, was predicted for a two-dimensional image system. A number of the images in the walking posture data set show a higher than expected value although only 15% lie outside the upper and lower limits. The higher values obtained tend towards the values expected for a standing posture. The results produced for the crouching postures show values which are consistently very close to the expected values. The error in the crouching posture data was smaller and more uniform than for the other two posture types. The apparent similarity between a few walking and standing postures caused the classifier some difficulties. A crouching posture is easier to identify from a two-dimensional image. Since crouching could be interpreted as potentially the most suspicious posture, the system developed shows higher performance at detecting the postures of more relevance to the task in hand.

The results are close to the expected response. This can also be used as a warning role as the MV can determine whether suspicious activity is present in an open scene under CCTV surveillance

8. Conclusions

MV application trend indicates that the advance of computation power and hardware developments allows the number and type of application to increase substantially in particular in the last 15 years.

The application of MV to variable objects requires the consideration of various factors to be accurate. Algorithms are required to obtain clear and detailed morphology including advance process using advance algorithms. In this type of application where information obtained in different planes it is useful to eliminate problems produced by variation of illumination. A good focus control based on a focus score allows the MV application to manipulate objects of small dimensions to gather more details of the characteristics of the object to be analysed.

The Machine Vision example presented in this chapter can perform automated analysis to determine whether or not micro-organism oocysts are present in treated water. The system can reliably determine the presence of micro-organisms and enable samples to be accurately and efficiently reviewed by an operator if required. The proposed approach allows a reliable detection of waterborne micro-organisms in large quantities of water. This provides an industrial system to monitor micro-organisms in the water industry. The implemented algorithm complies with the standard operating protocol provided by the water authorities in UK and satisfies the EU directive on drinking water quality

The MV second example presented in this chapter can improve the performance of automated analysis to determine whether suspicious activity is present in an open scene under CCTV surveillance. The system can determine the presence and movements of a person and provide indications of suspicious activity based on pathway taken, speed, direction; the system can also provide indication of suspicious activity based on human posture analysis. These enable efficient monitoring and accurate review of scenes by an operator. The system proposed can provide a warning role to reduce the problem of human operator's fatigue and shortened attention span. This greatly increases the ability to carry out properly the task of constant and distant monitoring.

9. Acknowledgment

The author wishes to thank the Scottish Parasitic Laboratory for providing samples of micro-organisms in water. Also I would like to thank my wife Vicky Grandon for her continual support and comprehension. Special thanks to my students Sorin Bota and John Freer.

10. References

BIDS (2011) Bath Information and Data Services, available from
  http:// www.bids.ac.uk
Braggins, D. (2000). Illumination for machine vision. *Sensor Review*, Volume 20, No1, pp 20-30.
Butler, B. E. (1980). Selective Attention and Stimulus Localization in Visual Perception. *Canadian Journal of Psychology*, Vol. 34, 1980 pp 119-133
Current, W.L. (1988). The biology of Cryptosporidium. *Am. Soc. Microbiology News*, 54 / 1988, pp. 605-611
Current, W.L. And Gracia. (1991). Cryptosporidiosis. *Clinical Microbiology Review*, 4/1991, pp. 325-358
Danielsson, P. (1980). Euclidean distance mapping. *Computer Graphics and Image Processing*, 14/1980, pp.227-248
EEC (1998). Council Directive 98/83/EC of 3 November 1998 on the quality of water intended for human consumption, *Official Journal* L 330 , 05/12/1998 pp. 0032 - 005
Ellenberger, S. & Ian T. Young, I. (2000). Microscope image acquisition, Image Processing and Analysis, Oxford University Press, pp.1-35
Eriksen, C. W., Murphy, T. D. (1987). Movement of attentional focus across the visual field: A critical look at the evidence., *Perception & Psychophysics*, Vol. 42, 1987 pp 229-305.
Eriksen, C. W., Hoffman, J. E. (1972). Temporal and spatial characteristics of selective encoding from visual displays, *Perception & Psychophysics*, Vol. 12, 1972 pp 201-204.
Fernandez- Canque, H. L.; Bota, S.; Beggs, B.; Smith, E.; Hintea, S. and Smith, H. V. (2000). Detection and Classification System for Water-Borne Micro-organisms Using Machine Vision. *Journal TABEMED 2000 Acta electrotehnica napocensis*. Romania. June 2000 ISSN 1224-2497 pp 105-111
Fernandez-Canque, H. L.; Hintea, S.; Csipkes, G.; Bota, S. and Smith, H. (2009). Machine Vision Application to the Detection of Water-Borne Micro-Organisms. *Intelligent Decision Technologies an International Journal*. IOS Press, ISSN 18724981,2009 Vol 3, Number 2. pp 93-100.
Fernandez-Canque, H. L.; Hintea, S.; Freer, J. And Ahmadinia, A. (2009). Machine Vision Application to Automatic Intruder Detection using CCTV. *Proceeding 13th International Conference, KES2009 Knowledge-Based Intelligent Information and Engineering Systems*. ISBN 13978364204594, Santiago, Chile September 2009. pp. 498-505.

Frazen, C and Muller, A. (1999). Cryptosporidia and Microsporidia – Waterborne Diseases in the Immunocompromised Host. *Diagn Microbiol Infect Dis*, 1999, 34: 245-262

Hanks, J. (1998). Using Edge Detection in Machine Vision Gauging Application. , *National Instruments* - 1998. Application Note 125.

Goodman, J.W. (1996). Introduction to Fourier optics, 2nd edition, McGraw-Hill, San Francisco, USA.

Goolkasian, P., (1991) Processing Visual-stimuli Inside and Outside the Focus of Attention. *Bulletin of the Psychonomic Society*. 1991 Vol. 29, No. 6, p 510.

Kalman, R.E. (1960). A new approach to linear filtering and prediction problems. *Journal of Basic Engineering* 82 (1): pp 35–45.

Luo, X., Jayas, D.S. and Symons, S. J.(1999) Identification of Damaged Kernels in Wheat using a Colour Machine Vision System, *Journal of Cereal Science*. 1999. 30 pp 49-59.

Pawley, J.B. (1995). Handbook of biological confocal microscopy, 2nd edition, Plenum Press, New York.

Russell, S. J.; Norvig, P. (2003), Artificial Intelligence: A Modern Approach 2nd ed., Upper Saddle River, New Jersey: Prentice Hall, pp. 111–114, ISBN 0-13-790395-2

Saarinen, J., Julesz, B. (1991) The Speed of Attentional Shifts in the Visual field. *Proceedings of the National Academy of Sciences of the United States of America*, Vol. 88, No. 5, pp 1812-1814.

Smith, H.V. and Rose, LB. (1990). Waterborne Cryptosporidiosis. *Parasitol Today* 1990. 6, pp. 8-12.

Smith, H.V. and Rose, LB. (1998). Waterborne cryptosporidiosis: Current status. *Parasitol Today. 1998. 14, pp.14-22.*

7

Reading Mobile Robots and 3D Cognitive Mapping

Hartmut Surmann, Bernd Moeller, Christoph Schaefer and Yan Rudall
University of Applied Science of Gelsenkirchen
Fraunhofer IAIS Sankt Augustin
Germany

1. Introduction

Cognition and perception forms a central basis for human intelligent behaviour. Humans are capable of building their own environment and adding several artefacts to it. It allows us to detect and localize objects, and based on that to perform tasks or to localize ourselves and furthermore to find persons who work e.g. in offices. Every year, since the last two decades, people have been forecasting breakthroughs of services robots on the service robot market (Siegwart et al., 200, Haegle et al. 2001). Nevertheless the reality is grey. Two of several reasons are a relatively high price and an unintelligent behaviour of the robot systems. At this point the contribution of this chapter starts. We will present a novel approach, on how a mobile robot actively creates a geometric 3D cognitive map with ROS[1] and consumer hardware, which forms a basis for further intelligent behaviours.

The 3D maps are created with a mobile robot, in this case a Roomba from iRobot[2], a Sick laser scanner LMS 100[3] and a Canon standard high resolution digital camera. In the first part of this chapter we present a new approach to create precise, high resolution, 360° 3D point clouds, which are not depending on the surface the robot stands on. Based on the 360° 3D point clouds we extract semantic information like floors, walls, ceilings and room dimensions (Nuechter et. al. 2005). Furthermore the second part of this chapter shows a novel approach on how to solve the localization problem for mobile robots, by reading doorplates as non-artificial font based landmarks in indoor environments. We present an extended OCR version, to recognize doorplates, and a method to detect doorplate candidates, based on reflection values of a 3D point cloud. After the generation of a 3D point cloud, the mobile robot actively drives to the doorplate candidates and takes high resolution images with a consumer digital camera (Lingemann et. al. 2005). The automatically read textual content of the doorplates are added to the doors in a 3D map. Our approach is not a single novel algorithm; it is a collection and intelligent integration of known technologies and approaches with consumer hardware. This makes it possible to keep the total costs for

---

[1] http://www.ros.org/wiki/

[2] www.irobot.com/Roomba

[3] http://www.sick.com/group/EN/home/products/product_news/laser_measurement_systems/Pages/lms100.aspx

the robot low. A certain highly interesting feature for architects and potential tenants is that the robot is able to build up maps which are similar to the maps google streetview creates, but indoors. A home inspection can thus be made quickly online without having to be present.

We have to account several topics to evaluate the state of the art our paper deals with. There are a few algorithms to create 2D and 3D-maps, e.g. Gmapping (Grisetti et. al. 2006, Thrun et. al. 2005), Karto[4], 6D-SLAM (Surmann et. al. 2004) and many more. These algorithms can be all put together in one concept called SLAM (Simultaneuos Localization and Mapping). Durrant-Whyte & Bailey gives a very good introduction to SLAM in their survey paper (Durrant-Whyte & Bailey 2006). SLAM includes all methods that work with 2D or 3D sensor data. This sensor data is put together by a comparison method to create a map. Given that the last position of the robot, after the scan is taken, is known, the position of the robot in map is known too. Therefore the position of the robot is calculated by the adjustment of the last measurement. Until now the fastest method to create 3D-Maps, is the continuously updated version of the 6D-SLAM method. An example for a mobile robot, which creates 3D-maps using a two-dimensional laser scanner, is the robot Kurt-3D (Holz et. al. 2010). Our current approach updated the former work in many different ways. At First we built a cheaper robot, by using a cheaper and lighter 2D scanner with better servos (dynamixels). Then secondly, the algorithm to generate 3D scans was optimized (section 4). Furthermore we added OCR techniques to get textual information of indoor environments. There are already some 3D-sensors which are capable of creating 3D-maps e.g. from Riegel[5], Leica[6] or Zoller&Froehlich[7]. They are very precise, but also very expensive. Other 3D sensors like the Microsoft-Kinect[8] are very cheap and useful for navigation, but also very imprecise and limited in their field of view. But current research tries to overcome these drawbacks. Stereo vision is also useful for robot mapping (Lowe & Little 2001) but cameras have a limited field of view and problems to generate dense 3D point clouds (May et. al. 2007). These approaches are time consuming and have problems in not structured environments e.g. corridors. Nevertheless all of these are used to generate 3D maps. 3D information is not only used to build maps, it is also used to find and classify objects and structures. One possible way to recognize objects in a point-cloud is to use the RANSAC algorithm[9]. RANSAC stands for Random Sample Consensus and grabs a sample out of the 3D-point-cloud and compares it with a mathematical model e.g. a plane equation. With the help of this algorithm, a route to the found object can be calculated and the robot is driven to the desired position.

It is natural for humans, to use visual information to sense the environment around them. Humans are capable of finding their path, with the help of their eyes. To make this easier in urban environments, there are many landmarks, like signs with street names or house numbers. For indoor environments, there are doorplates, direction signs and floor plans. With all this in mind, it seems logical to give robots the same capabilities of using those landmarks. Unfortunately there is only little work done in this area of robotics. Most work is done in the field of video mining (Weinman 2008). Video mining tries to read textual

---

[4] http://www.ros.org/wiki/karto
[5] RIEGL Laser Measurement Systems: http://www.riegl.com
[6] Leica Geosystems: http://www.leica-geosystems.com
[7] Zoller&Fröhlich: http://www.zf-laser.com
[8] http://research.microsoft.com/en-us/um/redmond/projects/kinectsdk/download.aspx
[9] http://en.wikipedia.org/wiki/RANSAC

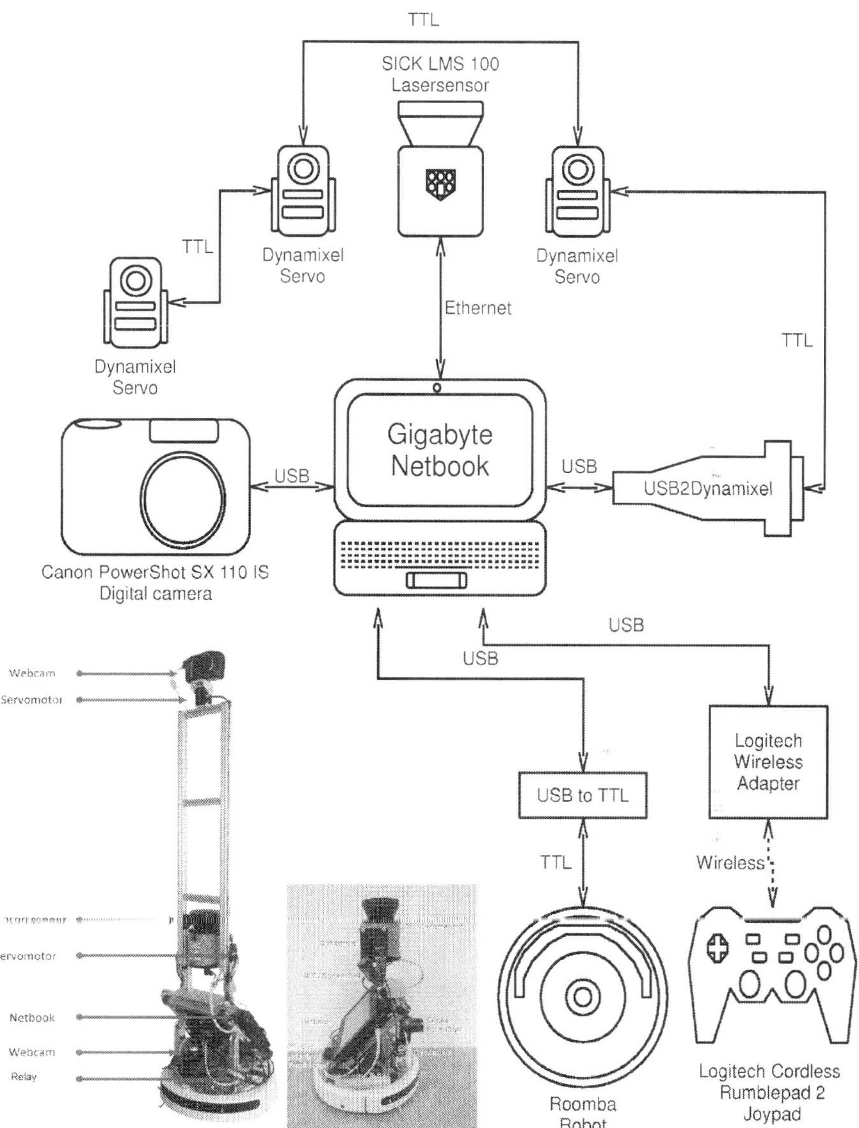

Fig. 1. a) Schematic overview of the hardware components and b) mobile robot with the 2D laser scanner (Sick LMS 100), the consumer camera (Canon Powershot SX 110 IS, 9-megapixel, 10x optical zoom) and the servo motors by Dynamixel. The scanner is in the start / end position. For the 3D scan it is turned perpendicular.

information out of video streams and first approaches are nearly 20 years old. Currently computers have barely reached the reading level accuracy of a second-grade child. Mostly the limited resolution of videos makes it difficult to read its text, but the approaches have interesting methods to detect text areas. A cogent survey of the document image analysis field, as represented by publications in the "Transactions on Pattern Analysis and Machine Intelligence", is given by Nagy. But why is it so difficult? Standard OCR needs around 300 dpi resolution pictures to achieve good conversion results. A 2-megapixel camera can cover an area of 4x6 inches, which is the size of a doorplate. But for a mobile robot it is difficult to move a camera so near to the object, that a precise picture can be taken. This lets us come to the conclusion that most of the known approaches from books, do not work with real mobile robots. A very time consuming way, to solve the problem, is to patch several images to one high resolution image (Mirmehdi et. al. 2001). Another solution suggests that robots should use a robot arm, to position the camera directly in front of the picture, but this is a very expensive way of solving the problem (Prats et. al. 2005). Other groups implement special techniques to read a couple of letters or numbers to avoid or substitute standard OCR (Baron 2002). Our approach to reading signs is different in a way that we use a real cheap mobile robot ($300) with a cheap consumer digital camera ($150), and combine it with a standard OCR algorithm, so that we have a really cheap and universal approach. The camera has a 10 x optical zoom and 9-megapixel resolution which allow us to focus objects from up to 3 meters distance at different angles. Distortion of the images could be removed because of the high quality and resolution of the images. In the upcoming sections the hardware setup, 3D measurement, tangents classification and the OCR approach will be described.

2. Hardware setup and system design

Special soft- and hardware is required to create 3D-measuremnts and to further process information. Software components are responsible to control the hardware, and in addition to store and process sensor data. Hardware components are used to position the robot and to capture room measurements. The following software represents libraries or algorithms which are used in this work. Some of these libraries and tools are offered by ROS, which stands for robot operating system, and comes with a lot of functionalities e.g. hardware drivers, visualisation tools and many more. Additionally 6D-SLAM is used, which is an extremely efficient SLAM (Simultaneous Localization and Mapping) algorithm to register 3D point-clouds based on ICP (Iterative Closest Point) (Besl & McKay 1992). 6D-SLAM calculates a correction of a transformation of two given 3D point-clouds. Point clouds are processed by the PCL (Point cloud library), which represent a library to process x-dimensional point clouds. To process image information the OpenCV (Open Source Compute-Vision library) is used, which contains over five-hundred algorithms for image processing. The hardware architecture is build up in many different components.

It contains a Roomba which is a vacuum cleaner built by iRobot. All hardware components are installed on the Roomba. A Netbook is used to deal with the huge amount of information processed by the 3D-point-cloud. One of the most important sensors used, is the LMS 100 2D-Laserscanner by Sick. It sends out a quick impulse of a laser beam and calculates the distance by measuring the time it needs to receive the laser beam. The laser scanner is moved by servomotors created by Dynamixel. In this way it is possible to build up 3D-maps by rotating the Roomba and the laser scanner. At last it uses a standard Canon

PowerShot SX110 IS digital camera to make an image of a doorplate. Figure 1 shows the setup. A video can be found at YouTube.[10]

3. 3D-measurement

A laser scan represents a 2D view of a certain area. To create a 3D laser scan, many two-dimensional laser scans have to be put together. To do this, the 2D laser scanner has to rotate over its own axis and record its laser scan continuously. The laser scans, which are in three dimensional spaces, are projected on a plane, which equates the coordinate plane. In ROS all laser scans are projected on a xy plane, at which x is equal to zero degrees. Furthermore each laser scan has a start and an end value, and the angular resolution represents the distance to an object. Afterwards the projected points are transformed into the coordinate system and added to the three dimensional point clouds. One task to solve is how to move the laser scanner to build up a 3D space. A well-established method is to rotate the laser scanner over one of its axis (e.g. Kurt3D). Another method is to align the laser scanner to a plane, from which the perpendicular is not 90 degrees to the direction of motion, because if this happens, the whole area will not be scanned properly. A third method is a combined measurement, where the robot moves and simultaneously the laser scanner is rotated over one of its axis. One huge advantage is that there is not much memory space required and if the surface is uneven, the scan doesn't have to be adjusted by the laser scanner. The transformation between the different measurements is calculated by the servomotors attached to the laser scanner and by the odometry of the robot. The trouble is that after calibrating the robot on a surface (e.g. carpet) the 3D scan will work correctly, but putting it onto another surface (e.g. wooden floor) will cause irregularities. To solve this problem an online correction has to be done. Here in this work the 3rd method is used. The laser scanner is perpendicular to the floor and the robot rotates. In a first step the orientation of the laser scanner is calculated by its odometry. The Sick LMS 100 laser scanner has a 270 degree opening angle, which leaves the robot not appearing in the scan taken. So how can precise 3D point clouds be acquired, based on imprecise odometry, especially at different surfaces? The trick is a reference measurement at the beginning and at the end of the 3D scan. Therefore the laser scanner will rotate (90 degrees) to take an initial horizontal 2D scan. After the initial scan is taken, the scanner is rotated to its perpendicular position and the robot starts turning. Only a 180° robot turn is necessary to take a complete 360° point cloud since the 2D laser has an open angle of 270°. Nevertheless the robot also turns 360° and acquires a few more perpendicular scans e.g. over a 190° turn and then moves back in its horizontal position. Now the second reference scan is taken and compared via ICP with the initial one. The ICP algorithm matches these two scans and results with the odometry position error during the turn. We estimate that this error is equally distributed during the rotation of the robot and the 3D point cloud is corrected e.g. reduced or enhanced with perpendicular 2D scans. Figure 2 visualizes the procedure and figure 3 shows an acquired 360° point cloud.

In addition to the distance values of the scanner, the reflected values among of light (remission values) are also acquired during the 3D scan. These remission values lead to a black and white panorama image (Figure 4). The remission value panorama image is used to calculate candidate positions of door plates (section OCR).

---

[10] http://www.youtube.com/watch?v=Il_aabmWeW8.

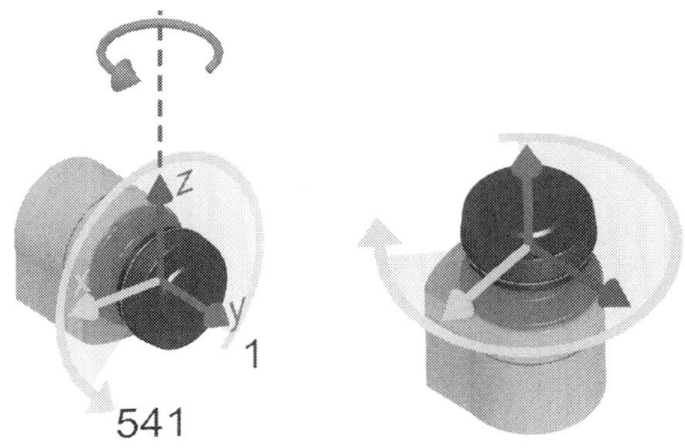

Fig. 2. a) Position of the laser scanner while turning the robot (3D scan). b) Start and end position of the laser scanner for pose (turning) error estimation.

Fig. 3. a) Scan results without and with pose correction. b) 3D scan with remission values.

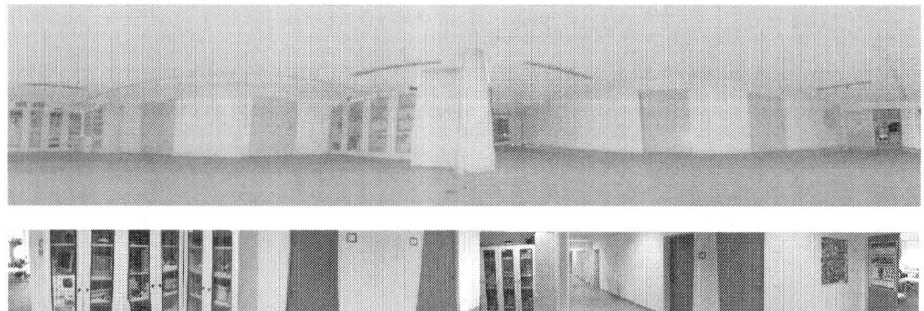

Fig. 4. Top: Panorama view generated with the remission values of the 3D scan. Bottom: Panorama generated by second turn of the robot with the panorama software hugin.[11]

---

[11] http://hugin.sourceforge.net/

3.1 Classification

The basic classification is done with the tangent segmentation. The tangent segmentation is a method to extract planar surfaces of a 3D point cloud. For each point of the point cloud a neighboring point is determined and the angle between these two points is calculated. For the determination of the neighboring point the original scan order of the scanner is used e.g. the information that the calculation of the 3D point cloud is based out of 2D scans (fig. 2). For a point *P1* of a 2D scan plan, a candidate point *P2* is a point acquired after *P1* and the Euclidean distance between *P1* and *P2* is larger than 20cm. A minimal distance between P1 and P2 is necessary to avoid angle oscillation since the precision of scan values is around 1 cm.

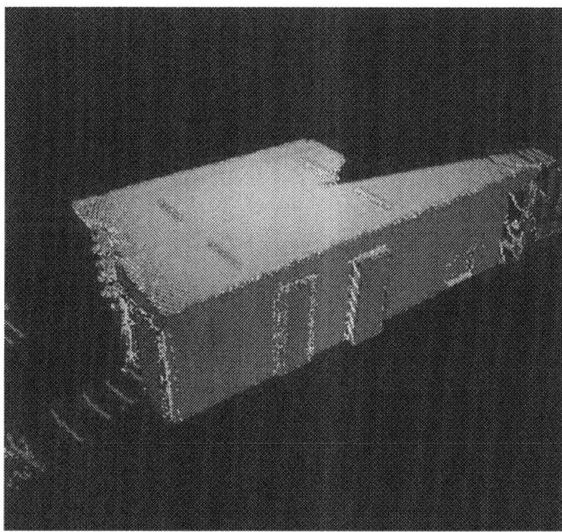

Fig. 5. a) Semantically labeled 3D point cloud from a single 360° 3D scan in an indoor environment. Green points mark the floor and ceiling, red and blue points mark the different walls, white points are unclassified.

The following formulas define the calculation of the two angles:

$$\Delta x = P1_x - P2_x, \; \Delta y = P1_y - P2_y, \; \Delta z = P1_z - P2_z$$

$$\theta_1 = \arctan((\Delta x^2 * \Delta y^2)^{1/2} / \Delta z), \; \theta_2 = \arctan(\Delta x / \Delta y)$$

The first angle represents the angle to the z-axis of the coordinate system and the second angle is the angle to the x-axis on the xy plane. Floor and ceiling points belong to angles θ_1 around 0° and 180°, walls belong to angles around -90° and 90°. θ_2 is used to determine the alignment of walls which allows to detect walls that are perpendicular to each other.

3.2 Histograms

Another important information, are the dimensions between walls or floors and ceilings. A histogram over the z-values has typically two maxima in indoor environments. One maxima represents the floor and the second one the ceiling. Figure 6 shows a typical histogram. Both maxima are used to estimate the height of the room.

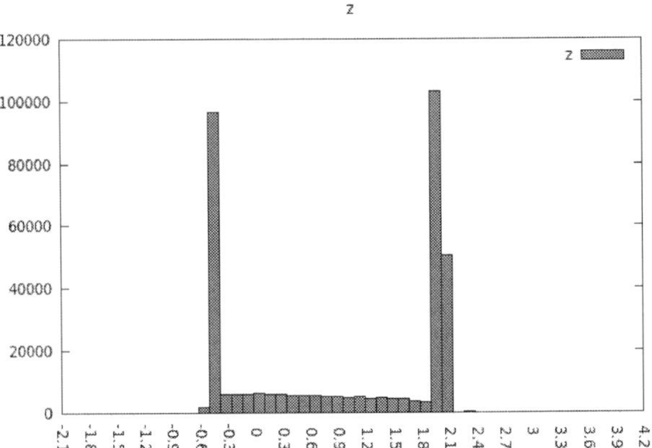

Fig. 6. Histogram over the z values of a 3D scan with 2 maxima. The maxima values belong to the floor and ceiling.

The histograms of the x and y axis could not directly be used as the z values since the robot is not aligned to the axis x or y while scanning. To align the walls of the 3D scan along the axis the maxima of the histogram over the angles θ are used since most angles are at the walls and have to be at -90° or 90°. After the alignment, the length and width could also be calculated by computing the difference of the two maxima in the histogram. Figure 7 shows an example.

4. OCR

Mobile robots have to know exactly where they are in an environment in order to plan where to go next. Therefore self-localization is one field of research in autonomous mobile robotics. Robots that work in outdoor environments have the advantage of using GPS. In indoor environments e.g. office environments humans typically use signs e.g. doorplates to localize themselves. Current mobile robotic approaches are focused on laser based SLAM techniques (section 3) but real applications need to read the visual signs made by humans. A typical order like, "goto Mr. Surmann's office" can then be executed by the robot. OCR in robotics is used to extract doorplate information and convert this information to text using, OCR engines. In office buildings doorplates are "natural" landmarks (actually doorplates are placed artificially in the environment, but the whole environment of an office, like a building is made by humans). Doorplates are used by humans to find their way through the corridors and rooms in unknown buildings.

Most doorplates contain a room number, which usually refers to a unique identifier for one room. There could be two or more doorplates with the same room number, if one room has more than one door. Often, doorplates contain additional information, like a room description, the name of the person who works in the room, or the name of the department, where the room is located. To detect a doorplate, a typical digital consumer camera is attached to the robot which will take high resolution images of the doorplate (see Fig. 1). This camera as well as many other digital consumer cameras can be completely controlled from the notebook via USB. An additional servomotor is attached to the camera to move it into the correct position. The camera is detached on the robot, and can be placed in several positions. Starting from a very low position (ground), and going up to table height. The camera has to be tilted quite a bit, to precisely read the textual information on the doorplate, at the bottom position.

Fig. 7. Example of the calculation of the space dimensions.

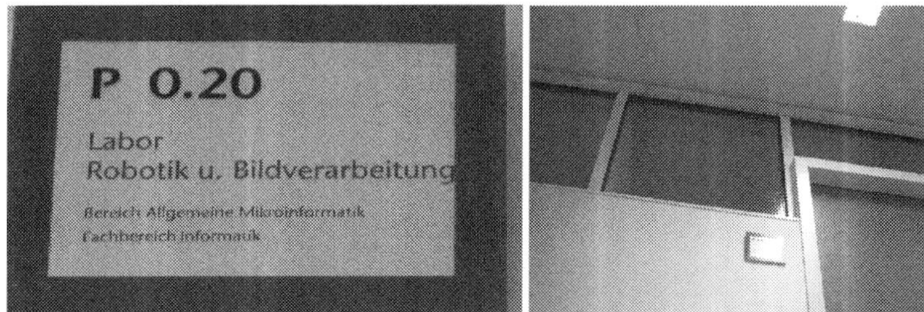

Fig. 8. a) Example of a typical doorplate (size 15 cm x 12 cm). b) View from the robot whereupon the digital camera is mounted at the bottom of the robot.

To localize the robot we developed two different methods. In the first method the robot only uses a digital camera. The robot moves in the environment, stops every two meters and scans for doorplate candidates while rotating the camera. If a doorplate candidate is found the camera focuses on the doorplate with the optical zoom and takes a full resolution image of the doorplate. A video of the approach can be found at YouTube.[12]

The second method combines a camera with a 3D scanner. First a 360° 3D laser scan is taken. Based on the remission values, the positions of doorplate candidates are extracted. The robot moves to all candidates and takes high resolution images, similar to method one. The

---

[12] http://www.youtube.com/watch?v=HQOBXeHXQ-A

information of the OCR extraction is added to the 3D point cloud. A video of the approach can also be found at YouTube[13].

4.1 Candidate search

The first part of the application is the accurate and reliable recognition of doorplates e.g. for a standalone camera based localization. The consumer camera was a Canon Powershot SX 110 IS with a 9-megapixel CCD sensor and 10x optical zoom. The camera has a weight of about 245g and is normally powered with 2 AA-size batteries, but it can also be powered alternatively with an external AC power supply. The camera delivers the display images (viewfinder) with a size of 320x240 (30hz) online. This viewfinder images are used to calculate the doorplate candidates. After that the candidates will be focused and a 9-megapixel image is taken. For robust candidate detection a simple 3 step filter is implemented. First the border color is selected in the YCrCb color space, and then the image is binarized with an adapted threshold, and preprocessed with closing and opening operations.

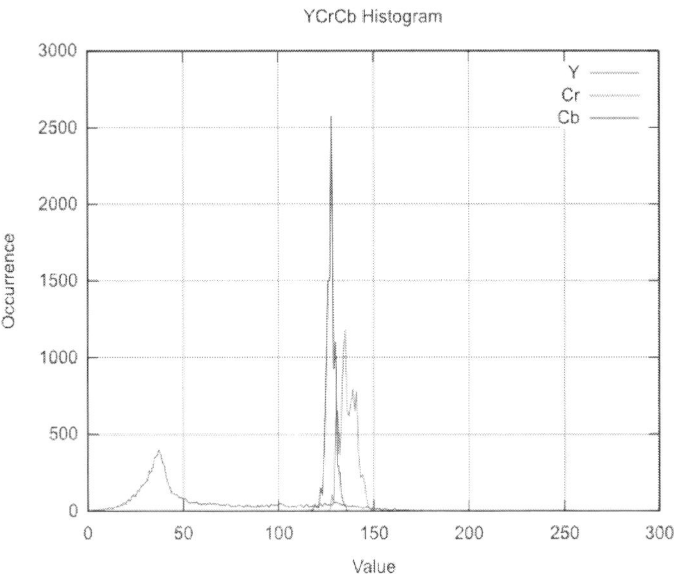

Fig. 9. Histogram of doorplate borders in YCrCb color space

Second, closed line contours are detected and approximated by simple polygons. Third, the aspect ratio of the contour area is measured. For our doorplates (15cm x 12 cm) the ratio between width and height has to be around 1.25. The filter is implemented with Intels OpenCV library and contains only 30 lines of code which could be easily adapted to other environments. The main advantage of the filter stage is the processing speed and accuracy.

---

[13] http://www.youtube.com/watch?v=Il_aabmWeW8

A core duo with 1.5 Ghz processes the filter in real-time (20ms). The false positive (type I error) is 0.01 and the false negative (type II error) is around 0.15 by a true positive of around 0.85 measured at one corridor with 32 doorplates.

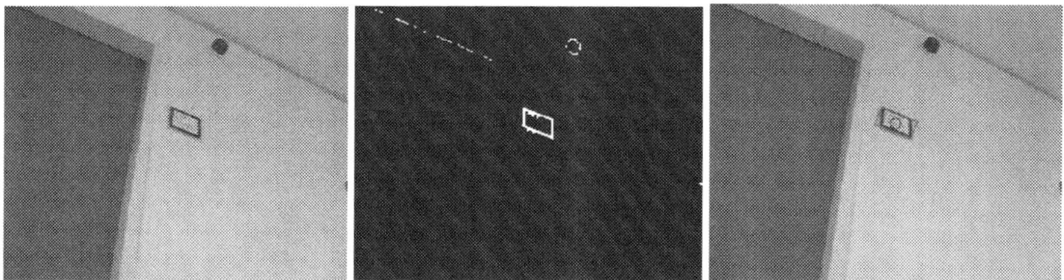

Fig. 10. Example of the filtering process. Left original image, middle binaries image and right annotated doorplate.

In contrast to the first part of the application, which deals with view finder images, the second application is different. For the integration of textual information in the 3D point cloud the doorplate candidates are calculated based on the panorama images of the remission values. Since the remission values directly correspond with the x-y-z values, only the region of height, where the doorplates are located is selected. Simple line detections with a Sobel operator and open and closing operations extract the doorplates candidates. A test in the corridor selects 4 out of 5 doorplates, but the number of experiments is not enough for a statistic (fig. 11).

Fig. 11. Selection of doorplates candidates based on 3D scan remission values. The candidates are marked red.

4.2 Doorplate reading

Two methods have been evaluated for reading the content of the doorplate based on the candidate calculation. First the mobile robot, the digital camera and the notebook is used. No laser scanner is detached in this version (cheap approach). The robot drives randomly through the environment, stops every two meters and searches for doorplate candidates as described above. If a candidate is found it is focused with the optical zoom. The size and orientation of the doorplate is calculated based on the 3 step filter (see above). After focusing the doorplate, a full resolution image is taken. The frame of the doorplate is cut out, based on the three stage filter and distorted, based on the hypothesis that the frame should be rectangular (see fig 8, 10, 13). Now the OCR process is started with this image. A topological map with the local position information at the edges of the graph between the doorplates is created (fig 12).

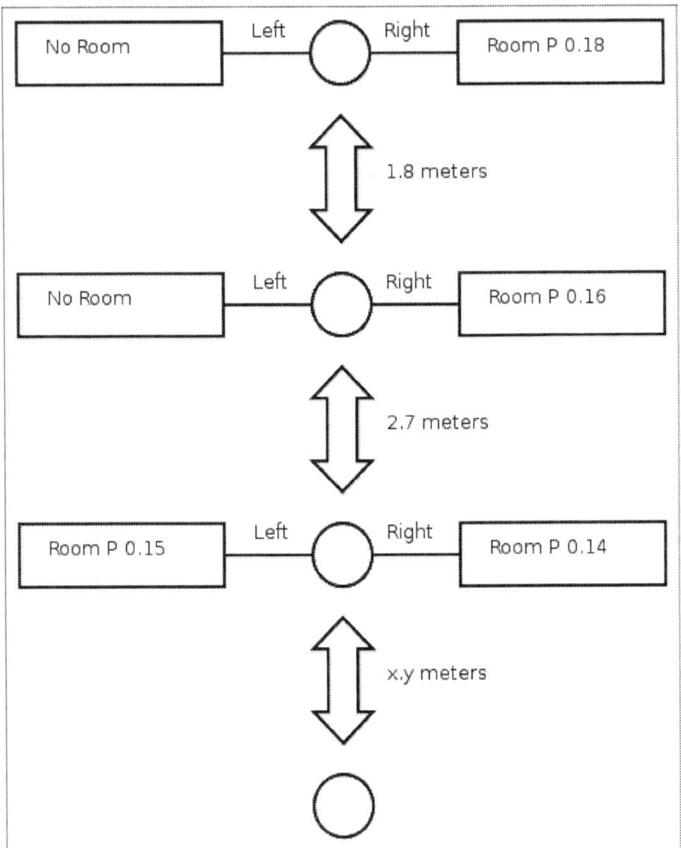

Fig. 12. Topological graph of a corridor based on the first camera only approach. The content of the doorplates is read and set to the squares. The local odometry of the robot is used to mark the edges. If no doorplate is found the square is empty.

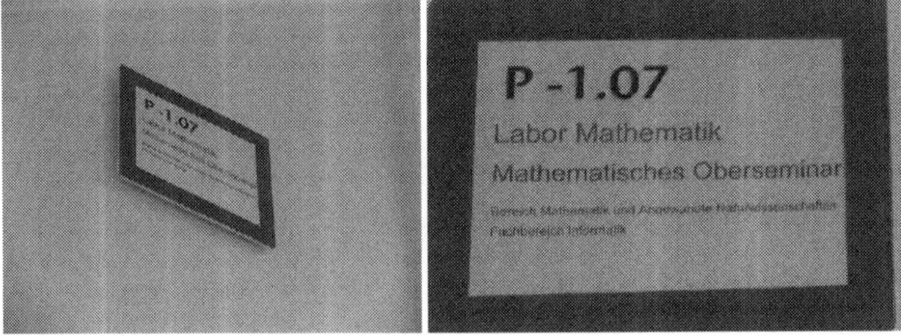

Fig. 13. Left: Original image of a doorplate. Right: Automatically corrected and cut out image of a doorplate.

The second method is evaluated with the mobile robot and the 3D laser scanner (fig. 1). After detecting the candidates in the panorama image, and based on the 3D geometrical data a good shooting position is calculated e.g. one meter in front of the doorplate. The mobile robot drives to all of these positions and takes high resolution images similar to method one.[14] The driving controller is a simple point based position controller. The content of the doorplate is set to the 3D point cloud based on the position of the robot and the 3D data of the candidate calculation. For the OCR process we evaluated different OCR engines.

4.3 Comparison of OCR engines

A lot of different OCR engines already exist so we define a test set of 46 images to test different engines. All of them can be used with the Linux operation system. The following table presents the timing results of these tests.

OCR Engine	Result	Time (total)	Average Time (per file)
Abbyy Finereader Engine 8 for Linux[1]	73.81%	158s	3.43s
Cuneiform 1.0 for Linux[2]	3.55%	100s	2.17s
GOCR 0.45[3]	22.38%	13s	0.28s
Ocrad 0.17[4]	23.91%*	9s	0.20s
OCRopus 0.3.1[5]	45.53%	43s	0.93s
Tesseract 2.04[6]	49.41%*	22s	0.48s

Table 1. Comparison of different OCR engines. The results of entries marked with an * have been achieved with grayscale images for the OCR process. For these engines, colored images produced lower quality results. The total time of each OCR engine relates to 46 test files, which have been processed in one batch.

The 46 images of the test set were taken autonomously by the robot with the help of a special application. The images have been automatically preprocessed by the application, so the doorplates have been cut out from the larger image and the shearing, which occurs because of the angle at which the camera was pointed at the doorplate, has been corrected.

To understand the results of the test and to evaluate or judge them in the right way, it is crucial to know how the measurement works. If a human reads a misspelled word, or a word with one character missing, he would most probably still understand the meaning of the word, this works, because the person who reads it, knows how it would be spelled correctly. A robot without any prior knowledge (like a dictionary) about the words can't achieve this. Considering this, a relatively strict rule of what is recognized correct and incorrect, was defined. To get some kind of reference data, all the images, which should be tested, have been reviewed and their content has been written into a text file. Words and lines are separated by a blank, in the same order as in the image. The example image as seen in figure 8 have the following reference data:

---

[14] http://www.youtube.com/watch?v=Il_aabmWeW8

P 0.20 Labor Robotik u. Bildverarbeitung Bereich Allgemeine Mikroinformatik Fachbereich Informatik

For this example the output of the OCRopus engine of this image was:

Labor
Robotik u. Bildverarbeitun
Bereich Allgemeine Nlikroinformatik
Fachbereich Informatik

Since it is time consuming to compare each file with its reference by hand, a little program was written to do the evaluation. The files get split up into several tokens, which are separated by blanks or line brakes respectively. Each token of the reference file, will be compared to each token in the OCR output and if it matches one of these, all characters and the blank will be counted as correct characters. If the reference token does not match any of the output tokens, the whole word and the blank will not be counted as correct characters. Table 2 to gives an example.

Reference Token	Found / Not found	Reason (if not found)	Character count
P	Not found	Missing in output	2
0.20	Not found	Missing in output	5
Labor	Found		6
Robotik	Found		8
u.	Found		3
Bildverarbeitung	Not found	missing 'g'	17
Bereich	Found		8
Allgemeine	Found		11
Mikroinformatik	Not found	Wrong characters	16
Fachbereich	Found		12
Informatik	Found		11

Table 2. Example of an evaluation of a doorplate. As a result 59/99 = 59,6% of the characters are correct.

The result would be 59 found characters of a total of 99 characters, so the output for this one file would be only 59.6 %, although only the P 0.20 was lost and the words "Bildverarbeitung" and "Mikroinformatik" have been misspelled. In general this is not that bad at all, with the rating of only 59.6 % misspelled characters. But overall, it is still a fair rating, because in this example some most probably relevant data, the room number, is lost completely and it is difficult to distinguish between relevant and irrelevant data, before you know the content. Nevertheless a dictionary or word data base or an evaluation based on n-gram will improve the output.

The Cuneiform OCR engine had problems with some files. Therefore it was not possible to process 24 of the 46 images at all, so the whole content of the corresponding reference files

could not be found in the OCR output which leads to the bad rating. Cuneiform shows a better performance with manual processed images. The Abbyy OCR engine shows the best performance concerning character recognition accuracy, but it is also the slowest engine. In this test it is the odd man out, because it is the only commercial engine. All the other engines are available for free and are under an open source license. The most promising open source OCR engines seem to be Tesseract and OCRopus. With better preprocessing and image enhancement, those two engines could deliver even better results (which is already implemented in the Abbyy OCR engine). Besides this, both engines are still under development.

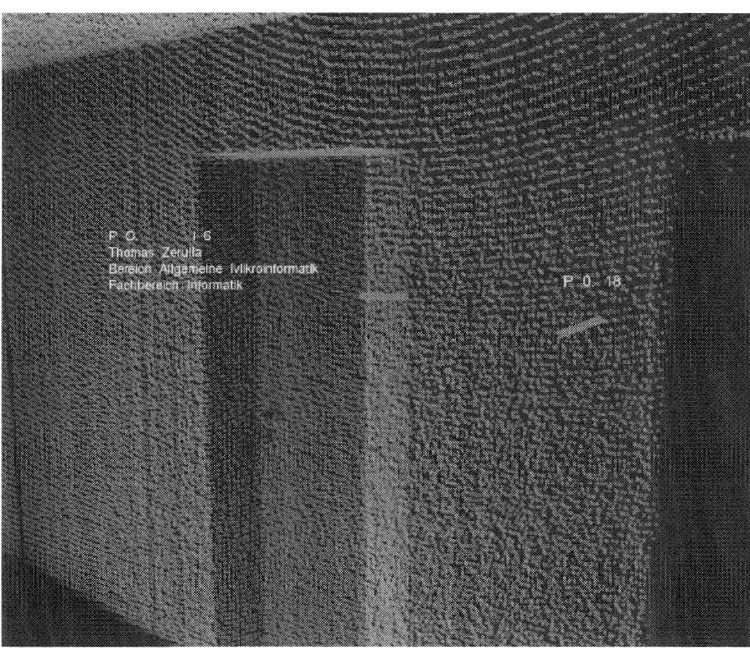

Fig. 14. Example of the extracted doorplate text mapped to the 3D point cloud in front of the door (ROS rviz viewer).

5. Conclusion

With a focus to real world indoor robotics we have presented two major things. First we have shown that mobile robots can use the same source of information as humans e.g. doorplates to localize itself. This is remarkable because only a cheap mobile robot (Roomba, $300), a consumer digital camera (Canon, $150) and a notebook (Gigabyte, $300) are needed to build a topological map with the textual information of the doorplates. Also remarkable is the fact that standard software can be used to implement our approach, mainly OpenCV and ROS is used. All modules are available as open source at our svn repository at the ROS website. The robot finds doorplates autonomously in its environment. It takes high resolution images of those doorplates with a camera and the quality of the images meet the requirements to process them effectively with standard OCR engines to extract the textual information. Unfortunately this process currently needs up to 30 seconds, manly focusing the doorplates, but there is much more potential for further improvements. However, the presented technique is a foundation for visual landmark based SLAM. The extracted data of the doorplates can be easily assembled to maps implemented as graphs. The maps are enhanced with additional geometric data, for example the distance of one doorplate to the other.

For our second contribution we extended the mobile robot with a 2D laser scanner (+$2000) and implemented an approach to acquire precise 3D scans. Odometry based position errors are eliminated by two additional horizontal scans at the start and end of the 3D scan. Comparison of our approach with a $100.000 Riegl VZ-400 laser scanner shows an average accuracy of 0.4 cm for one 3D scan. The acquired 3D point clouds are preprocessed to extract walls, ceilings and floors based on the tan segmentation. The OCR based reading of the doorplates is adapted to the 3D scan acquisition and the textual information is added to the segmented 3D point cloud. Further preprocessing of the 3D point clouds like CAD data is necessary. Also the kidnapped robot problem will be greatly simplified, because the robot needs to only find one doorplate to know its current position very precisely. Another great potential of this solution is the combination with e.g. googles search engine. With the help of the Internet, or some kind of local database, the robot is able to look up found names to get further information. For example if it reads the name of Mr. Surmann, the robot searches the web and parses the website to double-check if the read room number is correct or to find a corresponding phone number. For example afterwards the robot would be able to call Mr. Surmann and inform him about what is going on at his bureau. Another problem that can benefit from this technique is the anchoring problem. For example the robot does not need to know the exact form of a fire distinguisher, if it is red and the robot is able to read "Fire Distinguisher" on it, it probably is a fire distinguisher. Current work also includes the generation of HDR panorama images to support the tenants application.

6. Acknowledgment

This work has been funded by the European Commission under contract number FP7-247870-NIFTI. Furthermore, we would like to thank our current and former colleagues Sven Behnke, Rainer Worst, Thorsten Linder, Viatcheslav Tretyakov, Benjamin Fabricius, Benjamin Koenig, Ekkehard Schrey, Gregor Lux, Andreas Nuechter, Stefan May and Stefan Wilkes.

7. References

Baron W. (2002). *Camera-based text detection and OCR*, Master thesis, http://www.ai.rug.nl/nl/colloquia/tooncolloquium.php? afstudeerder=Wiebe+Baron&datum=26-06-2002.

Besl, P. J. & McKay, N. D. (1992). A Method for Registration of 3-D Shapes, IEEE Transactions on Pattern Analysis and Machine Intelligence 14(2): 239–256.

Clark, P. & Mirmehdi, M. (2002). *Recognising text in real scenes*, International Journal on Document Analysis and Recognition, Volume 4, Number 4, pp. 243-257.

Durrant-Whyte, H.; Bailey, T. (2006). *Simultaneous Localization and Mapping (SLAM): Part I The Essential Algorithms*. Robotics and Automation Magazine.

Durrant-Whyte, H.; Bailey, T. (2006). *Simultaneous localization and mapping (SLAM): part II.* Robotics and Automation Magazine.

Grisetti, G.; Stachniss, C. & Burgard, W. (2006). Improved Techniques for Grid Mapping with Rao-Blackwellized Particle Filters, IEEE Transactions on Robotics.

Haegele, M., Neugebauer, J. & Schraft, R. (2001). From Robots to Robot Assistants, Proceedings of the 32nd International Symposium on Robotics (ISR), Seoul, South Korea, pp. 404–409.

Holz, D.; Droeschel, D.; Behnke, S.; May, S. & Surmann, H. (2010). *Fast 3D Perception for Collision Avoidance and SLAM in Domestic Environments* Mobile Robots Navigation, Alejandra Barrera (Ed.), pp. 53-84, IN-TECH Education and Publishing, Vienna, Austria.

Lingemann, K., Nüchter, A., Hertzberg, J. & Surmann, H. (2005a). *About the Control of High Speed Mobile Indoor Robots*, Proceedings of the Second European Conference on Mobile Robots (ECMR), Ancona, Italy, pp. 218–223.

Lowe, D. & Little, J. (2001). *Vision-based mobile robot localization and mapping using scale-invariant features*. ICRA 2001.

May, S.; Pervoelz, K. & Surmann, H. (2007). *3D Cameras: 3D Computer Vision of wide Scope*, International Journal of Advanced Robotic Systems, pp. 181-202, Vol. 4, Advanced Robotic Systems (ARS), Vienna.

Mirmehdi, M.; Clark P. & Lam, J. (2001). *Extracting Low Resolution Text with an Active Camera for OCR*, Proceedings of the IX Spanish Symposium on Pattern Recognition and Image Processing.

Nagy, G. (2000). *Twenty years of document image analysis* in PAMI. IEEE Transactions on Pattern Analysis and Machine Intelligence 22, 1, 38–62.

Nuechter, A., Lingemann, K., Hertzberg, J., Wulf, O., Wagner, B. & Surmann, H. (2005). *3D Mapping with Semantic Knowledge*, Proceedings of the RoboCup International Symposium 2005: Robot Soccer World Cup IX, Osaka, Japan, pp. 335–346.

Prats, M.; Sanz, P.J. & del Pobil, A.R. (2005). *Model-based tracking and hybrid force/vision control for the UJI librarian robot*. IROS 2005.

Samarabandu, J. & Liu, X. (2002). *An Edge based Text Region Extraction*, International Journal of Signal Processing Volume 3 Number 4.

Siegwart, R., Arras, K. O., Bouabdallah, S., Burnier, D., Froidevaux, G., Greppin, X., Jensen, B., Lorotte, A., Mayor, L., Meisser, M., Philippsen, R., Piguet, R., Ramel, G., Terrien, G. & Tomatis, N. (2003). *Robox at Expo.02: A large-scale installation of personal robots*, Robotics and Autonomous Systems 42(3-4): 203–222.

Surmann, H.; Nuechter, A; Lingemann, K. & Hertzberg, J. (2004). *6D SLAM - Preliminary Report on closing the loop in Six Dimensions*, Proceedings of the 5th IFAC Symposium on Intelligent Autonomous Vehicles (IAV '04).

Thrun, S.; Burgard, W. & Fox, D. (2005). *Probabilistic Robotics*. MIT Press, Cambridge, MA.

Weinman, J. (2008). Unified detection and recognition for reading text in scene images. PhD. Thesis, http://www.cs.grinnell.edu/~weinman/pubs/weinman08unified.pdf

8

Transformations of Image Filters for Machine Vision Using Complex-Valued Neural Networks

Takehiko Ogawa
Takushoku University
Japan

1. Introduction

Neural networks expanded to complex domains have recently been studied in the field of computational intelligence. Complex-valued neural networks are effective for learning the relationships between complex inputs and outputs, and applications to complex analysis and complex image processing have been studied (Hirose, 2006). In addition, the effectiveness of the computational complexity and the number of training data has been confirmed when learning mappings in two-dimensional space (Nitta, 1997). Also, a method for complex-valued network inversion to produce an inverse mapping was proposed as a related technique using a complex-valued neural network (Ogawa, 2009). We can obtain forward mappings and inverse mappings in complex domains using these methods.

Image filters are important in bio-inspired systems, machine vision, and image processing. We can extract relevant information or remove unnecessary information from any given image using various image filters (Gonzalez & Woods, 2010; Pratt, 2007). In machine vision, image filters are effective for transforming, mapping, and making a required filter adaptive. In this work, we propose to adaptively map an image filter using a neural network to make an appropriate filter. We show that the mapping requires less training data when using complex-valued neural networks.

In this work, we examine the transformation of image filters using complex-valued neural networks. First, we conduct a simulation to learn the transformation, and demonstrate the capacity for forward and inverse mapping using complex-valued neural networks. We then demonstrate various transformations of image filters, such as Gaussian filters, using complex-valued neural networks. In addition, we present the results of image filtering using the transformed image filters.

2. Complex-valued neural networks

Complex-valued neural networks have recently been used to directly learn and recognize data in a complex region. These networks learn complex input–output relationships using complex weights and complex neurons. Various models have been proposed for representing these networks, such as the multilayer-type neural network (Benvenuto & Piazza, 1992), the self-organizing map (Hirose & Hara, 2003), and associative memory (Nemoto & Kubono, 1996), and a number of applications of these networks have also been studied.

Complex-valued neural networks are effective for processing data in a coordinate system where the phase rotates or for learning relationships in the frequency domain. Applications of complex-valued neural networks include adaptive design of patch antennas (Du et al., 2002), radar image processing (Hara & Hirose, 2004), and traffic-dependent optimal control of traffic signals (Nishikawa & Kuroe, 2004).

2.1 Complex-valued multilayer neural networks

In this study, complex-valued multilayer neural networks are used for filter transformation based on their capacity for mapping. Complex-valued multilayer neural networks are an extension of the usual multilayer neural networks to complex regions. This method determines the relationships between complex inputs and outputs using complex neurons and complex weights. They are typically composed of an input layer, some hidden layers, and the output layers. All functions can be realized in complex-valued multilayer neural networks if there is at least one hidden layer and a normal multilayer network. In this study, we used a neural network with three layers, namely, input layer, hidden layer, and output layer, for simulation.

In this study, we considered a multilayer neural network based on an error backpropagation learning method. This model learns complex input–output relationships using complex weights and complex neurons. Complex-valued neural networks are classified on the basis of their architecture and the type of neurons found in these networks. For instance, one type of complex-valued neural networks is based on the transfer function of the neuron, while another consists of real-type neurons. Here, we consider a neuron that independently applies a sigmoid function to the real and imaginary parts of the weighted sum of inputs. This neuron independently applies a complex sigmoid function to each real part and imaginary part, which can be defined as

$$f_C(s) = f(s_R) + if(s_I), \quad f(u) = \frac{1 - e^{-u}}{1 + e^{-u}} \tag{1}$$

where i and $s = s_R + is_I$ indicate the imaginary unit and the weighted sum of the neuron input, respectively. The architecture of the complex-valued sigmoid neuron is shown in Fig. 1. The neuron transforms the weighted sum $s = s_R + is_I$ of the input $x_n = x_{nR} + ix_{nI}$ and the weight $w_n = w_{nR} + iw_{nI}$ to the output $f_c(s) = f(s_R) + if(s_I)$ using the sigmoid function of equation (1). In this network, complex-valued neurons are used for the hidden layer and the output layer.

Complex-valued multilayer neural networks are usually used in two phases of learning and estimation, as shown in Fig. 2. In the learning phase, we provide the training input and output, and model the forward relation using the error backpropagation algorithm. During the estimation phase, we obtain the output for a given input by fixing the weights obtained in the leaning phase.

Next, we explain learning in a complex-valued neural network using the error backpropagation algorithm, which is enhanced for complex regions. Here, we consider a three-layer network with an input layer, a hidden layer, and an output layer. The output error $E = E_R + iE_I$ is defined by the squared error as

$$E_R = \frac{1}{2}\sum_r (y'_{rR} - y_{rR})^2, \quad E_I = \frac{1}{2}\sum_r (y'_{rI} - y_{rI})^2 \tag{2}$$

where $y'_r = y'_{rR} + iy'_{rI}$ and $y_r = y_{rR} + iy_{rI}$ are the r-th tutorial output and the network output, respectively. First, we formulate the weight update procedure between the hidden and output layers. The error signal $\delta_r = \delta_{rR} + i\delta_{rI}$ from the output layer is calculated by

$$\delta_{rR} = (y'_{rR} - y_{rR})(1 - y_{rR})(1 + y_{rR}), \quad \delta_{rI} = (y'_{rI} - y_{rI})(1 - y_{rI})(1 + y_{rI}). \tag{3}$$

Also, the gradient of the output error for the weight $w_{rk} = w_{rkR} + iw_{rkI}$ between the hidden and output layer is expressed by

$$\frac{\partial E_R}{\partial w_{rkR}} = \delta_{rR}v_{kR}, \quad \frac{\partial E_I}{\partial w_{rkR}} = \delta_{rI}v_{kI}, \quad \frac{\partial E_R}{\partial w_{rkI}} = -\delta_{rR}v_{kI}, \quad \frac{\partial E_I}{\partial w_{rkI}} = \delta_{rI}v_{kR} \tag{4}$$

where $v_k = v_{kR} + iv_{kI}$ indicates the input from the k-th hidden neuron. Therefore, the weights are updated by

$$w_{rkR}^{new} = w_{rkR}^{old} - \varepsilon_t\left(\delta_{rR}v_{kR} + \delta_{rI}v_{kI}\right), \quad w_{rkI}^{new} = w_{rkI}^{old} - \varepsilon_t\left(\delta_{rI}v_{kR} - \delta_{rR}v_{kI}\right) \tag{5}$$

where ε_t denotes a training gain. In this way, complex weights are updated between the hidden and output layers. Next, we formulate the weight update procedure between the input and hidden layers. The error signal $\delta_k = \delta_{kR} + i\delta_{kI}$ from the hidden layer is calculated by

$$\delta_{kR} = (1 - v_{kR})(1 - v_{kR})\sum_r \left(\delta_{rR}w_{rkR} + \delta_{rI}w_{rkI}\right),$$

$$\delta_{kI} = (1 - v_{kI})(1 - v_{kI})\sum_r \left(\delta_{rI}w_{rkR} - \delta_{rR}w_{rkI}\right) \tag{6}$$

Also, the gradient of the output error for the weight $w_{km} = w_{kmR} + iw_{kmI}$ between the input and hidden layer is expressed by

$$\frac{\partial E_R}{\partial w_{kmR}} = \delta_{kR}x_{mR}, \quad \frac{\partial E_I}{\partial w_{kmR}} = \delta_{kI}x_{mI}, \quad \frac{\partial E_R}{\partial w_{kmI}} = -\delta_{kR}x_{mI}, \quad \frac{\partial E_I}{\partial w_{kmI}} = \delta_{kI}x_{mR} \tag{7}$$

where $x_m = x_{mR} + ix_{mI}$ indicates the input from the m-th input neuron. Therefore, the weights are updated by

$$w_{kmR}^{new} = w_{kmR}^{old} - \varepsilon_t\left(\delta_{kR}x_{mR} + \delta_{kI}x_{mI}\right), \quad w_{kmI}^{new} = w_{kmI}^{old} - \varepsilon_t\left(\delta_{kI}x_{mR} - \delta_{kR}x_{mI}\right) \tag{8}$$

where ε_t is a training gain. In this way, the complex weights between the input and hidden layers are updated. The input-output relationship is learned by correcting each complex weight according to the above equations. In general, the afore-mentioned weight correction is repeated until a prescribed error value or repetition number. The principle of weight correction is based on the output error, as shown in Fig. 3.

The output is estimated from a given input using the learned complex-valued multilayer neural network. In the network studied, the output corresponding to the given input can be estimated by fixing the weights obtained during learning with a given input and obtaining the output.

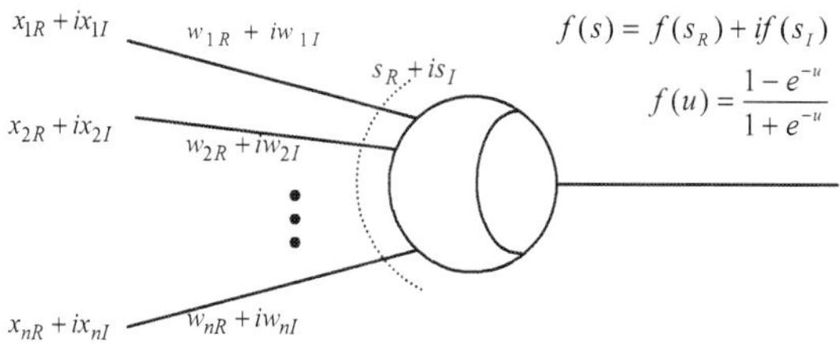

Fig. 1. A complex-valued sigmoid neuron.

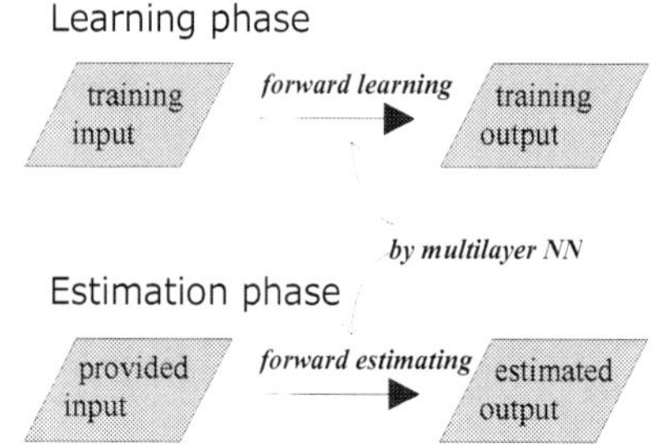

Fig. 2. Two-step estimation with complex-valued neural network.

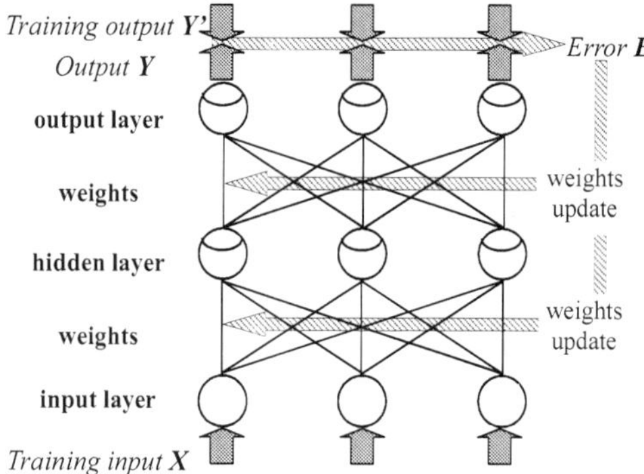

Fig. 3. Iterative correction of weights by error backpropagation learning.

2.2 Complex-valued network inversion

The inverse problem determines the inner mechanism or cause of an observed phenomenon. The concept of the inverse problem is shown in Fig. 4. The cause is estimated from a fixed model and a given result in the inverse problem, whereas the result is determined from a given cause by using a certain fixed mathematical model in the forward problem (Groetsch, 1993). We consider the estimation process with the neural network from the viewpoint of the direction of the problem. A multilayer neural network is a normal solution for the forward problem because it estimates the output from the input based on the forward relationship obtained by training. In contrast, an inverse problem can be solved using a multilayer neural network inversely with the forward relationship obtained during training.

A normal multilayer neural network can be used to solve the forward problem. Given a normal multilayer network where training is completed, the input-output relationship is given by $y = f(w, x)$, where x, y, and f are the input vector, the output vector, and the function defined by the interlayer weights w of the network, respectively. Given the input vector x, the network calculates the output vector y. Linden and Kindermann proposed a method for network inversion (Linden & Kindermann, 1989). Using this method, we can determine the observed output data y with f fixed after finding the forward relationship f by training. Then, the input x can be updated according to the calculated input correction signal, based on the duality of the weights and input. The input is actually estimated from the output by the iterative updating of the input based on the output error. In this way, the inverse problem for estimating input x from output y is solved with a multilayer neural network by using the forward relationship inversely. Further, network inversion has been applied to image restoration (Valova et al., 1995) and the inverse kinematics of robot arms (Ogawa & Kanada, 2010).

The network is used in two phases, forward training and inverse estimation, to solve the inverse problem by network inversion, as shown in Fig. 5. During the training phase, we provide the training input x and the training output y and calculate the output error E. Then, the weight w is updated by

$$w^{new} = w^{old} - \varepsilon_t \frac{\partial E}{\partial w} \tag{9}$$

where ε_t is the training gain, because the output error is due to maladjustments of the weights. The forward relationship is obtained by repeating this update procedure. This procedure is based on the usual backpropagation method. During the inverse estimation phase, we fixed the relationship obtained during training, given the random input x and the test output y, and we calculated the output error E. The input x is then updated by

$$x^{new} = x^{old} - \varepsilon_e \frac{\partial E}{\partial x} \tag{10}$$

where ε_e denotes the input update gain, because the output error is due to the error of the input. The input is estimated from the output by repeating this update procedure. The principle of input correction is shown in Fig. 6.

A complex-valued network inversion is an extension of the principle of the network inversion to a complex number. In a complex-valued network inversion, the network inversion technique extended to a complex number is applied to a learned complex-valued multilayer neural network to solve inverse problems. As a result, the complex input is estimated from a complex output, which is given to a learned complex-valued neural network. The network learns the input and output relationship using the error backpropagation algorithm extended to the complex region, which is explained in the previous section.

During the inverse estimation phase, the input is estimated from the given output. Thus, the provided initial random input is repeatedly updated by the output error, which is backpropagated to the input via the fixed weights. To provide an initial random input $x_m = x_{mR} + ix_{mI}$, the squared error $E = E_R + iE_I$ is calculated as

$$E_R = \frac{1}{2}\sum_r \left(y'_{rR} - y_{rR}\right)^2, \quad E_R = \frac{1}{2}\sum_r \left(y'_{rI} - y_{rI}\right)^2, \tag{11}$$

where $y_r = y_{rR} + iy_{rI}$ and $y'_r = y'_{rR} + iy'_{rI}$ indicate the network output and tutorial output, respectively. The error signals from the output and hidden layers are also formulated as

$$\delta_{rR} = \left(1 - y_{rR}\right)\cdot\left(1 + y_{rR}\right)\cdot\left(y'_{rR} - y_{rR}\right), \quad \delta_{rI} = \left(1 - y_{rI}\right)\cdot\left(1 + y_{rI}\right)\cdot\left(y'_{rI} - y_{rI}\right), \tag{12}$$

and

$$\delta_{kR} = \left(1 - v_{kR}\right)\cdot\left(1 + v_{kR}\right)\cdot\sum_r \left(\delta_{rR}w_{rkR} - \delta_{rI}w_{rkI}\right),$$

$$\delta_{kI} = \left(1 - v_{kI}\right)\cdot\left(1 + v_{kI}\right)\cdot\sum_r \left(\delta_{rI}w_{rkR} - \delta_{rR}w_{rkI}\right), \tag{13}$$

where $v_k = v_{kR} + iv_{kI}$ indicates the input from the k-th hidden neuron to the output neurons. Equations (12) and (13) are similar to equations (3) and (6), respectively. The error signal to the input layer is then calculated by

$$\delta_{mR} = \left(1 - x_{mR}\right)\cdot\left(1 + x_{mR}\right)\cdot\sum_k \left(\delta_{kR}w_{kmR} - \delta_{kI}w_{kmI}\right),$$

$$\delta_{mI} = \left(1 - x_{mI}\right)\cdot\left(1 + x_{mI}\right)\cdot\sum_k \left(\delta_{kI}w_{kmR} - \delta_{kR}w_{kmI}\right), \tag{14}$$

where $x_m = x_{mR} + ix_{mI}$ indicates the input from the m-th input neuron to the hidden neurons. The error signal $\delta_m = \delta_{mR} + i\delta_{mI}$ indicates a demand for input correction to the m-th input neuron, so the complex inputs are iteratively corrected as

$$x_{mR}^{new} = x_{mR}^{old} - \varepsilon_e\delta_{mR}, \quad x_{mI}^{new} = x_{mI}^{old} - \varepsilon_e\delta_{mI} \tag{15}$$

where ε_e is the inverse estimation gain. When the error reaches the target, the input correction is terminated and the obtained complex input becomes a solution. As a result, the complex input can be inversely estimated from the complex output by using the complex weight distribution obtained during training. This is similar to correcting the weights or the input iteratively during training and inverse estimation. However, the inverse estimation uses iterative corrections for a given pattern, which differs from training by repeated correction of plural patterns.

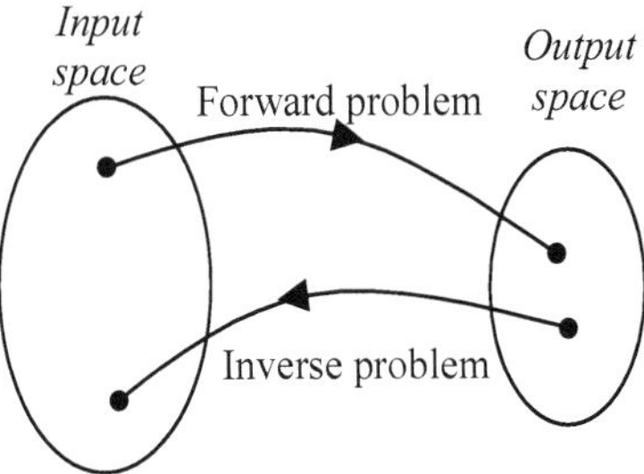

Fig. 4. Concept of inverse problems.

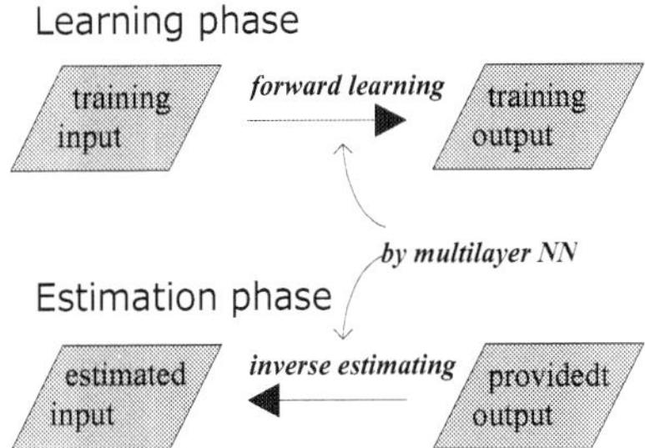

Fig. 5. Two-step estimation to solve inverse problems by complex-valued network inversion.

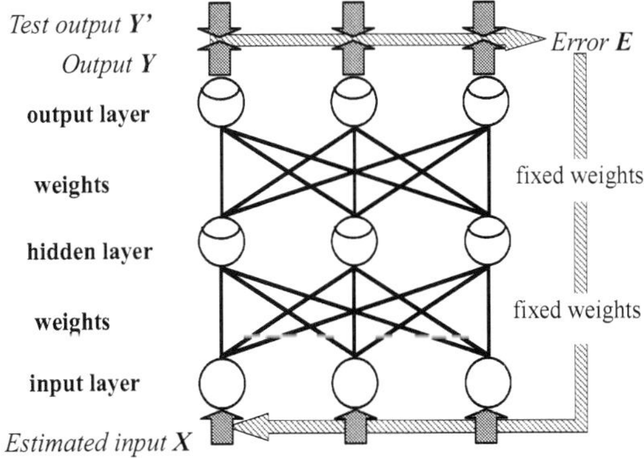

Fig. 6. Iterative correction of inputs by network inversion.

2.3 Learning of complex-mapping by complex-valued neural networks

A multilayer neural network can learn the nonlinear mapping relationships between inputs and outputs. A complex-valued multilayer neural network and a complex-valued network inversion can estimate, respectively, the forward mapping and the inverse mapping between an input and output. In this study, we examined the forward and inverse estimation problems using these networks. In the complex-mapping problem, it is important that learning is related to the mapping of points on a complex plane. A complex-valued neural network has the particular advantage of learning a map with a coordinate system that rotates. We consider the use of complex-valued neural networks by replacing the mapping with a transformation of the rotation with a mapping on a complex plane.

We consider the problem of mapping a point on a complex plane using a network with an input and an output. The network learns the input/output relationship using a given complex learning pattern for input and output learning. During the forward estimation of a complex-valued multilayer neural network, we provide the input to obtain the output by fixing the weights obtained in learning. During the inverse estimation of the complex-valued network inversion, we provide a complex random input pattern and iteratively correct the input from a given complex output pattern by fixing the weights obtained in learning.

Various kinds of information can be expressed by assigning meanings to the coordinates in complex mapping problems. In this study, we examined the allocation of the values of image filters to a complex plane and performed various conversions. We can generally implement filters that achieve non-symmetric filtering and direction-related filtering. These are effective tools in machine vision. In this study, we considered the conversion of an image filter using complex-valued neural networks.

We examined the linear transformation of expansion/compression and rotation, and general projective conversion, which are important methods for transforming image filters. First, we considered a figure $g(x, y)$ in two-dimensional space, where each value of the coordinates (x, y) is moved to coordinates (x', y') repeatedly. Generally, a linear transform is expressed by

$$\begin{pmatrix} x' \\ y' \end{pmatrix} = \begin{pmatrix} a & b \\ c & d \end{pmatrix}\begin{pmatrix} x \\ y \end{pmatrix} \tag{16}$$

using a matrix expression. Various linear transforms can be executed by choosing the four parameters a, b, c, and d. Here, we set the parameters $b = c = 0$ as

$$\begin{pmatrix} x' \\ y' \end{pmatrix} = \begin{pmatrix} a & 0 \\ 0 & d \end{pmatrix}\begin{pmatrix} x \\ y \end{pmatrix} \tag{17}$$

to consider the transform of expansion/compression shown in Fig. 7 (a). The parameters a and d indicate the rate of expansion/compression in the x-direction and y-direction, respectively. Expansion is indicated if these parameters are larger than 1.0, whereas compression is indicated if they are lower than 1.0. The transform of rotation is given as

$$\begin{pmatrix} x' \\ y' \end{pmatrix} = \begin{pmatrix} \cos\theta & -\sin\theta \\ \sin\theta & \cos\theta \end{pmatrix}\begin{pmatrix} x \\ y \end{pmatrix} \tag{18}$$

where θ denotes the counterclockwise angle around the origin, as shown in Fig. 7 (b). These are linear transforms, and they are realized by simple parameter estimation; however, we need to learn and estimate these transforms to illustrate the procedure for complex-valued neural networks used in this study. More general geometric transforms include a projective transform. A projective transform is expressed by

$$x' = \frac{a_{11}x + a_{12}y + a_{13}}{a_{31}x + a_{32}y + a_{33}}, \quad y' = \frac{a_{21}x + a_{22}y + a_{23}}{a_{31}x + a_{32}y + a_{33}},$$

(19)

which includes nine parameters a_{ij}. An example of a projective transform is shown in Fig. 7 (c). In this study, we consider these three transforms as geometric transforms on a complex plane, and we use them for estimation with complex-valued neural networks.

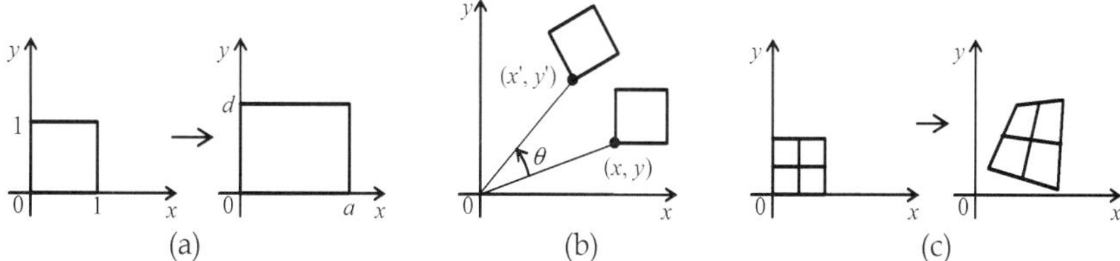

(a)   (b)   (c)

Fig. 7. Examples of geometric transforms: (a) expansion and compression, (b) rotation, and (c) projective transforms.

3. Image filters

Image filters are an important tool in the fields of bio-inspired systems, robot vision, and image processing. Relevant information is extracted or unnecessary information is removed from a given image with various image filters. In robot vision, it is useful if the image filter can transform or adaptively map when making a necessary filter. In this section, we propose to adaptively map an image filter using a neural network to make an appropriate filter. Complex-valued neural networks are known to effectively map using less training data.

A Gaussian function is often used as an expression of the frequency domain of a filter. For example, let $H(u)$ denote the 1-D frequency domain Gaussian filter as

$$H(u) = Ae^{-u^2/2\sigma^2}$$

(20)

where σ is the standard deviation of the Gaussian function. This function can be used as a one-dimensional low pass filter. Moreover, let $H(u, v)$ denote the 2-D frequency domain Gaussian filter as

$$H(u,v) = e^{-D^2(u,v)/2\sigma^2}$$

(21)

where $D(u,v) = \left(u^2 + v^2\right)$ and the origin, $u = v = 0$, is considered as the center of the filter.

Various filters can be made by applying the Gaussian function using the above-mentioned function, which basically provides a low-pass filter. For instance, a high-pass filter is produced by assuming $1 - H(u,v)$. Moreover, a filter of the lateral inhibition type can be produced based on the difference of two Gaussian functions with different standard deviations. This is called the DOG function and it can be used as an edge enhancement filter.

Moreover, an orientation selectivity filter can be produced from the rotated elliptic function by compressing and rotating a Gaussian function. This filter can extract a line segment or filter an image in a specific direction. A filter with various features can be produced by variously compressing and rotating the Gaussian filter. Thus, linear transformations and nonlinear transformations can be produced by learning using neural networks. As an example, we consider a nonlinear conversion, such as a projective transform. Fig. 8 shows examples of the plot of 2-D filter functions related to Gaussian functions: a low-pass filter, a high-pass filter, a lateral inhibition filter based on the difference of Gaussian functions, and an orientation selectivity filter that is obtained using an elliptical Gaussian function.

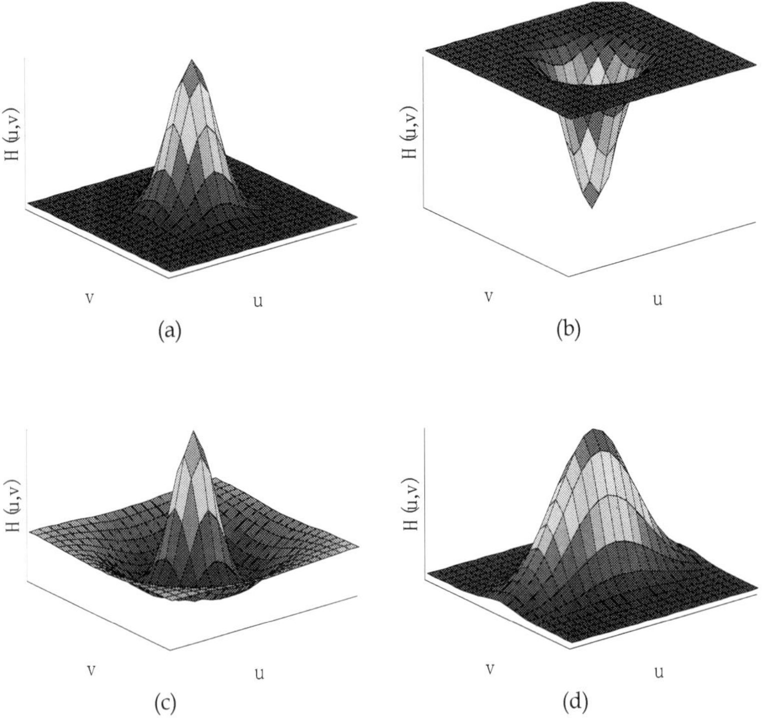

Fig. 8. Plots of 2-D filter functions related to Gaussian functions: (a) low-pass filter, (b) high-pass filter, (c) lateral inhibition filter based on the difference of Gaussian functions, and (d) a directional filter obtained using an elliptical Gaussian function.

4. Simulation

We conducted a simulation of a forward and inverse transform of the filter using forward and inverse mappings with a complex-valued multilayer neural network and a complex-valued network inversion. First, we examined the geometric conversions namely, the expansion/compression, rotation, and projective conversions, on a complex plane to demonstrate the learning procedure and the estimation of the complex mapping. The result was a transformation of the geometric figure, the movement vector on the complex plane, and a conversion of the filter. In addition, we filtered the image with the transformed filter and showed the effect of the filter conversion with complex-valued neural networks.

We use a network with an input and an output, and we considered the problem of mapping one point to another on a complex plane. We provided complex input and output patterns and made the network learn the input/output relationship during learning. Then, we examined the forward estimation of the multilayer neural network and the inverse estimation using the network inversion of the learned network. Thus, we obtained an output from a given input by using the learned relation as it was and obtained the input from the given output by using the learned relation inversely. The network parameters and network architecture are presented in Table 1 and Fig. 9, respectively. The following section shows the results of the expansion/compression conversion, the rotational transformation, and the projective conversion.

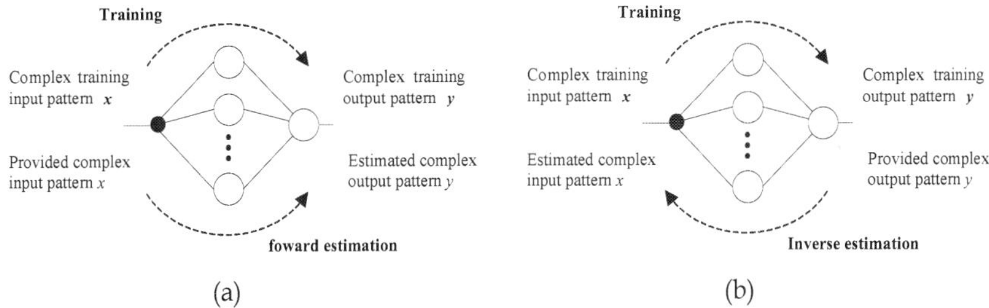

Fig. 9. Network architectures for (a) forward estimation and (b) inverse estimation.

	Expansion/compression		Rotation	Projective transform
	(symmetry)	(asymmetry)		
Input neurons	1			
Hidden neurons	10			
Output neurons	1			
Training rate ε_t	0.01			
Input correcting rate ε_e	0.1			
Maximum number of training epochs	50000	10000	50000	50000
Maximum number of estimation epochs	10000	10000	10000	10000
Criterion for learning convergence	0.0001	0.0001	0.0001	0.0001
Criterion for estimation convergence	0.001	0.001	0.001	0.001

Table 1. Network parameters.

4.1 Expansion/compression transform

We examined the learning, forward estimation, and inverse estimation of the expansion/compression transform on a complex plane with the complex-valued neural networks. Both symmetric and non-symmetric transforms along the vertical and horizontal axes are important for transforming an image filter such as the orientation selectivity filter.

Thus, symmetric transforms and non-symmetric transforms are examined here. As the learning data, we provided 22 pairs of data that satisfied $x' = ax$, $y' = dy$, $y = x$, $y = -x$, where a and d are constants, and (x, y) and (x', y') are points before and after the transform, respectively. We prepared the 11 points $x = (-1.0, -0.8, ..., 1.0)$.

First, we examined the learning, forward estimation, and inverse estimation of the symmetric expansion/compression transform by setting parameters $a = d = 0.5$. The forward mapping vector by forward estimation and the inverse mapping vector by inverse estimation are shown in Figs. 10 (a) and (b), respectively. Based on these results, it was confirmed that the transform vectors were correctly obtained. In Fig. 11, we show the results of the forward and inverse estimation of the expansion/compression transform of a circle, whose radius and center are 0.5 and the origin, respectively. Based on these results, it was confirmed that the forward and inverse estimations were correctly conducted. In addition, Fig. 12 shows the results of the forward and inverse estimation of the expansion/compression of the Gaussian function. Based on these results, it was found that the expansion/compression is correctly conducted. Therefore, it was shown that a complex-valued neural network can realize the forward and inverse transforms of expansion/compression.

Next, we examined the learning, forward estimation, and inverse estimation of an asymmetric expansion/compression transform by setting parameters $a = 1.0$, $d = 0.2$. Fig. 13 shows the forward mapping vector and the inverse mapping vector obtained by learning. Based on these results, it was found that the expansion/compression was applied only along the y-axis. Fig. 14 shows the results of the forward and inverse estimation of the expansion/compression transform of a circle, whose radius and center are 0.5 and the origin, respectively. Based on these results, it was found that the forward and inverse estimations of the expansion/compression were correctly shown to be an oval distribution of the estimated points. In addition, Fig. 15 shows the results of the forward and inverse estimation of the expansion/compression of the Gaussian function. Therefore, it was shown that a complex-valued neural network can realize the forward and inverse transforms of the asymmetric expansion/compression.

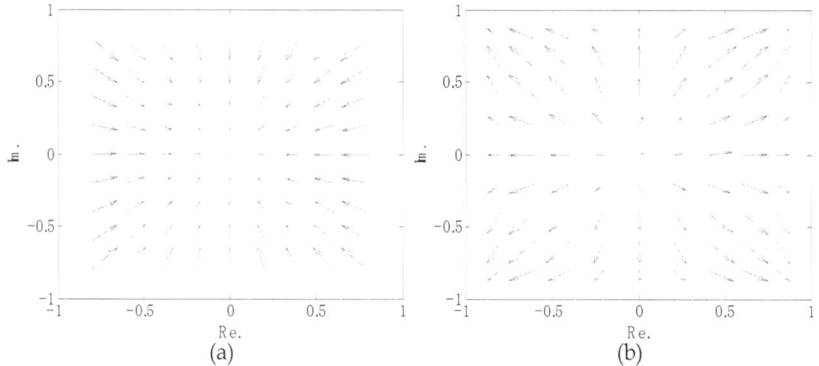

Fig. 10. Transform vector obtained by learning of the symmetric expansion for (a) forward estimation and (b) inverse estimation.

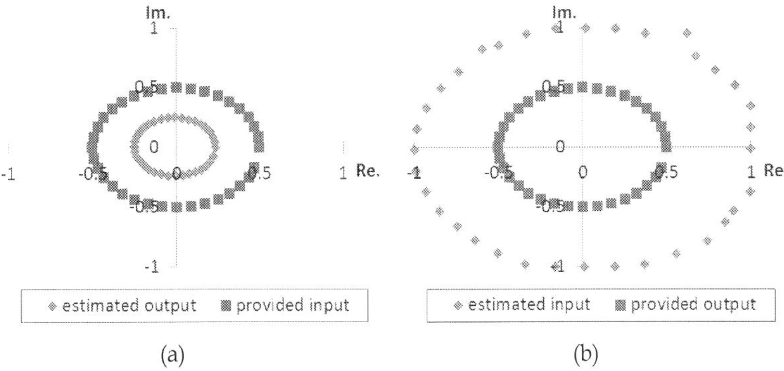

Fig. 11. Results of symmetric expansion of a circle by (a) forward estimation and (b) inverse estimation.

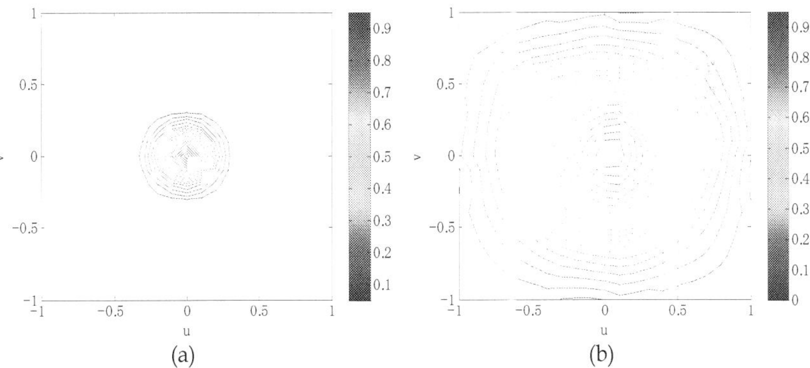

Fig. 12. Results of symmetric expansion of a Gaussian function by (a) forward estimation and (b) inverse estimation.

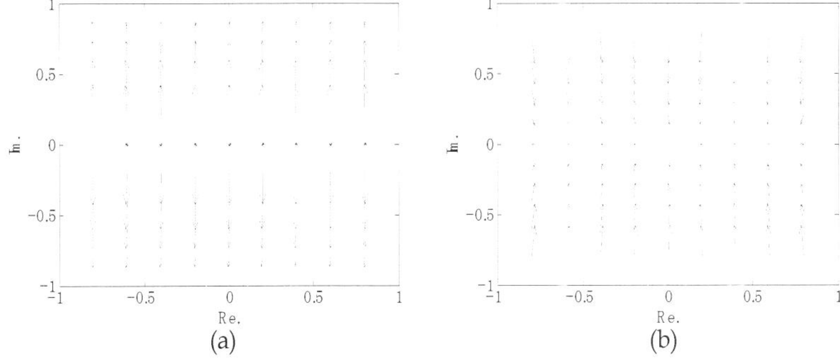

Fig. 13. Transform vector obtained by the learning of asymmetric expansion with (a) forward estimation and (b) inverse estimation.

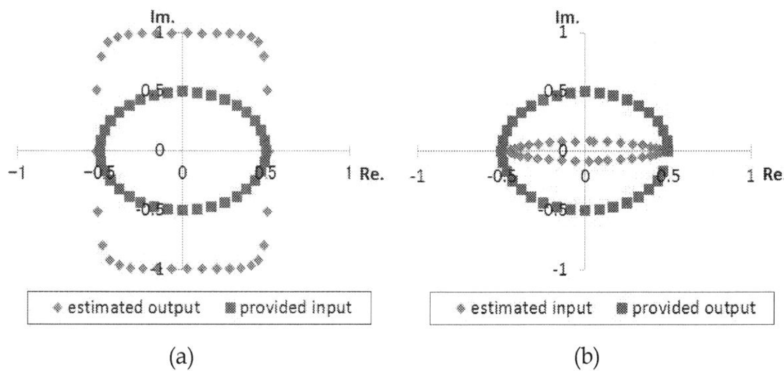

Fig. 14. Results of the asymmetric expansion of a circle by (a) forward estimation and (b) inverse estimation.

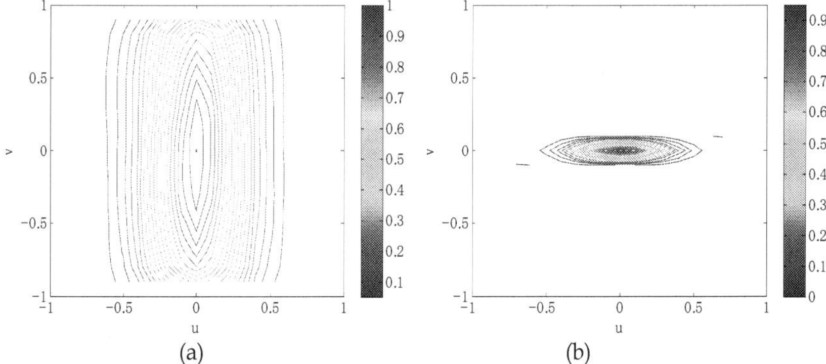

Fig. 15. Results of asymmetric expansion of a Gaussian function by (a) forward estimation and (b) inverse estimation.

4.2 Rotation transform

We examined the learning, forward estimation, and inverse estimation of the rotation transform on a complex plane with complex-valued neural networks. As learning data, we provided 22 pairs of data that satisfied $y' = x\sin\theta + y\cos\theta$, $y = x$, $y = -x$, where (x, y) and (x', y') are the points before and after the transform, respectively. We prepared the 11 points $x = (-0.5, -0.4, ..., 0.5)$.

We examined the learning, forward estimation, and inverse estimation of the rotation transform by setting parameter $\theta = 45°$. Fig. 16 shows the forward mapping vector and the inverse mapping vector obtained by learning. Based on these results, it was confirmed that the transform vectors were correctly obtained. Fig. 17 shows the results of the forward and inverse estimation of the rotation transform of an ellipse whose major axis, minor axis, and center were 0.5, 0.125, and the origin, respectively. Based on these results, it was confirmed

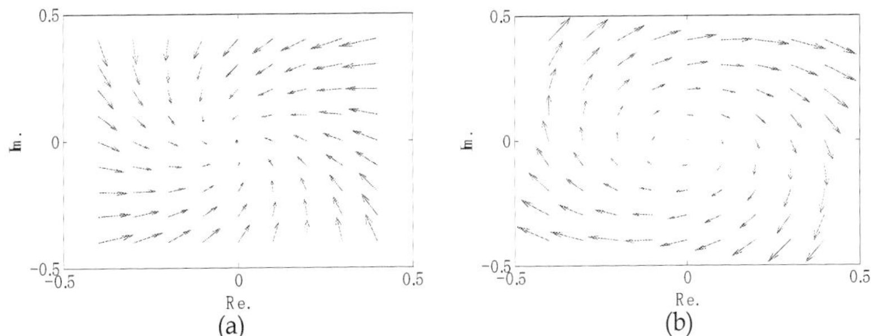

Fig. 16. Transform vector obtained by learning of the rotation with (a) forward estimation and (b) inverse estimation.

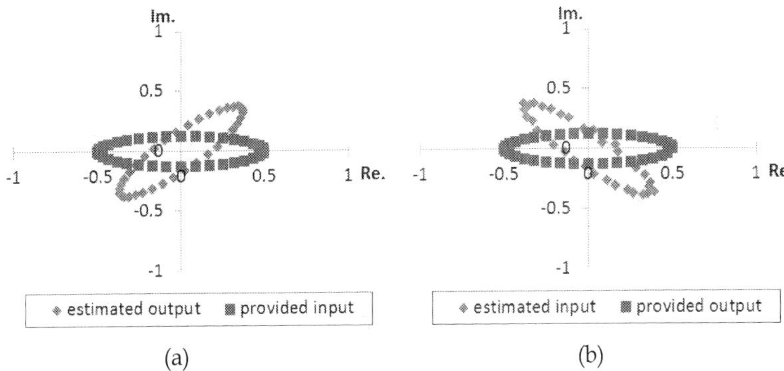

Fig. 17. Results of the rotation of an ellipse by (a) forward estimation and (b) inverse estimation.

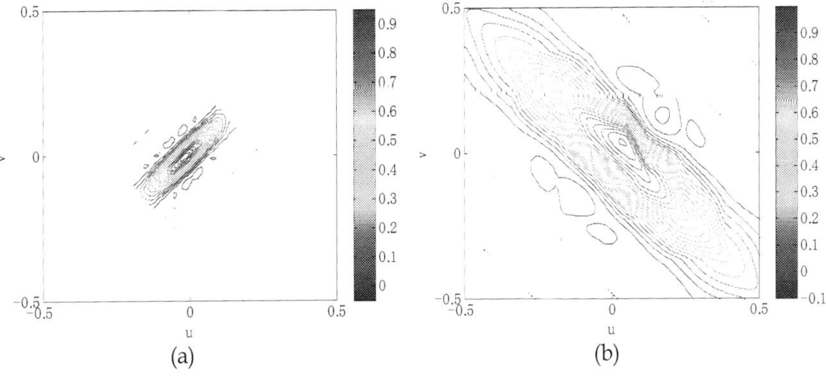

Fig. 18. Results of the rotation of an elliptic Gaussian function by (a) forward estimation and (b) inverse estimation.

that the forward and inverse estimations were correctly conducted. In addition, Fig. 18 shows the results of the forward and inverse estimation of the rotation of an elliptic Gaussian function. Based on these results, it was found that the rotation was correctly conducted. Therefore, it was shown that a complex-valued neural network can realize the forward and inverse transforms of the rotation.

4.3 Projective transform

We examined the learning, forward estimation, and inverse estimation of a projective transform on a complex plane with complex-valued neural networks. As learning data, we prepared 22 pair of data on $y = x$ or $y = -x$ that satisfied equation (19), where (x, y) and (x', y') were the points before and after the transform, respectively. We prepared the 11 points $x = (-0.5, -0.4, ..., 0.5)$.

First, we examined the learning, forward estimation, and inverse estimation of a projective transform by setting the parameters $a_{11} = 3$, $a_{12} = 0$, $a_{13} = 0$, $a_{21} = 0$, $a_{22} = 3$, $a_{23} = 0$, $a_{31} = 0$, $a_{32} = 6$, and $a_{33} = 6$. Fig. 19 shows the forward mapping vector and the inverse mapping vector

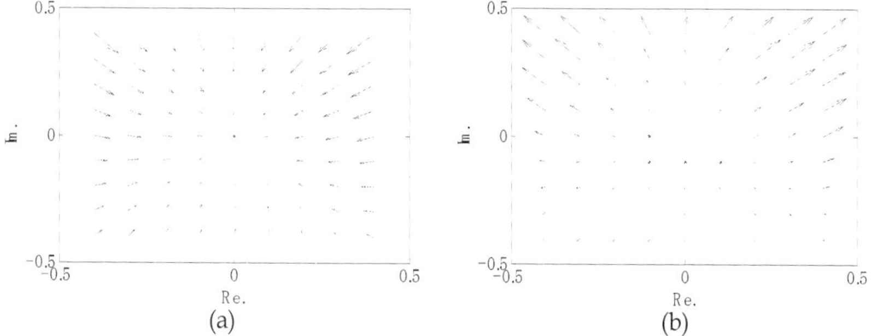

(a)   (b)

Fig. 19. Transform vector obtained by learning a projective transform with (a) forward estimation and (b) inverse estimation.

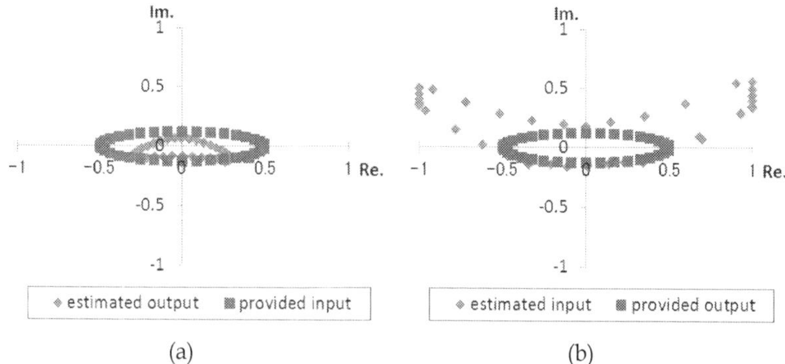

(a)   (b)

Fig. 20. Results of the projective transform of a circle by (a) forward estimation and (b) inverse estimation.

obtained by learning. Based on these results, it was confirmed that the transform vectors were correctly obtained. Fig. 20 shows the results of the forward and inverse estimation of the rotation transform of an ellipse whose major axis, minor axis, and center were 0.5, 0.125, and the origin, respectively. Based on these results, it was confirmed that the forward and inverse estimations were correctly conducted. In addition, Fig. 21 shows the results of the forward and inverse estimation of the rotation of an elliptic Gaussian function. Based on these results, it was found that the rotation was correctly conducted. Therefore, it was shown that a complex-valued neural network can realize the forward and inverse transforms of a projective transform.

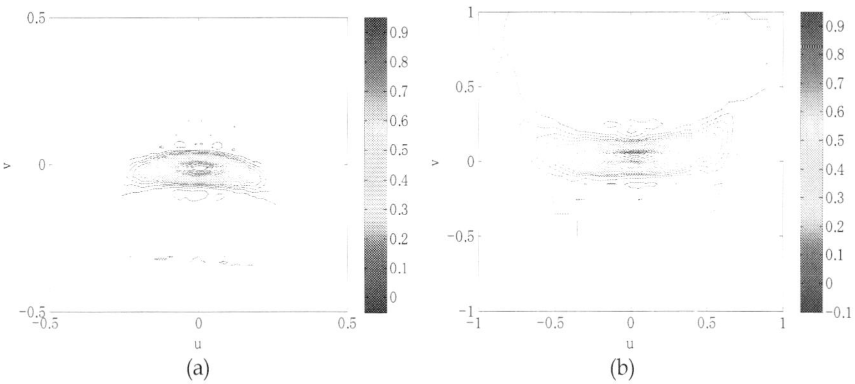

Fig. 21. Results of the projective transform of an elliptic Gaussian function by (a) forward estimation and (b) inverse estimation.

4.4 Filtering images using transformed filters

We performed image filtering using the transformed filter estimated in the previous simulations and examined the results. We used four transformed filters: an expanded Gaussian low-pass filter with forward estimation, an expanded Gaussian low-pass filter with inverse estimation, a rotated elliptic Gaussian filter with forward estimation, and a rotated elliptic Gaussian filter with inverse estimation. The transformed image spectrum $I'(u, v)$ can be described as the product of the transfer function $H(u, v)$ and the original image spectrum $I(u, v)$; that is,

$$I'(u,v) = H(u,v)I(u,v) \qquad (22)$$

The standard image on which the filtering was performed is shown in Fig. 22(a). Fig. 22(b) shows simple line segments that indicate the orientation selectivity of the rotated elliptic

Gaussian filter. The results for the standard image are shown in Fig. 23. Fig. 24 shows a magnification of the upper-left part of Fig. 23. Part (a) in Figs. 23 and 24 shows the standard image filtered using the expanded Gaussian low-pass filter with forward estimation; part (b) shows the case for expanded Gaussian low-pass filter with inverse estimation. In Fig. 23 (c) and (d), a striped pattern flowing from upper left to lower right and from upper right to lower left, respectively, is observed; this indicates that orientation selection was performed. To clearly demonstrate the effects of the orientation selectivity, the simple line segments were filtered by transformed elliptic Gaussian filter, as shown in Fig. 25. It was found that the line segments at 45° and -45° were selectively extracted, as shown in Fig. 25 (a) and (b), respectively. This result confirmed that directional selectivity had been achieved.

The above results confirm that the low-pass filter and orientation selection filter can be correctly realized by transforming image filters using a neural network. We can obtain a low-pass filter and an orientation selection filter having arbitrary characteristics by appropriate scaling and rotation of a Gaussian filter. An advantage of the neural network based method is that arbitrary filter characteristics can be obtained by learning of the input/output relation.

The advantage of the transformation of the image filter by a neural network is the adaptive composition of the filter by learning. As shown in the above simulation, the use of a neural network enables the easy realization of not only linear transformations, such as scaling and rotation, but also a nonlinear transformation, namely, projective transformation. Because neural networks can obtain a transformation only by a mapping between input and output, any transformation is realizable if input and output are known. Moreover, the use of neural networks enables the realization of an inverse filter by a network inversion method, which can be applied to areas such as image restoration and bidirectional image processing. The advantage of transformation by complex-valued neural networks is that the mapping on a plane, especially one that has undergone rotation, can be expressed well. Moreover, complex-valued neural networks afford lower computational complexity than conventional real-valued neural networks because, in the former, two-dimensional information can be expressed by a neuron.

In machine vision, the advantage of filter transformation by the proposed neural network is as follows. Neural networks are often used as part of the recognition system in a machine vision system. The filter transformation proposed in this work corresponds to the pre-processing stage in machine vision. Because neural network based pre-processing is compatible with a neural network based recognition system, we will be able to integrate the pre-processing and recognition system when designing a machine vision system. Furthermore, the model of a recognition neural network, such as the neocognitron (Fukushima, 1988), includes an orientation selection cell. Therefore, we expect that the proposed method can be directly applied to such a model.

The experimental results indicate that the proposed filter afforded most of the expected advantages. The disadvantage of the proposed neural network based method is that its computational complexity is slightly high. However, it is expected that this can be resolved by further refinement of the computer, system, and calculation method.

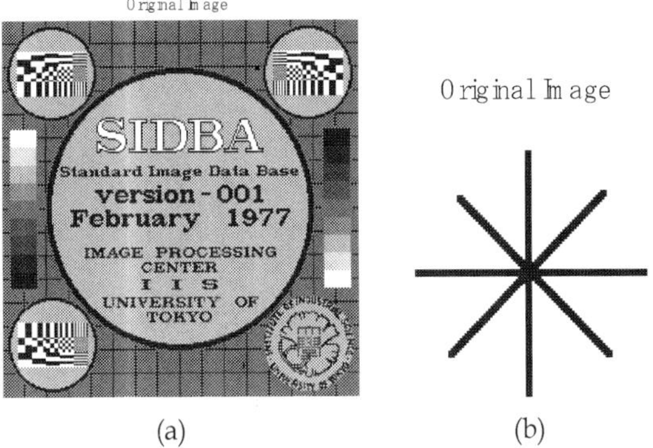

Fig. 22. Original images used in the simulation: (a) standard image (b) simple line segments.

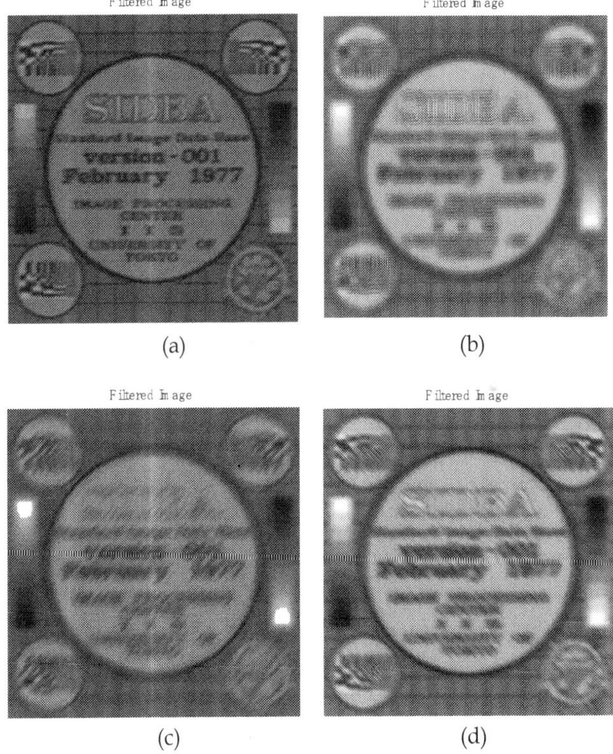

Fig. 23. Images filtered using (a) an expanded Gaussian low-pass filter with forward estimation, (b) an expanded Gaussian low-pass filter with inverse estimation, (c) a rotated elliptic Gaussian filter with forward estimation, and (d) a rotated elliptic Gaussian filter with inverse estimation.

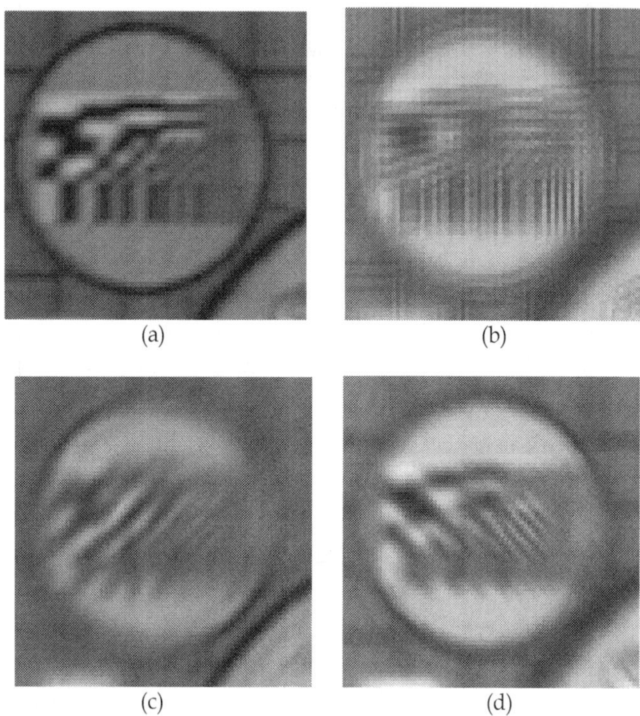

(a)   (b)
(c)   (d)

Fig. 24. Magnified images of the upper left part of Fig. 23.

Fig. 25. Image of simple line segments filtered using (a) a rotated elliptic Gaussian filter with forward estimation, and (b) a rotated elliptic Gaussian filter with inverse estimation.

5. Conclusion

In this study, we showed the mapping ability of a complex-valued neural network and proposed its use in the transform of an image filter. We introduced a complex-valued multilayer neural network for solving forward problems and a complex-valued network inversion for solving inverse problems and explained each principle of operation in detail. Moreover, to demonstrate the mapping ability, we handled complex mapping problems, i.e., the linear geometric transforms, namely, expansion/compression, rotation, and projective transforms. We confirmed the estimation procedure by simulation. In addition, we applied this mapping capacity to the transform of an image filter, and we demonstrated the geometric transform of various filters, such as the Gaussian filter. Moreover, we examined image filtering with a filter that was transformed using a complex-valued neural network and confirmed its effectiveness.

As the future work, we will apply complex-valued neural networks to nonlinear transforms of various image filters. Moreover, we will introduce processing with complex-valued neural networks into an actual robot vision system based on the results of this study.

6. References

Benvenuto, N. & Piazza, F. (1992). On the Complex Backpropagation Algorithm, *IEEE Trans. on Signal Processing*, vol.40, no.4, pp.967–969.

Du, K. L., Lai, A. K. Y., Cheng, K. K. M. & Swamy, M. N. S. (2002). Neural Methods for Antenna Array Signal Processing: A Review, *Signal Processing*, vol.82, pp.547–561.

Fukushima, K. (1988). Neocognitron: A hierarchical neural network capable of visual pattern recognition, *Neural Networks*, vol 1, pp. 119-130.

Gonzalez, R. C. & Woods, E. W. (2010). *Digital Image Processing*, Pearson Education International, ISBN: 978-0132345637, New Jersey.

Groetsch, C. W. (1993). *Inverse Problems in the Mathematical Sciences*, Friedr. Vieweg and Sohn Verlags. mbH, ISBN: 978-3528065454, Stuttgart.

Hara, T. & Hirose, A. (2004). Plastic Mine Detecting Radar System Using Complex-Valued Self-Organizing Map That Deal with Multiple-Frequency Interferometric Images, *Neural Networks*, vol.17, no.8–9, pp.1201–1210.

Hirose, A. & Hara, T. (2003). Complex-Valued Self-Organizing Map Dealing with Multi-Frequency Interferometeric Data for Radar Imaging Systems, *Proc. of WSOM 2003*, pp. 255–260.

Hirose, A. (2006). *Complex-Valued Neural Networks*, Springer, ISBN: 978-3540334569, New York.

Linden, A. & Kindermann, J. (1989). Inversion of Multilayer Nets, *Proc. Int. Joint Conf. on Neural Networks*, pp.425–430.

Nemoto, I. & Kubono, M. (1996). Complex Associative Memory, *Neural Networks*, vol.9, pp. 253–261.

Nishikawa, I. & Kuroe, Y. (2004). Dynamics of Complex-Valued Neural Networks and Its Relation to a Phase Oscillator System, *Proc. of ICONIP 2004*, pp.122–129.

Nitta, T. (1997). An Extension of the Backpropagation Algorithm to Complex Numbers, *Neural Networks*, vol.10, no.8, pp.1392–1415.

Ogawa, T. & Kanada, H. (2010). Solution for Ill-Posed Inverse Kinematics of Robot Arm by Network Inversion, *Journal of Robotics, Hindawi Publishing*.

Ogawa, T. (2009). *Complex-Valued Neural Network and Inverse Problems*, in *Complex-Valued Neural Networks: Utilizing High-Dimensional Parameters*, (Dr. Nitta, T. ed.), IGI-Global, ISBN 978-160566214-5, New York, Chapter 2, pp.27-55.

Pratt, W. K. (2007). *Digital Image Processing,* John Wiley & Sons, ISBN: 978-0471767770, New Jersey.

Valova, I., Kameyama, K. & Kosugi, Y. (1995). Image Decomposition by Answer-in-Weights Neural Network, *IEICE Trans. on Information and Systems,* vol.E78-D-9, pp.1221–1224.

9

Boosting Economic Growth Through Advanced Machine Vision

Soha Maad[1], Samir Garbaya[2], Nizar Ayadi[3] and Saida Bouakaz[4]
*[1]IGROW Integrated Technologies and Services for Sustainable
Growth European Economic Interest Grouping (EEIG)
Invent DCU, Dublin City University, Glasnevin, Dublin
[2]ENSAM - Arts et Métiers ParisTech, Image Institute
[3]International Program Director, University of Alicante, Alicante
[4]Laboratoire d'InfoRmatique en Image et Sytemes d'Information (LIRIS),
Université Claude Bernard Lyon 1
[1]Ireland
[2,4]France
[3]Spain*

1. Introduction

In this chapter, we overview the potential of machine vision and related technologies in various application domains of critical importance for economic growth and prospect.

Considered domains include healthcare, energy and environment, finance, and industrial innovation. Visibility technologies considered encompass augmented and virtual reality, 3D technologies, and media content authoring tools and technologies.

We overview the main challenges facing the application domains and discuss the potential of machine vision technologies to address these challenges.

In healthcare, rising cases for chronic diseases among patients and the urgent need for preventive healthcare is accelerating the deployment of telemedicine. Telemedicine as defined in the EU commission staff working paper on "Telemedicine for the benefit of patients, healthcare systems and society" (COM-SEC, 2009) is the delivery of healthcare services at a distance using information and communication technologies. There are two main groups of telemedicine applications: (1) applications linking a patient with a health professional; and (2) applications linking two health professionals (such as tele-second opinion, teleradiology). Machine vision technologies, coupled with reliable networking infrastructure, are key for accelerating the penetration of telemedicine applications. Several examples will be drawn illustrating the use of machine vision technologies in telemedicine.

Sustainable energy and environment are key pillars for a sustainable economy. Technology is playing an increasing vital role in energy and environment including water resources management. This would foster greater control of the demand and supply side of energy and water. On the demand side, technologies including machine vision, could help in developing advanced visual metering technologies. On the supply side, machine vision technologies could help in exploring alternative sources for the generation of energy and water supply.

In the finance domain, financial crises and the failure of banking systems are major challenges facing the coming decade. Recovery is still far from reach entailing a major economic slowdown. Machine vision technologies offer the potential for greater risk visibility, prediction of downturns and stress test of the soundness of the financial system. Examples are drawn from 3D/AR/VR applications in finance.

Innovation could be seen as the process of deploying breakthrough outcome of research in industry. The innovation process could be conceived as a feedback loop starting from channelling the outcome of basic research into industrial production. Marketing strategies and novel approaches for customer relationship management draw a feedback loop that continuously update the feed of breakthrough research in industrial production. In this respect, machine vision technologies are key along this feedback process, particularly in the visualisation of the potential market and the potential route to market.

CYBER II technology (Hasenfratz et al, 2003 and 2004) is described in section 6 as a machine vision technology that has a potential use in the various application domains considered in this chapter. CYBER II technology is based on multi-camera image acquisition, from different view points, of real moving bodies. Section 6 describes CYBER II technology and its potential application in the considered domains.

The chapter concludes with a comparative analysis of the penetration of machine vision in various application domains and reflects on the horizon of machine vision in boosting economic growth.

2. Machine vision in healthcare

2.1 Challenges facing the healthcare domain

All healthcare and scientific authorities worldwide are realising the importance of developing global healthcare infrastructures and access, at least at information and communication technology levels, for exchange of patient and healthcare data, services and to provide wider opportunities for clinical research. The US National Research Council (NRC-US, 2008) has stressed the need to invest in information technology and infrastructure for efficient communication among players in the global health arena. Adopted healthcare models in Australia, Canada, France, Germany, Netherlands, Sweden, UK and USA suggested an added value from adopting an integrated health care model incorporating international healthcare practices (Banta, 2004). The Irish health policy is influenced by the developments at the international level and by the standards set by the World Health Organisation (WHO). In recent times, the Irish health policy has emphasised the importance of prevention, healthy living, more active lifestyles and community-based services and noted that these are highly influenced by globalisation. In particular, the 2001 Irish government strategy for the development of primary care services proposed a wider availability of general practitioners (GP) services through teams and GP co-operatives and the establishment of multi-disciplinary primary care teams (Harvey, 2007; Government of Ireland, 2001).

In the wider European arena, the policy "Better Healthcare for Europe" is an EU policy, research and development agenda involving eHealth policy development, development of EU public health portal (EU Portal, 2009; Health-EU) and eHealth interoperability (i.e., cross-border interoperability of electronic health records, telemedicine, healthcare and society, eHealth Resolution).

Globalisation is influencing to a large extent social behaviour and fosters a greater diversity of local communities. The adoption of open economies, markets and systems created an unprecedented impact on the culture and practices of individuals including their health knowledge and behaviours. Various research studies has been undertaken to assess the impact of globalisation on healthcare. It is widely recognised that globalisation is a complex, multidimensional phenomenon that has already influenced the way in which hospitals operate and will increasingly impact the healthcare landscape and patients experience worldwide. Globalisation is a key context for the study of social determinants of health (e.g., the conditions in which people live and work) (Labonté et al, 2007).

The tools of the modern digital world, in conjunction with the novel technologies, especially those in the biological and medical sciences have dramatically changed the potential for obtaining and using new information. In the field of global health, the benefits can be seen in many ways, e.g. how medical research is conducted; how new information is published, stored, retrieved and used; how scientists and clinicians communicate; how diseases are monitored and tracked; and how medicine is practiced. In regional development agenda, IT solutions for life sciences are considered at a global infrastructural level (Maad et al 2012; Maad et al 2009).

2.2 Potential application of machine vision in healthcare

Machine vision has a great potential in the advance and development of telemedicine. The EU commission working paper on telemedicine (COM-SEC, 2009) defines the main classes of telemedicine applications and discusses the potential benefits accruing from the implementation of these systems. The benefits can potentially be felt by many different levels of society through the empowerment of individual patients, healthcare systems and the EU marketplace more generally. This document also identifies significant barriers to

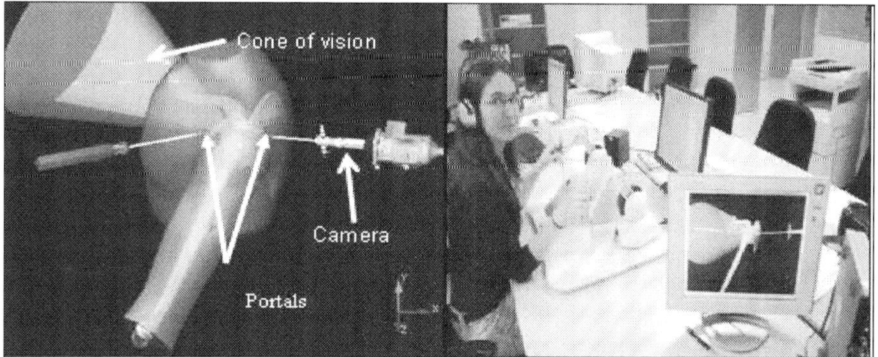

Fig. 1. The Application of virtual reality assisted medical gesture developed at the ENSAM-Image Institute.

successful implementation of consistent levels of telemedicine facilities throughout different EU member states.

A potential application of machine vision in healthcare is the one developed at the Image Institute in France. It covers visualization for medical applications, training and assisted surgery. Since 2008, the research group is developing applications for medical rehabilitation (Van Hanh et al, 2010) using virtual reality and training junior doctors in performing surgical gestures (see Figure 1). The Virtual Reality Assisted Triangulation Gesture is one the most important project which led to important results obtained in collaboration with medical schools in Spain and in France.

3. Machine vision for sustainable growth

3.1 Challenges facing sustainable growth

The Europe 2020 strategic agenda highlighted the extent of the crisis that wiped out progress bringing Europe Gross Domestic Product (GDP) growth to -4% in 2009 and industrial production to -20% with skyrocketing unemployment levels. The Europe 2020 Strategy, the EU's growth strategy for the coming decade draws the road to the exit from the crisis to a lasting recovery by focusing on three priorities for sustainable growth and jobs: 1) growth based on knowledge and innovation; 2) inclusive high employment society; and 3) green growth (Europe-2020).

The Annual G20 World Economic Forum, held in Davos, Switzerland on the 27th of January 2011 addressed the challenge of global risks, developed risk mitigation strategies and captured related opportunities. A Risk Response Network was launched to improve global risk management.

UN secretary general urged the need of revolutionary thinking and policy to bring about sustainable economic growth that can both protect the environment and raise living standards. He emphasised the global nature of the challenges and the need for a global, multinational response.

The world is facing scarcity in environmental resources. For instance, the world statistics on water (UN-Water) reveals that the world average water requirement is about 6,000 cubic meters per person per year. Water problems create opportunities to develop new water producing technologies and industries. Extensive flooding put great pressure on developing integrated waste water systems. There is an urgent need to speed up investment in water projects. Foreign investors experiencing the negative effects of recession on prestigious assets may now be more ready to put their money into sectors such as power and water where future demand is assured. Throughout the world, governments are realizing water is a scarce resource, especially as population grow and emerging market countries industrialise. China recently declared water to be a strategic resource and is planning to spend billions of dollars on water infrastructure to underpin its rapid growth.

While abundant oil and gas reserves may provide wealth in Gulf Cooperation Council GCC countries, they cannot substitute for that most basic of commodities: water. Forecasts of severe shortages by 2015 are concentrating the mind of officials eager to increase supplies and reduce consumption.

Mobilising the regions capital resources to support joint ventures and private investment in water demand as well as water supply could help insure the security and sustainability of a commodity vital to health and life as well as prosperity.

3.2 Potential application of machine vision for sustainable growth

Machine vision has a great potential in visualizing water and energy demand and could be useful in depicting and controlling the supply infrastructure.

Figure 2 depicts the potential of machine vision in conveying better understanding of the water cycle. It shows an animated visualization of the water cycle. The application depicted in the figure is developed by WssTP[1], the Water supply and sanitation Technology Platform. WssTP was initiated by the European Commission in 2004 to promote coordination and collaboration of Research and Technology Development in the water industry. Through our Strategic Research Agenda we provide strategic answers for the water research future challenges. WssTP has 61 members and 210 contributors from Industries, Academics, Research, Policy Makers and Water Utilities

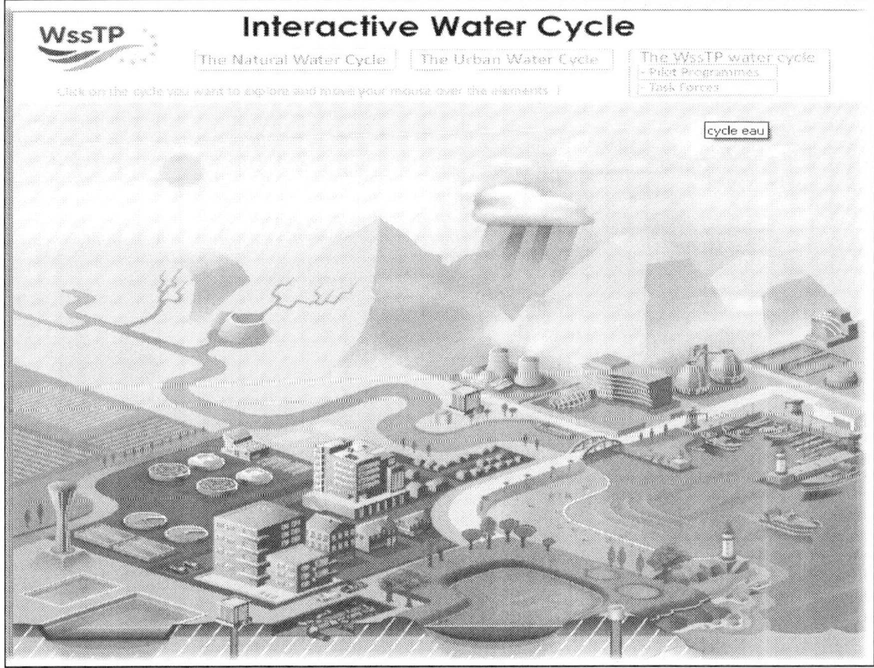

Fig. 2. Advanced interactive visualization of the water cycle developed by WssTP

[1] http://www.wsstp.eu/content/default.asp?PageId=688&LanguageId=0

4. Machine vision in finance

4.1 Challenges facing the finance domain

The recent financial crisis and its aftermath motivate our re-thinking of the role of IT as a driver for change in the global financial enterprise and a critical factor for success and sustainability. We attribute the recent financial crisis that hit the global market, causing a drastic economic slowdown and recession, to a lack of state visibility, inadequate response to events, and a slow dynamic system adaptation to events. There is evidence that ICT is still used mainly as the tool to store and process data, but not yet as a tool to create business value and business intelligence capable of counteracting devastating events.

Machine Vision technologies offer a great potential in supporting the dynamics of global financial systems and in addressing the grand challenges posed by unexpected events and crisis. Advanced high end state visualization supported by dynamic networking, e-infrastructures, system adaptation and multimodality can support a greater potential for intelligent financial analysis and perception and increase business value of IT.

4.2 Potential application of machine vision in finance

Below we describe two potential applications for machine vision in finance:

1.   Financial state visibility application;
2.   financial education

The technology focus is on 3D Internet technologies (image processing, advanced visualisation, augmented and virtual reality).

4.2.1 Financial state visibility

The urgent economic problem, linked to the financial crisis, challenges current research and technological development. The scale of the fiscal crisis that undermined the credibility of the financial system motivates the consideration of "Global Financial State Visibility" as a key global challenge that validates research and technological development activities to support the engineering dynamics of automatically adaptable software services along the "global financial supply chain" (Maad et al, 2010-A; Maad, 2010-B). Financial state could be conveyed in various ways:

- perception the state of financial risk
- perception of financial events
- perception of the financial activity
- perception of the financial system and regulatory framework

Our aim is to align the prevalent thinking in terms of mediating the financial state using reports or static models to mediating the financial state using advanced visualisation and interaction technique. Key issues to consider are who will access, manipulate, and govern the financial state. Various entities (policy makers, regulators, auditors, accountants, investors, consumers, suppliers, producers, individuals) need to access /govern / adapt Financial state Visibility depending on service level agreements Service Level Agreement SLA (see Figure 3 below).

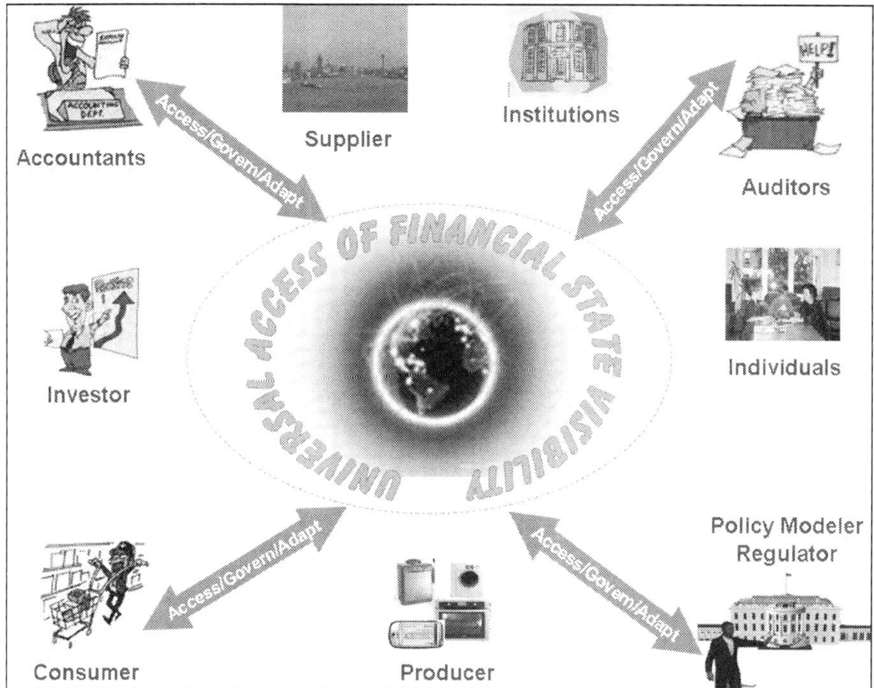

Fig. 3. Actors that need to access / govern / adapt Financial state Visibility

The Financial state visibility challenge has various dimensions:

- *Domain knowledge dimension:* this involves building the financial state knowledge base (the development of techniques to store and manipulate the semantic representation of the financial state by various stakeholders including regulators, investors, and central banks worldwide); and the visual rendering (using techniques such AR/VR) of the financial state knowledge base.
- *Converged ICT and media dimension:* this involves the development of an interoperability layer at the service infrastructure and interface levels to guarantee instant access to financial state via various converged ICT and media devices.
- *Global factors dimension:* financial state knowledge is stored and manipulated in different languages and different structures and formats. This raises geographical cultural, and accessibility technical challenges. Rendering of the financial state needs to adapt to "global context on demand".
- *Governance dimension:* There is an urgent need to support the governance of the financial state with greater perception and manipulation capability tools.

Various financial state visibility services, depicted in Figure 8 below, could be developed taking into account the above considered dimensions. These services can be grouped into various levels and categories:

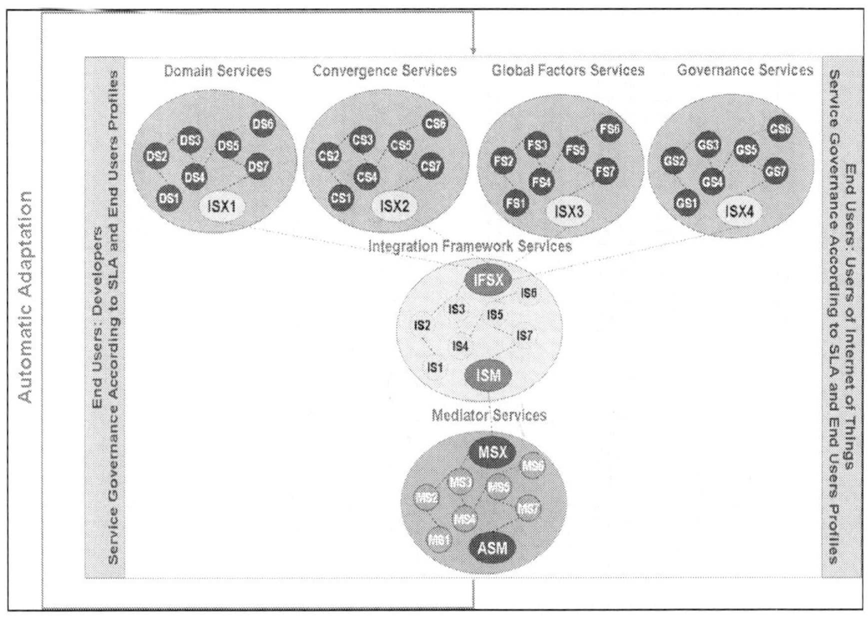

Fig. 4. Financial state visibility services

4.2.2 Financial education

This section describes a virtual reality application in financial trading developed by the author at the University of Warwick in UK in collaboration with Laboratoire de Robotique de Paris (Maad et al, 2001). The virtual reality application, depicted in Figure 5 below, involves a user playing the role of a dealer who sets his/her bid/ask spread to attract buyers and sellers. The presence of the dealer in the rendered virtual reality scene is a simulated presence. As such the virtual reality simulation is fully detached from the real world. The user needs to wear a head mounted display to have a feeling of immersion in the virtual reality scene. Moreover the interaction with the virtual world is carried out using a pair of Pinch™ Gloves. The dealer manipulates bid and ask prices (red and blue cylinders) to attract buyers and sellers (informed and uninformed traders).

While an improved perception of the financial market activity and of the role of the dealer in manipulating the true price of a security is gained from the use of Virtual Reality in the financial trading application, the isolation from the real world and the constrained interaction (the user needs to wear a head mounted display and a pair of Pinch™ Gloves to acquire a feeling of immersion in the virtual world) made the experience lived by the user (dealer) less realistic (Maad et al., 2001).

Fig. 5. The Virtual Reality simulation

5. Machine vision in innovation

5.1 Challenges facing Innovation

The EU policy challenge for smart, sustainable, and green growth (2020 Strategic priorities) requires bringing the competences of various sectors together to develop innovative services from an end-to-end perspective in ways that may not have been possible before. It has been widely acknowledged that the effort required to do this, measured in terms of investment or skills, is not within the reach of a single company, a single sector, or a single country. Consequently, the complexity of the EU policy challenge largely exceeds the individual capabilities of today's European stakeholders (higher education institutions, businesses, vertical and application markets and public authorities). There an urgent need in developing innovation in education design and delivery, innovation in service modelling and delivery, and the promotion of entrepreneurial skill (Digital Agenda-EU, Innovation Union-EU, Future Internet-EU).

5.2 The potential application of machine vision for innovation

Machine vision has the potential to depict various stages along the innovation process. The following figure 6, developed within the framework of the Sprint-Start program[2] funded by Dublin City Enterprise Board, visualize the challenges facing a new business. In this respect three key views of the company are considered: Business, Leadership, Personal.

---

[2] http://www.dceb.ie/networking/sprint-start

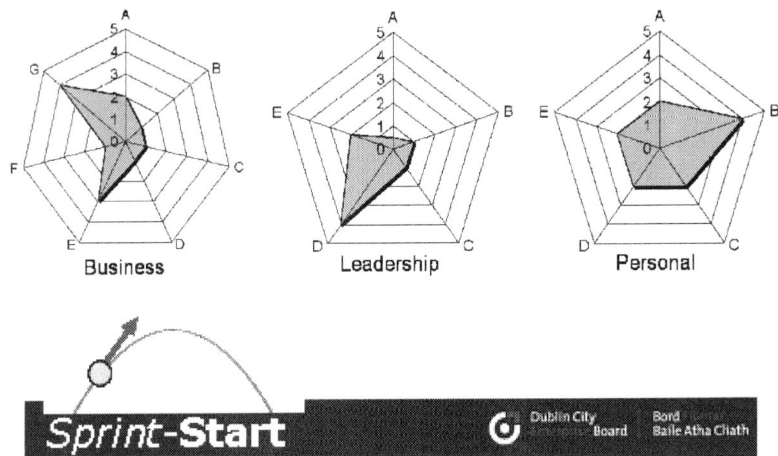

Fig. 6. Visualization of the various company views (source: Sprint-Start Program funded by Dublin City Enterprise Board)

6. CYBER II: A machine vision technology for various application domains

This section describes CYBER II technology as a machine vision technology with potential application in the various considered domain. Section 6.1 overviews the CYBER II technology and section 6.2 unveils its potential in various application domains.

6.1 Description of CYBER II technology

The CYBERII project (Hasenfratz et al 2004; Hasenfratz et al, 2003) aims at simulating, in real-time, the presence of a person (e.g. a TV presenter or a teacher) in a virtual environment. Novel paradigms of interaction were proposed within the context of the project. These paradigms involve full body interaction with the virtual world in real time. This goes beyond traditional modes of interaction involving the use of mouse, remote control, power gloves, or human sensor equipments.

The CYBERII project adopts a five steps technique to insert one or several humans in a virtual interaction space. It uses the notion of "Active Regions" to initiate the interaction with the virtual world. Actions are triggered upon body interaction with "Active Regions". This interaction may take the form of touching the "Active Region" and may be technically sensed using image analysis techniques that identify a body presence in the "Active Region". As described in (Hazenfratz et al., 2004; Hazenfratz et al., 2003), the CYBERII project adopts the following five steps :

- Multi-camera image acquisition, from different view points, of real moving bodies (see Figure 7 - left image).
- Reconstruction, modelling, and motion tracking of the acquired bodies and the surrounding environment (see Figure 7 - right image).
- Rendering of the reconstructed bodies and their surrounding.

- The creation of patterns of interaction in the rendered world using "Active Regions" as shown in Figure 8. Examples of "Active Regions" in a virtual interaction space include: the On/Off Button "Active Region" (see Figure 8 - left image) and the moving slider (see Figure 8 - right image).
- Data management and distributed parallel computing to meet the real time and realistic rendering constraints.

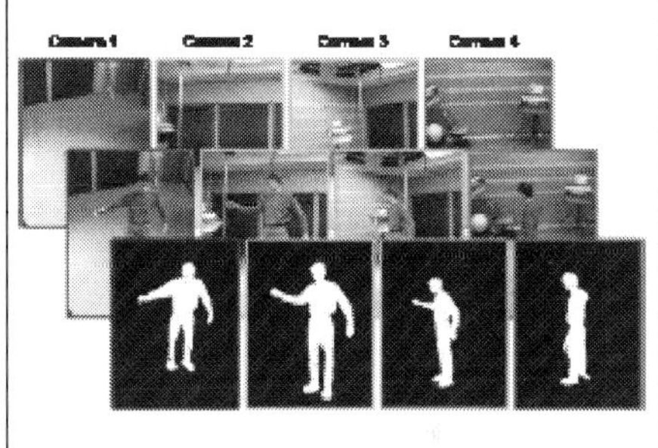

Fig. 7. CYBER II technology: image capturing (left image); image-based reconstruction (right image)

Fig. 8. CYBER II technology: Interaction with: an on/off button (left image); Interaction with a slider active region (right image)

The CYBERII project targets various industries including: (1) the TV industry (e.g. virtual sets and online presentations) ; (2) the game industry (e.g. inserting real persons in the game world); and education and entertainment (e.g. allowing visits and presentation of remote places). The proposed novel paradigm of interaction developed within the scope of the CYBERII project, namely full body interaction with active regions, promises universal accessibility to media content. For instance, physically impaired users may find a greater convenience in full body interaction with a virtual scene instead of interaction with a mouse, a keyboard, or a remote control.

6.2 Use of CYBER II technology in various application domains

In this section we briefly describe the potential use of CYBER II technology in various health, water, finance, and innovation.

6.2.1 CYBER II in healthcare

Preventing the elderly from falling has been a priority on the EU healthcare agenda COM-SEC (2009). Telemedicine application involving CYBER II technology could be used to track elderly motion and report directly any risk of falling.

Figure 9 shows the use of CYBER II of Multi-camera image acquisition of real moving bodies to detect the risk of falling for the elderly. The healthcare professional could be monitoring the motion tracking of the elderly and real time data on risk of failure could be generated as shown in the healthcare profession screens.

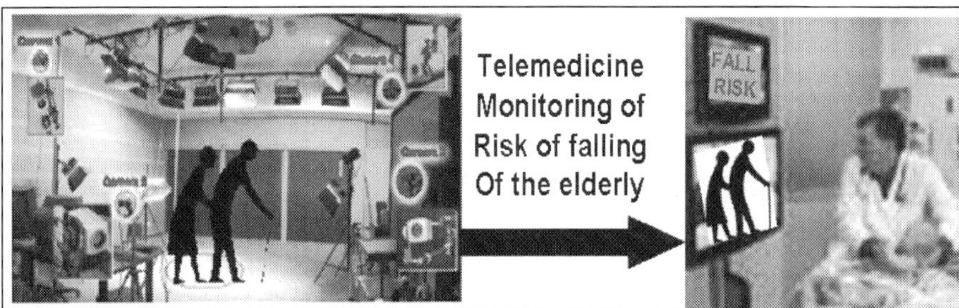

Fig. 9. CYBER II technology used in healthcare telemedicine to detect the risk of failure of the elderly

6.2.2 CYBER II in water management

CYBER II technology could be used to provide immersive interaction with utility, for instance water data, generated by SCADA systems. SCADA stands for Supervisory Control and Data Acquisition. It generally refers to the control system of the industry which is a computer system that controls and monitors a process. This process can be infrastructure, facility or industrial[3]. SCADA systems are used in energy and water resources management.

For instance CYBER II interaction with slider active region could be interfaced with SCADA System water or energy data to inform the user (the consumer) about his water and energy consumption in an interactive way. A slider active region could be the indicator of water consumption of the user.

Figure 10 depicts the potential of CYBER II technology to transform visual data on water and energy that may be produced by SCADA systems, into an immersive knowledge consumption environment based on CYBER II slider active region techniques. The consumer will have better conveyed knowledge about his water and energy consumption levels through immersive interaction.

---

[3] Definition extracted from http://www.scadasystems.net/

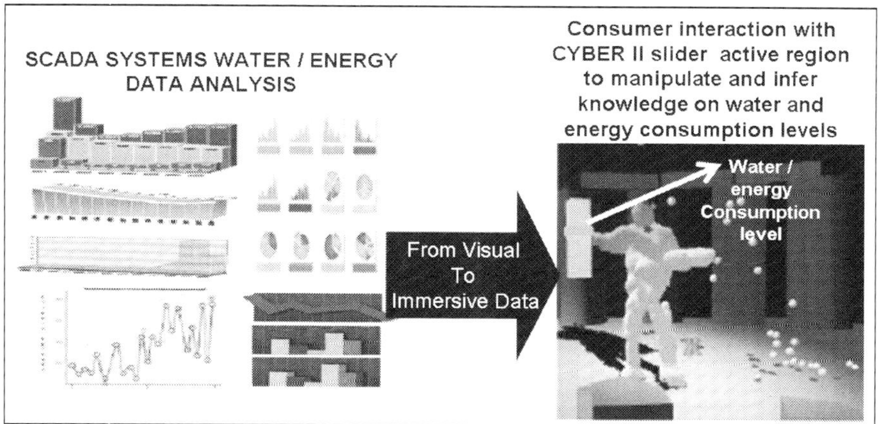

Fig. 10. CYBER II technology to transform visual data on water and energy into immersive knowledge consumption environment based on CYBER II slider active region techniques

6.2.3 CYBER II finance

Reference to the AR/VR financial application described in section 4.2.2, advanced machine vision in finance could be further deployed using the CYBERII technology to extend the functionality of the financial trading application. The CYBER II financial application, depicted in Figure 11 and 12 below, involves the insertion of a user (playing the role of a financial dealer) in a virtual world, and the use of the technique of sliders "Active Regions" to enable the body interaction of the user (dealer) to set his/her bid/ask prices for attracting buyers and sellers (Maad et al, 2008). The flow of buyers and sellers is abstractly represented by synthetic objects generated in the augmented scene following the user interaction with active regions. Figure 6 shows how the technique of slider "Active Regions" can help the dealer adjust his quotes to attract buyers and sellers. The flow of buyers and sellers is represented by red balls (for sellers flow) and yellow balls (for buyers flow). This flow is triggered through body interaction with the sliders "Active Regions". This illustrates how the CYBERII concept of full body interaction with a virtual environment and the technique of slider "Active Regions" could be used for greater engagement and unconstrained immersion in a virtual world of financial indicators. The simulation augments the real world with perceptual knowledge about bid-ask spread variation and about the flow of traders (buyers and sellers) as a result of this variation.

6.2.4 CYBER II for innovation

Similarly, CYBER II technology could be used to immerse the business entrepreneur in a virtual immersive environment where he/she can have better perception of the challenges facing a new business. CYBER II novel interaction techniques of active regions and slider bars can be used to interact with the company the three company views identified in section 5.2 above as Business, Leadership, and Personal (see Figure 13 below).

Fig. 11. The CYBERII financial application

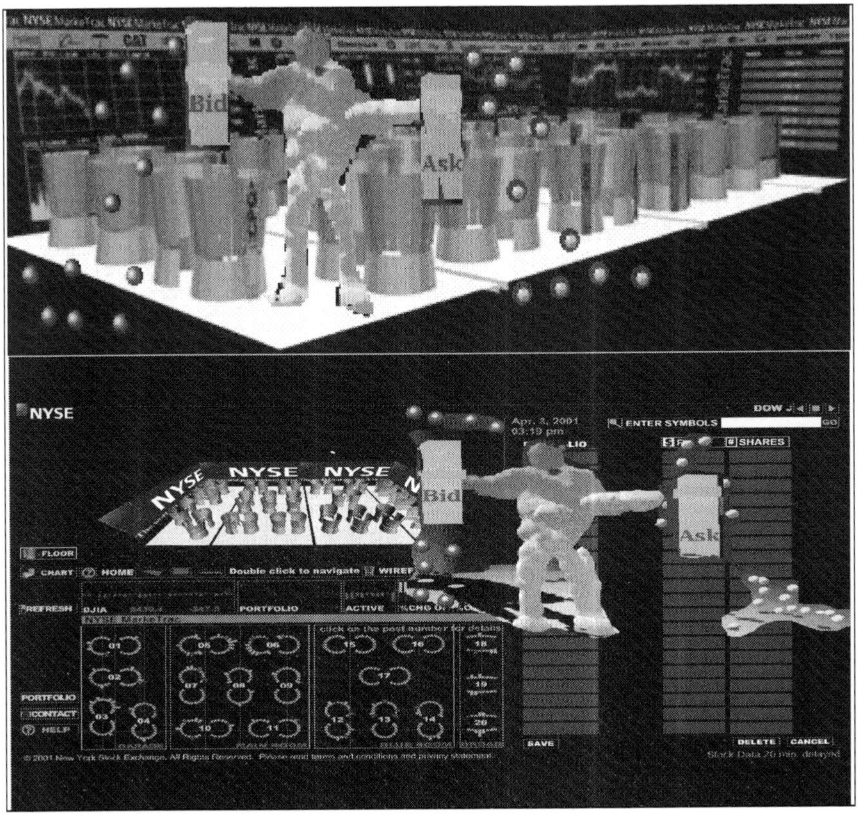

Fig. 12. CYBERII incrustation in a Virtual World of Financial indicators (illustrative example)

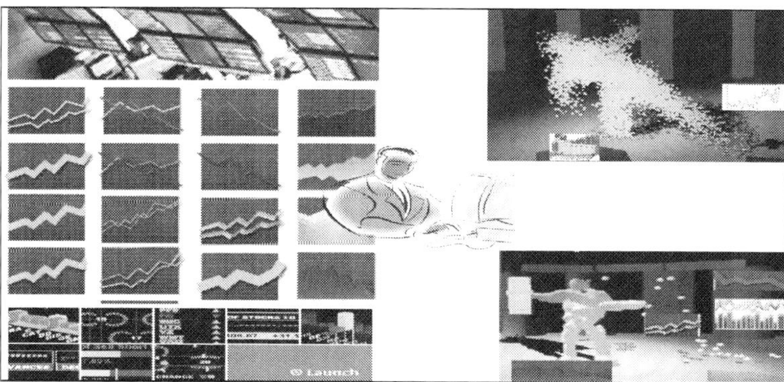

Fig. 13. CYBERII interaction with three company views: Business, Leadership, Personal

7. Conclusion

This chapter reflected on the potential of machine vision in various application domains. Various examples are drawn for the use of machine vision in the considered domains. The chapter reveals that there is a great potential to be harnessed in the use of machine vision technologies, including Augmented and Virtual Reality and rich visual media technologies, in various application domains.

Machine vision would support application domains to a various extent in providing:

- rich medium for education and knowledge building
- greater visibility of risks and events
- alternative environment for safe interaction
- a tool for policy modelling and decision
- a medium for innovation

While machine vision found a greater penetration in application domains such as e-health and finance, a great potential is foreseen for the application of machine vision in sustainable growth and in depicting and advancing the innovation process.

Various advantages could be drawn from the deployment of machine vision in various application domain including enhanced knowledge and perception of state leading to better planning and decision support.

8. References

Banta H. (2004) Health Care Technology and Its Assessment in Eight Countries. DIANE Publishing.

COM-SEC (2009), Telemedicine for the benefit of patients, healthcare systems and society, COMMISSION STAFF WORKING PAPER SEC(2009)943 final June 2009 http://ec.europa.eu/information_society/activities/health/docs/policy/telemedi cine/telemedecine-swp_sec-2009-943.pdf (accessed December 2011)

Cortinois AA, Downey S, Closson T, Jadad AR (2003) Hospitals in a globalized world: a view from Canada, Centre for Global eHealth Innovations, University Health Network, Toronto, Ontario, Canada. HealthcarePapers, 4(2), 14-32.

DigitalAgenda-EU, http://ec.europa.eu/information_society/digital-agenda/index_en.htm

EU Portal (2009) Europe's Information Society Thematic Portal. eHealth: Better Healthcare for Europe 2009. Activities: Information and Communication Technologies for health. http://ec.europa.eu/information_society/ activities/health/index_en.htm

Europe-2020, http://ec.europa.eu/europe2020/index_en.htm

Future Internet – EU, http://initiative.future-internet.eu/publications.html

Government of Ireland (2001), Department of Health and Children, Primary Care, A New Direction, Quality and Fairness - A Health System for You, Health Strategy, Government of Ireland 2001

Harvey B. (2007) Evolution Of Health Services And Health Policy In Ireland.

Hasenfratz, J. M., Lapierre, M. and Sillion, F. (2004), A Real-Time System for Full Body Interaction, Virtual Environments 2004.

Hasenfratz, J. M., Lapierre, M., Gascuel, J. D. and Boyer, E. (2003), Real-Time Capture, Reconstruction and Insertion into Virtual World of Human Actors VVG-, Vision, Video and Graphics – 2003

Health-EU. The Public Health Portal of the European Union. Health-EU. http://ec.europa .eu/health-eu/index_en.htm

Innovation Union-EU, http://ec.europa.eu/research/innovation-union/index_en.cfm

Labonté R, Schrecker T (2007). Globalization and social determinants of health: The role of the global marketplace (in 3 parts). Globalization and Health, 3:6.

Maad S (2010-B), Augmented Reality, edited by Soha Maad, The Horizon of Virtual And Augmented Reality: The Reality of the Global Digital Age, ISBN 978-953-7619-69-5, 230 pages, Published by Intech, Publishing date: January 2010.

Maad S, Dimitrov D B, Fahey T (2012), A concept for a long-term scalable bioengineering model of primary care, Int. J. Value Chain Management (in press).

Maad S, Beynon M, Garbaya S (2001), Realising Virtual Trading: What Price Virtual Reality?, Usability Evaluation and Interface Design: Cognitive Engineering, Intelligent Agents and Virtual Reality, M.J. Smith, G. Salvendy, D. Harris, R.J. Koubek (editors), Lawrence Erlbaum Associates, Mahwah, N.J., ISBN: 0-8058-3607-1, Volume 1, 2001, Part II: Virtual Reality, pp. 1007.

Maad S, Dimitrov B, Fahey T (2009), A Concept for a Long-Term Scalable Primary Care Model, CD-ROM/Online Proceedings of the European and Mediterranean, Conference on Information Systems (EMCIS), 2009, 13-14 July, The Crowne Plaza, Izmir, Turkey, Editors: Prof Zahir Irani, Dr Ahmad Ghoneim, Dr Maged Ali, Dr Sarmad Alshawi, Assistant Prof Omur Y.Saatcioglu, Prof A.Güldem Cerit , ISBN: 978-1-902316-69-7

Maad S, Garbaya S, Bouakaz S (2008), From Virtual to Augmented Reality in Finance : A CYBERII Application, Journal of Enterprise Information Management 2008; 21(1):71-80.

Maad S, McCarthy JB, Garbaya S, Beynon M, Nagarajan R (2010-A), Service Software Engineering For Innovative Infrastructure For Global Financial Services, Proc. European and Mediterranean Conference on Information Systems 2010 (EMCIS10), Abu Dhabi, United Arab Emirates, April 12-13, 2010, CDROM.

NRC-US (2008), The U.S. Commitment to Global Health: Recommendations for the New Administration, Committee on the U.S. Commitment to Global Health, National Research Council, ISBN: 0-309-12767-X, 2008, http://www.nap.edu/catalog/12506.html

UN-Water, http://www.unwater.org/statistics.html

Van Hanh Nguyen, Frédéric Merienne, Jean-Luc Martinez (2010), TRAINING-BASED ON REAL-TIME MOTION EVALUATION FOR FUNCTIONAL REHABILITATION IN VIRTUAL ENVIRONMENT", to appear in special issue of "Image and graphics for virtual reality in medicine" - IJIG Jounal, Vol. 10 (No. 2), pp. 235-250, Avril 2010